Performance Consulting

Performance Consulting

Moving Beyond Training

Dana Gaines Robinson & James C. Robinson

Berrett-Koehler Publishers
San Francisco

Berrett-Koehler Publishers, Inc.
155 Montgomery St.
San Francisco, CA 94104-4109
Tel: (415) 288-0260   Fax: (415) 362-2512

ORDERING INFORMATION

Individual sales. Berrett-Koehler publications are available through most bookstores. They can also be ordered direct from Berrett-Koehler at the address above.

Quantity sales. Special discounts are available on quantity purchases by corporations, associations, and others. For details, contact the "Special Sales Department" at the Berrett-Koehler address above.

Orders for college textbook/course adoption use. Please contact Berrett-Koehler Publishers at the address above.

Orders by U.S. trade bookstores and wholesalers. Please contact Publishers Group West, 4065 Hollis Street, P.O. Box 8843, Emeryville, CA 94662; Tel: (510) 658-3453; 1-800-788-3123. Fax: (510) 658-1834.

Library of Congress Cataloging-in-Publication Data
Robinson, Dana Gaines, 1944–
    Performance consulting: moving beyond training / Dana Gaines
    Robinson & James C. Robinson — 1st ed.
        p.   cm.
    Includes bibliographical references and index.
    ISBN 1-881052-84-2
    1. Employees, Training of.   2. Performance.   3. Business
    consultants.   I. Robinson, James C., 1930– .   II. Title.
    HF5549.5.T7R526   1995
    658.3'124—dc20   94-47066
                                                                                    CIP

First Hardcover Printing: March 1995

First Paperback Printing: January 1996

07 06 05 04 03   19 18 17 16 15 14 13 12 11 10

This paperback edition contains the complete text of the original hardcover edition.

Book Production: Pleasant Run Publishing Services
Composition: WESType Publishing Services, Inc.

To Dana's mother, Lindy Larson

and Jim's children
Bill Robinson
Susan Schwartz
Lynn Marrable

Contents

Preface

Consider these facts:

- In North America in 1994, more than $50 billion was spent on formal training and development of employees. These are direct costs only; if the cost of having employees attend training off the job is added into the equation, the figure rises to more than $300 billion.

- To remain competitive in today's world, organizations must have a highly skilled, adaptive, and motivated work force. There *must* be a return for the investment made in training.

- On the average only 10 to 20 percent of training transfers to the job so that the performance of the employee has been changed and enhanced (Broad and Newstrom, 1992, p. 7).

Unfortunately, what we in the human resource development (HRD) field have been doing for many years is *not working*, if "working" is defined as changing human performance. As Gloria A. Regalbuto (1992, p. 31) has observed: "Organizations do not ask us to deliver what they need; they ask us to deliver what they believe we can provide. . . . And what we are asked to provide—

training—is often ineffective, unnecessary, and expensive. Occasionally it is even harmful. We do just what we are asked to do—deliver training. We do not do what we are not asked to do—improve human performance in the workplace."

In this book we advance the concepts and techniques described in our first book, *Training for Impact: How to Link Training to Business Needs and Measure the Results* (Robinson and Robinson, 1989). That book described the how-to's of delivering a specific training program so that it results in performance change. Thousands of people have read that book; hundreds have written or called us to discuss it. A message we have repeatedly heard is that the book is right on about what should be done, followed by a sincere question as to how a trainer could ever work with management that way. As one individual said, "If I tried to talk to managers about their performance and business needs, they would think I was a busybody. After all, my job is to run training programs."

What struck us was the number of people in the HRD field who think of themselves as *Traditional Trainers,* focusing on the identification of what people must learn and then responding to that need. When people see themselves this way, they often find it uncomfortable or impossible to do what is required if training is to result in performance change. And, as noted at the start of this Preface, research clearly indicates that the results from this role are insufficient if we, as professionals in the HRD field, are to be truly helpful to our organizations. An alternative role is that of *Performance Consultant,* where the purpose and focus of the role is to partner with management to identify and achieve performance excellence.

In this book we provide practical and specific techniques for how you can make the transition from:

- The role of Traditional Trainer to the role of Performance Consultant

- Being held accountable for the delivery of training programs to a responsibility that focuses on changing human performance and having an impact on the organization

■ Being viewed as "just a trainer" to being valued as a partner to management in the achievement of performance and business needs

For Whom Is This Book Written?

This book is primarily written for individuals for whom the development of human resources is at least a part of their job responsibilities. This book is for you if your job title or function sounds like any of the following:

■ Trainer (technical trainer, sales trainer, management development trainer, and so on)

■ Training specialist

■ Training coordinator

■ Instructional designer

■ Instructional systems designer

■ Internal or external consultant

■ Career developer

■ Organizational developer

■ Media specialist

The book is also for anyone who directly or indirectly manages these types of positions. Therefore, training managers, human resource managers, and other managers who have people with training responsibility reporting to them will benefit from this book.

Scope of This Book

In this book, we will be providing both a conceptual framework and practical techniques relevant to the role of Performance Consultant. The use of the term *role* is purposeful. We are not describing a job title but a function. One individual can fill several roles: instructor, manager, program designer, needs analyst. Our belief is that the Traditional Trainer role must evolve into the Performance Consultant role. It is not that the Traditional Trainer role is "bad"; rather, it is no longer sufficient to address the needs of our organizations. Times have changed—and so must we.

In the book, you will learn how to:

■ Identify performance requirements that are directly linked to the operational and business goals of an organization

■ Contract with management to take all the actions that are needed if the identified performance is to be successfully implemented

■ Work in a consultative manner with critical people so that you become a valued business partner

■ Move from focusing on delivery of training services to focusing on performance

Overview of the Contents

The book is divided into four sections. Part One discusses why the role of the Performance Consultant is important at this time. Additionally, the skills of consulting and identifying needs are discussed in depth.

Part Two introduces the performance relationship map. Performance Consultants can use this map to design and complete performance assessments. When we are asked, "What is a key skill for a consultant to have?" we respond by indicating that consultants must "ask the right questions right." This map provides guidance as to what the "right" questions are if performance is to be improved or changed; it also illustrates the interrelationship between training, performance, work environment, and business needs. Front-end assessments are a requirement, not an option, for working in the role of Performance Consultant. Part Two provides many techniques for conducting successful performance assessments as opposed to training assessments. Additionally, techniques are provided for effectively influencing your partners to realize that training alone will not change performance.

Part Three discusses the subject of contracting. The term *contract* refers to a social agreement, not a legal document. Performance Consultants must form contracts on two occasions: (1) when agreeing to do performance assessments and (2) when determining the actions to be taken to change on-the-job performance. Although we provide techniques for forming successful implementation contracts, the book does not provide in-depth guidance in managing the change process. That guidance can be found in other books, many of which are acknowledged in the Resources section at the back of this book.

Part Four looks at the traditional training function in its entirety, rather than at any single individual within that function. What must be done to ensure that the function is a performance improvement department and not a training department? What must be different? How can you make the transition from your current situation to one desired for the future? Answers to those questions are provided in this section of the book.

Performance Consulting Tools and Exercises

Our intent is to make this book as practical and filled with how-to's as possible. We provide many exercises (or self-tests), which you can elect to complete as a way of measuring your learning progress. In addition, we offer several tools designed for your use, including checklists and interview guides. Adapt and use these tools as you wish.

Acknowledgments

This book would not be a reality without the support of many people. First, we wish to thank our many clients from whom we have learned so much. It is in their organizations that we have been able to form, test, and improve the concepts described in this book. Additionally, we want to thank the members of the Partners in Change, Inc., team: Veronica Bartosik, Karen Brewer, Lori Calhoun, Karen Saccoccia, and Linda Venturella. These

individuals work in our company. Because they are so competent, we were able to remove ourselves from the day-to-day business and write a book with full confidence that everything was
going smoothly in the office. A special thanks to Terri Lutz, of
our firm, for her many hours in front of the word processor as
she worked on our manuscript. Her attention to detail and commitment to quality have been invaluable.

We also want to thank Roger Addison, Veronica Bartosik,
Stephanie Jackson, Bill Kahnweiler, Chuck Kormanski, Marc
Rosenberg, and Rosaline Tsai, who read the book manuscript
and provided us with feedback; their comments definitely enhanced the quality of the finished product. A very sincere thank-
you to Steven Piersanti, our editor and publisher. This is the
second time we have worked with Steve; we value his encourage-
ment, guidance, and patience.

Finally, we want to thank those individuals who have pre-
ceded us on the journey from training to performance. We, and
our profession, owe much to Tom Gilbert, Joe Harless, Pat
McLagan, Robert Mager, and Geary Rummler.

Pittsburgh, Pennsylvania   Dana Gaines Robinson
January 1995   James C. Robinson

Introduction:
The Need for
Performance Consulting

"Remember, training is not what is ultimately im-
portant, . . . performance is."
—Marc Rosenberg, 1990–91 President, National
Society for Performance and Instruction

Have you ever been in any of these situations?

Nancy McDowell, a training professional in a manufacturing company, receives a phone call from an
operations manager, who indicates that there is
conflict in her work team. She wants Nancy to conduct a team effectiveness workshop as soon as possible. Nancy has a concern that this workshop, by
itself, may be insufficient to improve team relations. She begins to ask the manager questions,
such as "When did this problem begin?" and
"What exactly is happening that causes you concern?" After a few questions, the manager becomes
irritated, saying that she thought Nancy worked in
the *training* department and she wants a *training*

program. The manager concludes with the question: "Are you going to help me or not?"

Harold Jones has just read an electronic message on his computer from a supervisor in the customer service department with whom he worked about six months ago. At the time, the supervisor asked Harold to conduct a course for the customer service representatives in the department. This course, entitled "Consultative Customer Skills Workshop," provided skills in identifying customer service needs and addressing customer problems. The course was conducted because customer satisfaction scores for service had been declining. As Harold recalled, the course was successful; the reaction evaluations were positive. However, according to the electronic message Harold has just read, the customer satisfaction ratings for service are even lower than they were six months ago. The message indicates that the supervisor is very upset and ends with the statement: "Whatever you did certainly didn't work."

Rhonda Thompson is very perplexed. It seemed as though everyone in the organization has been talking about empowerment for some time. When she attended a major trade conference about eight months ago, she spent time going through the exhibits just to find out what programs were available in the area of empowerment. She found a terrific course and negotiated a contract with the supplier. The course was put into the training catalog and has been offered on two occasions to all supervisors and managers in the company. Each time it has been a struggle to fill the class. Supervisors and managers are not eager to sign up, and there are many last-minute cancellations. It looks as if the next time this program is offered only half of the available spaces will be filled.

Scenarios like these are occurring daily in our organizations. What these situations have in common is that a *training* solution is being used to address a *performance* need. Sometimes a training solution is selected because management requires it (such as the situation with Nancy McDowell); at other times it is chosen because we naively believe that training alone will solve the problem. Whatever the reason, the lack of results is the same. As reported in the book *Transfer of Training*, by Mary Broad and John Newstrom (1992, p. ix), "Most of [the] investment in organizational training and development is wasted because most of the knowledge and skills gained in training (well over 80 percent by some estimates) is not fully applied by those employees on the job." Timothy Baldwin and Kevin Ford (1988, p. 63) report, "Not more than 10 percent of these expenditures [in training] actually result in transfer to the job." Clearly the traditional training approaches do not work.

Part of the problem is that the traditional training process confuses training activity with performance improvement. In our earlier book, *Training for Impact: How to Link Training to Business Needs and Measure the Results* (Robinson and Robinson, 1989, pp. 3-9), we describe the activity approach to training, in which the focus is on what people must learn versus what they must do on the job. While the activity approach to training focuses on developing excellent learning experiences, it does not address the transfer of the newly learned skills and knowledge onto the job.

The concept of making the transition from a training approach to a performance approach is not a new one. In 1970, Joe Harless (Dixon, 1988, pp. 65-68) coined the term "front-end analysis." In his work then and now, Harless clearly believes that lack of skill and knowledge is *not* the most frequent cause of existing performance problems. He advocates using front-end analysis to focus on what people are expected to accomplish on the job versus what they are expected to learn. In 1970, Bob Mager and Peter Pipe (1970, p. v) also advocated a structured approach to analyzing performance problems. They indicated that solutions to performance problems should be based upon a thorough analysis of causes of the problem and said, "Solutions to problems are like keys and locks; they don't work if they don't fit. And if solutions aren't the right ones, the problem doesn't get solved." They also advocated that trainers differentiate between skill and knowledge deficiencies and other work environment factors that affect performance.

For over three decades, Tom Gilbert has advocated performance analysis based upon rigorous examination of exemplary performers. He has argued that it is not enough to ask exemplary performers what they do; instead, the analyst must observe their performance. In his book, *Human Competence: Engineering Worthy Performance,* published in 1978, Gilbert presents "a model for engineering human competence—for finding out why it is lacking and what to do to get more of it" (p. v).

Geary Rummler (1989, pp. 43, 44) states that "training alone is almost never an appropriate cure." He advocates that trainers "use a rigorous approach of a systems engineer to analyze organizational behavior and design programs that change or improve human performance" (Dixon, 1988, p. 3). He continues by indicating that the work environment within which employees operate has a tremendous impact upon their job output.

What is of concern to us is that these performance-oriented technologies are in little evidence today. There are some training functions that have worked with management to successfully enhance performance. For example, *Fortune* magazine (Henkoff, 1993) identified several such organizations, including Motorola, Federal Express Corporation, General Electric Aircraft Engines, and Corning. However, these are the exceptions, not the rule.

This situation cannot continue. In today's right-sized, delayered, and reengineered organizations, people are being asked to do more and more. The performance demands placed on employees are growing; the work they are asked to do is changing. As Robert Reich (1994, pp. 1, 3) states, "There is no doubt that our economy is changing in fundamental and far-reaching ways.

The challenge we face is to take full advantage of change, to expedite the movement from 'old work' to high-wage, higher-skill 'new work.' New work means fewer repetitive tasks and more problem solving. New work . . . cannot be instantly duplicated by other countries because it depends on the one resource within the nation that remains durably *here* with us—our minds."

The Conference Board, a nonprofit business membership and research organization based in New York, conducted a research study of member organizations in 1994. The overall finding was that "despite major investments in technology, downsizing, restructuring and re-engineering to cut costs and improve competitive advantage, 98 percent of companies responding [to the study] report a need to gain more productivity and higher performance from their work force" (Csoka, 1994, p. 7). This report went on to say that the majority of human resource executives who were interviewed explained the primary reason for a lack of performance results from human resource initiatives to be "a failure to look at human performance systemically, to involve all aspects of the organization, and then to apply comprehensive solutions to performance problems."

So our challenge can be summed up this way:

1. The competitive advantage, and perhaps the survival, of an organization demands that employees perform at a high level.

2. Traditional training approaches in support of performance change are not working, primarily because they are not system-oriented in their approach to resolving performance problems—this despite the fact that significant leaders in the field have been writing about performance approaches for thirty years.

If Not Us, Who? If Not Now, When?

This situation provides a tremendous opportunity for those in the training and development field at this time. Management and others will seek out those people who can partner with them to install the performance required by the organization. Those who work effectively in the future must be able to:

- Develop collaborative working relationships with key managers and other partners
- Clearly understand the vision and strategies that management is striving to achieve
- Identify the performance required of employees if the organization is to thrive
- Determine the conditions in the work environment that must be modified if needed performance is to take root
- Work with people in and out of management to determine *all* the interventions required if high performance is to be achieved

Clearly, these activities are outside those of the traditional training processes.

We must evolve from a training to a performance perspective. If we do not rise to the occasion now, others will. We will have missed an opportunity to be viewed as a value-added partner and will risk being seen as peripheral to the mainstream of the business.

The time is now. Opportunity waits for no one. Performance consulting is the process by which we can work with management and others to identify and achieve performance excellence linked to business goals. The theme that threads throughout this book is quite simply this: *think performance, not training!*

PART ONE

THE ROLE OF THE PERFORMANCE CONSULTANT

When people ask you what you do, how do you respond? Are you: . . .

____ An HRD professional?   ____ Instructional designer?
____ Training specialist?   ____ Media specialist?

For too long the HRD or training profession has focused on the *activity* of training; people in the profession thought of themselves as specialists associated with some aspect of learning, such as designing the courses, delivering the programs, or identifying the needs. That focus will no longer suffice in today's business environment. We must shift from focusing on what people need to learn (training) to what they must do (performance). In the next two chapters, some key concepts and principles associated with the role of Performance Consultant are discussed.

1

How Performance Consulting
Moves Beyond Training

Jim Robinson was having lunch with a plant manager and the training manager of a manufacturing facility. It was a "getting-to-know-you" lunch. Jim was on-site for the first time to have preliminary discussions about the needs of these managers and ways in which he could be of assistance.

Partway through lunch Jim asked the plant manager, "What are your primary initiatives for the next year?" The plant manager responded, "We need to improve our metal-recovery operations. We have technology that is capable of recovering 98.5 percent of the metal from the ore, but we're currently recovering only 94.5 percent." He felt that the 4 percent gap could be closed only through improvement of operator and supervisor performance. The plant manager also discussed other initiatives of concern to him, including better cost control, increased consistency in the quality of raw ingredients brought into the plant, and improved maintenance.

Later during the lunch, Jim asked the training manager about his initiatives for the coming year. He responded that in addition to the training programs already offered in the catalog, he hoped to provide additional training in the areas of new-employee orientation, meeting facilitation, and team building.

"Wait a minute," Jim thought. "What about the metals recovery need of the plant manager? Why is there no mention of any work being done to support that business need?" The training manager saw himself as a provider of training programs and not as someone who was to work with management to improve performance in support of business needs.

Key Differences Between the Roles of Traditional Trainer and Performance Consultant

A skillful Performance Consultant would have listened to the comments of this plant manager and thought, "Here's a business need I can support. The manager wants to increase the percentage of metal recovery and believes that it will only occur through increased performance by supervisors and operators. I can help him to identify the *specific* performance that is required for each group—the decisions they need to make, the analyses they need to do; I can also help to identify the actions that must be taken if that performance is to change." Someone in the role of Performance Consultant thinks in terms of what people must *do* if business goals are to be achieved. This is different from the traditional training process of focusing on what people must *learn*.

We have purposely used the phrase "role of Performance Consultant." Throughout this book we will describe the techniques we espouse for the role of Performance Consultant. We will contrast this role with the one we refer to as Traditional Trainer. For us, a role, as opposed to a job, is defined by the outputs that are produced. One individual can fulfill several roles; in fact, someone can work in the roles of both Traditional Trainer and Performance Consultant. Unfortunately, at the present time too few people are working in the Performance Consultant role. Table 1.1 contrasts these two roles.

As mentioned in both the Preface and the Introduction of this book, the Traditional Trainer role is not "wrong" or "bad"; rather, it is insufficient for the needs of our organizations in today's highly competitive, reengineered, customer-focused world. The Performance Consultant requires the skills of a trainer or access to people who have those skills. But the role requires more.

**Table 1.1. The Traditional Trainer Role
Contrasted with the Performance Consultant Role.**

Element	Traditional Trainer Role	Performance Consultant Role
Focus	Identifies and addresses learning needs of people.	Identifies and addresses performance needs of people.
Output	Produces structured learning experiences such as training programs, self-paced packages, and computer-based training programs. Views training as an end; if people have learned, then the desired outputs from the Traditional Trainer role have been achieved.	Provides services that assist in changing or improving performance. These can include training services but should also include formation of performance models (that is, performance needed to achieve business goals) and guidance in addressing work environment obstacles. Views training as a means to an end. People must transfer what they learn to the job. Only when performance has changed in the desired direction has the output from the Performance Consultant role been completed.
Accountability	Held accountable for training activity. Measures include number of participant days, instructor days, and courses. Frequently, the axiom under which this role operates is "More is better."	Held accountable for establishing and maintaining partnerships with managers and others in the organization. The contribution to improving the performance of people in the organization is measured.
Measures	Training evaluations are completed for participant reaction and learning.	The results of training and nontraining actions are measured for performance change and cost benefit.
Assessments	Assessments typically identify only the *training* needs of employees.	Assessments are completed to determine *performance* gaps and the reasons for these gaps; in this manner the work environment's readiness to support required performance is identified.
Relationship to Organizational Goals	Training function is viewed as a cost (not an investment). Training programs and services have a limited, acknowledged linkage to business goals.	The function is viewed as producing measurable results, such as cost savings. Completed work has a high linkage to the organization's goal.

Specifically, four key areas of knowledge and skill are needed if the Performance Consultant is to be successful:

1. Business knowledge
2. Knowledge of human performance technology
3. Partnering skill
4. Consulting skill

Business Knowledge

> "If you want to bring something to the party when meeting with managers, you have to understand the financial and marketing language that they deal with every day. Once you begin talking their language, then you can begin establishing some joint partnerships."
> —Jerold Tucker, Director of Corporate Education, GTE, as stated in Steinburg, 1991, p. 30

While Performance Consultants must have an in-depth knowledge of the disciplines associated with human resource development, it is imperative that they also become immersed in the "business of the business" they support. In essence, Performance Consultants are businesspeople who specialize in human performance rather than finance, marketing, or operations.

Performance Consultants can:

■ Read the annual report of their organization and *understand* it.

■ Discuss knowledgeably with managers and others the ratios used to measure the operational health of the organization in order to compare the current performance of the organization against goals. Is the return on equity what it should be? Is operating revenue on target? If not, what are the primary causes for the difference? What business actions must be taken to close the gap?

- Identify the primary forces, outside the control of the organization, that will challenge the organization's ability to meet its business goals.

- Discuss the strategies and actions being taken by competitors and the implications of those actions for the organization.

- Skillfully use the business terminology of the organization. Performance Consultants make sure that their language is no different from that of those who work throughout the organization.

A Performance Consultant must continually seek out information about the business. Reading an annual report once a year will not be sufficient. An organization's business challenges and goals change; a Performance Consultant takes the initiative to remain current in this area. Some of the approaches that have been used with success include the following:

- *Reading trade journals relevant to the organization:* In essence, Performance Consultants read the same journals as the people they are supporting. Examples of reading material would be the business section of daily newspapers, business magazines such as *Fortune* and *Business Week,* trade journals, governmental publications, and reports related to the organization's own industry.

- *Reviewing organizational documents that provide information about the organization's vision, mission, strategic goals, and performance:* Such items as business plans, marketing plans, annual reports, plans for new ventures, research-and-development achievements, customer service reports, and operating statements are needed. Performance Consultants ensure that this type of information is made available to them.

- *Volunteering to serve on task forces or committees formed to address a particular business issue:* Such teams are being formed frequently for purposes of quality initiatives, customer service initiatives, market penetration, or human resource initiatives. As busy as a Performance Consultant may be, time spent on such committees provide contact with business colleagues and an opportunity to learn of their concerns; partnerships are also formed in the process.

- *Volunteering to work on a special assignment in areas of the organization such as Manufacturing, Customer Service, or Maintenance:* Working on this type of assignment for several months or a year and then returning to the role of Performance Consultant increases knowledge and insight into the workings of the operation. Trust can also be developed with business partners in a substantive manner through such an assignment.

- *Identifying key performers in a business unit or division and asking permission to "shadow" them for a few days:* In the process of observing what they do, many questions will form about the business goals and challenges faced by these performers. Discussions with these individuals can be an invaluable source of information.

Knowledge of Human Performance Technology

There are several definitions for the phrase "human performance technology." The one we value defines human performance technology as "a systematic approach to analyzing, improving, and managing performance in the workplace through the use of appropriate and varied interventions" (American Society for Training and Development, 1992, p. 1). This technology acknowledges that human performance is a function of many influences: feedback, accountability, rewards or incentives, and motivation, to name just a few. One of these influences— but only one—is the skill and knowledge required of people to perform. Another concept associated with human performance technology is the idea that these influences are interdependent; it is the combination of these factors that results in the desired performance. For example, if it is important for customer service representatives to resolve customer complaints, then many factors need to be aligned toward this performance goal. For example, the representatives need:

- The skill and knowledge required to resolve complaints

- Incentives or rewards (that is, resolving complaints must become part of their job performance rating and accountability)

- Both coaching and feedback to assist them in increasing their effectiveness in dealing with customers who have problems

It is not that incentives are the most important factor; rather, the interrelationship and alignment of all factors must be acknowledged and achieved.

Performance Consultants must possess knowledge of this technology and operate from a systems approach each time a problem or performance challenge is presented to them. They are bias-free concerning any particular solution; rather, they strive to understand what the system currently *is* and what it *must be* if the desired performance is to occur. Additionally, the *causes* of any performance gap must be identified. Performance Consultants operate from the basic assumption that performance is a function of a system and not of any one element. Therefore, solutions to performance problems will be systemic in nature and not unidimensional (that is, training alone will not be the solution). This book will provide many techniques for putting human performance technology into operation.

Partnering Skill

Performance Consultants take the initiative to meet, work with, and gain the trust of managers and others within their organization. It has frequently been said that building trust takes time; it does not happen overnight. Performance Consultants actively forge these relationships. Partnerships can, and should, be formed with various people in an organization: senior managers, other managers and supervisors, and thought leaders and subject matter experts, whatever their title. Partnerships are also forged with customers and suppliers to the organization.

Assigning members of the performance improvement function to form a liaison with specific managers and/or key personnel is an effective way to create these partnerships. More will be discussed about this in Chapter Twelve, but let us provide an example from one of our client organizations to illustrate.

This organization has ten major business units that organizationally report to the president. Four individuals work as Performance Consultants. Each of these individuals has two or three business units with which he or she is partnered. The Performance Consultants regularly meet with the key personnel responsible for the operational results in each business unit; in some instances the Performance Consultants have also been invited to participate in the regularly scheduled planning meetings of managers within the business unit. This access provides the Performance Consultants with information about the current and future performance needs of the business unit as well as with an opportunity to educate and raise the awareness of those they support about the implications of their plans for employee performance. These Performance Consultants represent a "one-stop-shopping" benefit to their partners; when the partners have a training or performance need, they call their Performance Consultant. The Performance Consultant, in turn, works to identify the need and find a way to address it; at times, this means acting as a broker in finding an external resource. Over time, these partnerships are becoming stronger and stronger as trust is built.

Networking is another technique used to forge partnerships. Our research has shown that effective Performance Consultants are skillful networkers. By networking we mean the identification of people throughout the organization, in various positions and levels, with whom ongoing contact would be mutually beneficial. In networking, information is both given and received. People in the Performance Consultant's network provide that consultant with a means of staying current regarding strategic plans, departmental objectives, and initiatives. They also provide a way of assessing current morale and concerns.

Consulting Skill

We define consulting as a synergistic process by which the expertise of both the client and the consultant is maximized. In essence, it is as though the consultant represents a value of "1," the client represents a value of "1," and together they accomplish a "3" result; this is due largely to the synergistic nature of working together in a partnered manner. (The term *client* is discussed in Chapter Two. The term refers to the person or people with whom the Performance Consultant is partnered for a specific project in support of a business need.)

Peter Block (1981, pp. 18–22) has identified three consulting styles that are used with frequency: the pair-of-hands, expert, and collaborative styles. Only one of these, the collaborative style, will yield results for a Performance Consultant. Let's look more closely at each of these three styles.

The Pair-of-Hands Style

In this style the client retains almost all of the control for the project. The client determines the problem and the solution, and the Performance Consultant implements these decisions. An example would be a call from a manager who says, "My supervisors are not prioritizing their work effectively. You have that program on time management. Please give me a call to indicate when you could run it for the six people reporting to me."

In this scenario, the client has identified the problem (lack of prioritization of work) and determined the solution (a training program on time management); the Performance Consultant is expected to implement that decision as a pair of hands for this manager. The advantages and disadvantages of this style are illustrated below.

Virtually every professional works in the pair-of-hands style at times. What is important to realize is that this style will not be successful when the goal is to change performance.

Advantages	*Disadvantages*
1. It is responsive; action can be taken shortly after initial communication.	1. The wrong action may be taken. The client could have made the wrong assessment and requested an inappropriate action.
2. It relieves the Performance Consultant of any decision-making responsibility; the client makes all the decisions.	2. The probability that the performance problem will be resolved is low. Usually performance problems have multiple causes, so a request for only one action (in this instance, training) will be insufficient to produce change.
3. It is viewed as supportive; the Performance Consultant is doing what the client has requested.	3. When change does not occur, the Performance Consultant will most likely be held accountable; blame will be diverted toward the implementer of the action.
	4. The actions and accountabilities of the client are not identified in this style; the Performance Consultant assumes all the responsibility for implementation.
	5. When a Performance Consultant is approached by a client in a pair-of-hands manner and does little or nothing to renegotiate the relationship, the Performance Consultant is implicitly endorsing the solution advocated by the client.

The Expert Style

In this approach the Performance Consultant assumes the majority of control for the project. Although the client may make suggestions, the Performance Consultant makes recommendations and tells the client what would be best to do.

For example, suppose that a manager is experiencing problems with quality in the production process. The Performance Consultant listens and may obtain some additional information, then tells the manager what actions are required to "fix" the problem. In essence, the Performance Consultant determines the cause of the problem, makes recommendations for action, and (assuming that the recommendations are accepted) implements most or all of these actions. The following list illustrates the advantages and disadvantages of this style:

Advantages	*Disadvantages*
1. The Performance Consultant retains a great deal of control, which can enhance the consultant's self-esteem.	1. There is a strong possibility that the client will have limited or no investment in the actions. The ideas are the Performance Consultant's; emotional ownership is lacking for the client. Over time, the client's sponsorship of the project may dissipate.
2. When the Performance Consultant assumes the majority of the control, decisions can be made quickly.	2. An inaccurate diagnosis is possible. As skillful as the Performance Consultant may be, it is her or his perspective that is brought to the situation. The subtleties and complexities of the situation may be unknown to the Performance Consultant and may not

be considered when mak-
ing recommendations.

3. The client's responsibilities and accountabilities
regarding the project are
rarely articulated; the Performance Consultant as-
sumes all the responsibility. If the project fails, the
Performance Consultant
will receive the blame.
(They were the Perfor-
mance Consultant's ideas,
after all!)

Again, the expert style is one in which most professionals
work at times. However, it will not be appropriate when changing employee performance is the goal.

The Collaborative Style

Peter Block (1981, pp. 21, 22) indicates that the collaborative
style is the most effective approach because it is the only one that
utilizes both the consultant's specialized knowledge (for example, of human resource development) and the client's knowledge
of the operation and the process. It brings to life the formula of
$1 + 1 = 3$.

In the collaborative style, decisions regarding actions to
take and implementation plans are all shared responsibilities.
The advantages and disadvantages of this style are shown below:

Advantages	*Disadvantages*
1. The probability of an ac-curate diagnosis is high. The input and thoughts of both the Performance Consultant and the client are sought and utilized.	1. This style requires more time by both the Perfor-mance Consultant and the client. They will need to meet frequently; agree-ments must be reached

2. The client is invested in supporting the decisions that are made because he or she was a party to making those decisions.

3. The probability that the project will yield the desired results is increased because *all* actions (by both the Performance Consultant and the client) are identified and are being taken.

4. Learning occurs throughout the project for both the Performance Consultant and the client. This learning is generic in the sense that it can be drawn on in future projects.

5. A relationship is established throughout the course of the project; mutual trust and respect are developed. This provides some long-term benefits.

and differences resolved. (Of course, it can also be said that this style requires less time because it has the greatest probability of achieving results, following the principle that "doing it right the first time" ultimately takes *less* time.)

2. A client who prefers to "tell" or "be told" (as in the pair-of-hands or expert styles) will resist this approach. Not all clients want to be "collaborated with."

Performance Consultants develop finely honed collaborative consulting skills, many of which will be further described in this book.

Summary

1. Performance Consultant is a role and not a job. It is distinguished from the role of Traditional Trainer by its focus on what people must *do* rather than on what they must *learn*.

2. Performance Consultants develop four sets of skills and knowledge and utilize these techniques daily:

   ■ Business knowledge

   ■ Knowledge of human performance technology

   ■ Partnering skill

   ■ Consulting skill

2

Identifying Needs
Proactively and Reactively

Consider this scenario. You return from a business trip and find the following message from a production manager on your voice-mail: "Communication between the day and night shifts during changeover is very poor. Day supervisors aren't giving complete and accurate information to those who are coming on shift; night shift supervisors don't do much better. Also, there seems to be a lot of hostility between the two shifts. I'd like to talk to you about what training program you have that could increase communication and build more of a team here. Give me a call when you get back."

There are two very different ways to respond to this request: as a Traditional Trainer or as a Performance Consultant. Certainly, the nature of the call places the responder into a pair-of-hands relationship with the manager. Frequently, someone responding as a Traditional Trainer will accept the diagnosis of the manager (that increased communication skills would correct the problem) and will respond with a training program. Unfortunately, it is improbable that any one training program will change the performance deficiencies identified by this manager. So while actions will be taken, little impact will result.

However, someone responding as a Performance Consultant will respond quite differently. One of the primary differences is that a Performance Consultant identifies four kinds of needs: business, performance, training, and work environment.

Four Kinds of Needs

If performance change in support of business needs is to occur, the performance and business needs must be identified together with any training needs. In addition, any changes needed in the work environment of the performers must also be identified. While all of these needs are related, they are different. Table 2.1 illustrates the four kinds of needs for a manufacturing organization and a service organization. Let's look at each kind of need in depth.

Business needs are the goals for a unit, department, or organization. They are expressed in operational terms, which are the hard data measures used to monitor the "health" of the organization. Each of the business needs can be measured in quantifiable terms. In the manufacturing organization, lack of the three business needs can be measured with hard data; for example, waste is measured as a percentage of output (that is, waste is 1.5 percent of production). In the service organization, revenue and response time can also be measured in quantifiable terms; for example, customer satisfaction can be measured through analysis of customer satisfaction surveys. What percentage of customers are indicating satisfaction with service and how does this compare to the goal that has been established?

Performance needs are the on-the-job behavioral requirements of people who are performing a specific job. These needs describe what people need to *do* if the business needs are to be met.

Training needs identify what people must *learn* if they are to perform successfully. *Work environment needs* identify what systems and processes within the work environment of the performer must be modified if the performance needs are to be achieved. Combining the training and work environment needs leads to actions to be taken to achieve the performance needs.

Table 2.1. Business, Performance, Training, and Work Environment Needs.

Type of Organization	Business Needs	Performance Needs	Training Needs	Work Environment Needs
Manufacturing Organization	Production waste needs to be reduced.	Operators need to determine if the product is produced according to specifications; if it is not, they need to stop the process and determine the cause of the problem.	Operators need to learn statistical process control techniques.	The authority to stop production needs to be clearly communicated to operators; a process for putting this decision into action needs to be formed.
	Safety goals need to be achieved.	Employees need to operate forklift equipment in a safe manner.	Employees need to learn the most common problems in forklift operation and actions to take if these problems occur.	Supervisors need to coach employees and provide feedback to them on safe driving techniques.
	Run time of equipment needs to be increased.	Operators need to follow preventive maintenance procedures for the equipment they operate.	Operators need to learn how to discriminate between normal equipment noises and noises that indicate a potential problem.	The tools required to do preventive maintenance need to be provided.
Service Organization	Customer satisfaction needs to be increased.	Customer service representatives (CSRs) need to take ownership for resolving any customer problem that comes to their attention.	CSRs need to learn who to contact within the organization for customer problems that may be outside their personal responsibility.	Incentives and rewards need to be provided for taking time to work with a customer to resolve problems.
	Sales revenue needs to be increased.	Sales representatives need to position the benefits of a product against the specific needs of the customer.	Sales representatives need to learn how to ask need-based questions by customers.	Sales representatives need to be given coaching and feedback by their manager following a meeting with a prospect.
	Response time needs to be reduced.	Clerks need to enter requests for service into the data file in an accurate manner.	Clerks need to learn how to see, recall, and enter nine-digit account numbers without making transposition or other errors.	An on-screen service request form needs to be developed and formatted to facilitate ease of input and reduce the number of keystrokes.

Will there be a training course? If so, what will be its learning
objectives? Does the work environment need to be modified? If
so, what specifically must be done?

Visually, these four types of needs nest together like boxes
in a box. Figure 2.1 illustrates the relationship between the four
types of needs. Business needs are the largest box. They are the
raison d'être of an organization. Training and work environment needs are linked to business needs through the performance needs box. In focusing on performance, it is critical to
identify both training and work environment needs. Training
needs represent areas where performers lack the skill or knowledge to perform satisfactorily. Work environment needs represent the aspects of the system that must be modified to ensure
that the needed performance is adequately supported.

In a traditional training environment, training needs are
identified; affirming any of the other needs is optional. An example from our consulting practice may illustrate this. Recently,
a manager in an organization phoned to ask if we would measure the impact of a diversity training program that the organization had conducted. It seems that management had determined

**Figure 2.1. Relationship of Business,
Performance, Training, and Work Environment Needs.**

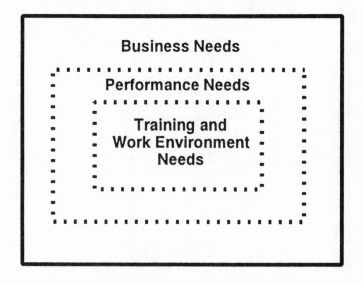

some time earlier that a business need existed in the area of diversity. Even though the organization was actively recruiting people of diverse backgrounds and making efforts to mentor and support them early in their careers, too many of these individuals were leaving the organization within twelve to eighteen months of hire. The primary reason given was that the environment in which they worked was perceived to be hostile; their diversity was viewed as a disadvantage.

The management response had been to conduct a training program for all five thousand employees in the area of diversity. Now management wanted to measure the program for its impact. Unfortunately, as Figure 2.2 illustrates, although the training and business needs had been identified, no attempt had been made to identify the *performance* or *work environment* needs. As a result, the manager could not answer the question: "What do you expect people to be doing differently on the job?" Unfortunately for this manager, a traditional training response to a business need had been used.

A Performance Consultant approach would have identified the performance requirements of managerial and nonmanage-

Figure 2.2. Traditional Training Response
to a Diversity Business Need.

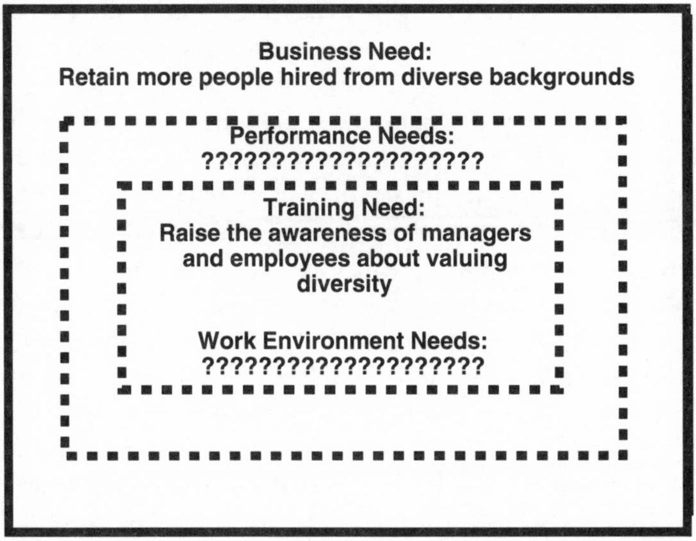

Business Need:
Retain more people hired from diverse backgrounds

Performance Needs:
????????????????????

Training Need:
**Raise the awareness of managers
and employees about valuing
diversity**

Work Environment Needs:
????????????????????

rial personnel. What decisions do they need to make? What actions do they need to take? What must be different in their day-to-day behavior if people of diverse backgrounds are to value working in the organization? And what actions, other than training, may be required if that performance is to be achieved (in other words, what are the work environment needs)? In this instance a tremendous investment (in excess of $300,000) had been made with virtually no resulting change.

The Two Kinds of Business Needs

Business needs focus on the operational goals and initiatives of the organization. There are two types of business needs: problems and opportunities.

Business problems define a gap between what should be occurring operationally and what is actually occurring at the present time. Examples would be excessive waste, low sales, high production costs, or reduced customer satisfaction ratings. Business problems exist when two criteria are met:

1. There is a deviation between what should be occurring operationally and what is occurring.

2. Someone in management feels "pain" about the deviation and is, therefore, motivated to address the problem.

An example we encountered some time ago illustrates how a deviation can be present with no business "pain." Dana Robinson called on the vice president of store operations for a retail chain. In the course of the meeting, the conversation turned toward the issue of employee turnover. It is known that in retail stores the position of retail clerk traditionally has a high turnover rate. The VP indicated that the current turnover in this position was approximately 70 percent a year. By only considering the deviation between an *assumed* goal and what was actually occurring, it would appear that this chain had a business problem. However, the VP mentioned this figure as a source of pride! In the past the turnover had been close to 100 percent, but through concerted efforts it had been reduced. The VP felt no "pain" about this number; other business issues were of greater concern to him.

Business opportunities focus on a future operational goal. No current problem needs to be fixed; instead, an opportunity needs to be optimized. Examples of opportunities occur when one organization acquires another; a return is expected with such a large investment. Or perhaps a company is bringing a product into the marketplace after much research and development; again, an opportunity can be maximized.

Business opportunities exist when the following two criteria are met:

1. Operationally defined goals exist that are expected to be met from the business opportunity.

2. Some members of management desire to maximize the gain from the opportunity. In essence, while business problems require pain, business opportunities leverage off perceived gain.

Before proceeding with this chapter, you may want to complete Exercise 2.1. The purpose of the exercise is to assess your skills in discriminating between the four kinds of needs we have been discussing: business, performance, training, and work environment needs.

Identifying Clients

If a Performance Consultant is to work successfully, he or she must consult to someone else. How do you identify that someone? "Look for the manager who has a Maalox moment when things go wrong," says one of our colleagues. "Look for someone who gives a damn," says another. More specifically, a client owns the business, performance, and work environment needs. This is the individual who has the most to gain or lose when these needs are addressed. The client also has the authority to make or implement the decisions and interventions associated with these needs. As we know, these decisions can concern train-

Exercise 2.1. | DISCRIMINATING BETWEEN BUSINESS, PERFORMANCE, TRAINING, AND WORK ENVIRONMENT NEEDS

Instructions:

1. Each of the following statements should be considered as coming from a manager who is requesting your service. The statements have been sent to you (by voice-mail, electronic mail, memo); therefore, you can only discriminate based upon the stated information. Do not make assumptions!

2. Each of the statements identifies one or a combination of the following needs:

BN = *Business need:* Defines what is required of the organization at an operational level.

PN = *Performance need:* Describes what people must do on the job.

TN = *Training need:* Describes what people must learn. (Hint: When someone requests a specific training program, that request is actually a training need. The individual wants people to *learn* what is in the program.)

WN = *Work environment need:* Describes a system or process within the work environment of the performer that is not adequately supporting the desired performance.

Identify the need or needs you believe are being described; then check your answers against those immediately following the exercise.

1. _____ *"I want our customer service people to become more customer-oriented. Could you conduct that workshop you have on identifying customer needs?"*

2. _____ *"I just looked through your catalog. That course on team effectiveness seems like just what our people could use. Call me so we can set up some time for you to conduct that course."*

3. _____ *"I saw this guy on 'Good Morning America' who wrote a book about customer service in our country*

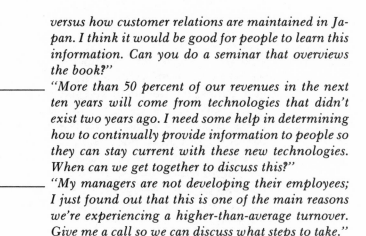

versus how customer relations are maintained in Japan. I think it would be good for people to learn this information. Can you do a seminar that overviews the book?"

4. _____ *"More than 50 percent of our revenues in the next ten years will come from technologies that didn't exist two years ago. I need some help in determining how to continually provide information to people so they can stay current with these new technologies. When can we get together to discuss this?"*

5. _____ *"My managers are not developing their employees; I just found out that this is one of the main reasons we're experiencing a higher-than-average turnover. Give me a call so we can discuss what steps to take."*

Answers

1. **PN/TN**   *Rationale:* The initial statement (wanting people to become more customer-oriented) describes what people must do on the job. Therefore, it is a *performance need*. In a conversation it will be important to identify the behaviors that comprise "customer orientation" in order to make the need more discrete. The individual continues by requesting a specific course ("Identifying Customer Needs"); this is a *training need*. In the mind of the requester, if people learn what is in the course, they will become more customer-oriented.

2. **TN**   *Rationale:* The identification of a course is shorthand for identification of a *training need*. By definition, the individual is indicating that people need to *learn* what is in the course. There is no statement indicating either what people must do on the job as a result of the course or what impact it will have upon operational goals. Therefore, it is only a *training need*.

3. **TN**   *Rationale:* While the requester discusses customer service, it is *not* in terms of what is or is not happening in the company or in the performance of employees. The comment is made in a conceptual manner, comparing customer relations in the United States with those in Japan. The requester would like people "to

learn this information"; therefore, this is only a *training need.*

4. **BN/WN**   *Rationale:* Revenues of a company are *the* critical business need; anything that holds potential for increasing those revenues definitely focuses on an operational measure. Therefore, the first sentence in the request refers to a *business need* (specifically, it is a business opportunity). The second sentence indicates that a new system must be formed that will provide needed information to people on a continual basis. This is an information *system;* as such, it is referring to a needed change in the *work environment* of the performers.

5. **BN/PN**   *Rationale:* Turnover of employees is a business problem (which means that it is a *business need*). By saying that managers are not developing employees, this individual is describing something managers are *not* doing on the job. Therefore, this part of the statement is identifying a *performance need.*

---

ing and/or the work environment. This individual can obtain the needed resources and will *make* things happen.

Frequently, this individual is not the person who calls. The person who actually calls is often someone we refer to as the contact. Many times the contact is a well-intentioned messenger. She or he may be the individual with authority over the training need but may not own the business and performance needs. The rationale is that if the individual is calling someone in the training function, it is for the purpose of meeting a training need; the contact may not be thinking about the bigger picture. This is when the Performance Consultant's expertise at raising awareness becomes critical.

The process of raising awareness is best accomplished through asking questions. In Chapter Nine, in-depth information is provided regarding management of an initial meeting with a contact when raising awareness is key. Here are three ways to determine whether the individual with whom you are speaking is a contact, a client, or part of a client team:

1. If the request comes as a training need, ask questions about the business and performance needs that are behind that request. The person may be a contact if he or she either cannot answer the questions or continues to mention other specific individuals as the people who do have this information.

    For example, suppose that someone calls to request that a course in customer relations skills be offered to service representatives. You could respond by asking questions such as "What have you observed that leads to the conclusion that a course in customer relations skills would be beneficial?" or "What, if any, actions have been taken already to improve relations between the representatives and our customers?" If the individual with whom you are talking lacks answers to these questions, she or he may be a contact rather than a client or a member of a client team.

2. Ask questions regarding the work environment and how it must support the performance and/or business needs. The person may be a contact if he or she cannot answer the questions or lacks the authority to take the actions that are being identified.

    For example, continuing with the same scenario regarding service representatives, perhaps you ask a question such as "Do these representatives have the authority to take the type of actions you want them to take?" If the individual with whom you are speaking either cannot answer that question or suggests that someone else would need to get involved if authority limits are to be modified, then that "someone else" is probably a client.

3. If, in general, the individual does not believe that she or he can make decisions regarding the project's scope and/or process, then the individual is probably a contact. In this instance, ask who *would* be able to make these decisions.

In today's organizations, it is doubtful that a client will be only one individual. We have found that the successful achievement of specific business needs requires the involvement of not only the owner of the problem but also others who can provide essential resources and who have something to gain from the project. Organizations are becoming less reliant on managerial authority to get things done; therefore, client teams may be composed of a variety of people. These could include any or all of the following:

- Senior managers or other key managers within a business unit
- Suppliers to the organization
- Customers to the organization
- Subject matter experts throughout the organization

   It is vital, however, that the client team include:

- The owner of the business and performance needs
- Someone who is within the chain of command of the performer group
- The individual who must legitimize the project to others (particularly the performers)

Typically, we have found that some or all of the members of the client team are two or more levels above the performer group. Rarely are direct managers of performers the client because many of the decisions that need to be made go beyond the scope of these individuals.

Identifying Business Needs: The Reactive Approach

Business needs can be identified in two ways: reactively and proactively. In the reactive approach we respond (react) to a request for help; in the proactive approach we initiate contact for the purpose of identifying needs before they come to us. Each of these will be discussed in this chapter; however, it has been our experience that the majority of the time, Performance Consultants operate in a reactive manner, so we will begin there.

   In the reactive approach we typically are brought into the

picture when we receive a request to meet a training need, for example, "I'd like you to conduct that Effective Negotiation course for my people" or "When is the next time you are running the Safety Awareness program?"

In these situations, you are beginning with a training need; the challenge is to move out to other "boxes" and identify other needs. Figure 2.3 illustrates how these three boxes relate to each other in a reactive approach. This "movement out" will be accomplished through a questioning process. If you do not ask the right questions in the initial meeting, it is probable that you will remain within the training needs box (and operate in a traditional training manner).

Two steps must be completed in order to identify the other types of needs.

1. Identify the needs that have been provided in the initial request. A rule of thumb is to begin asking questions by focusing on the highest-level need you have been provided.

Figure 2.3. Identifying Business Needs Reactively.

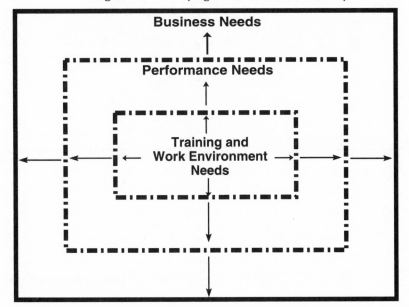

2.   Prepare questions to ask in an initial meeting that will ensure a focus on performance, business, and work environment needs.

Let's return to the scenario that began this chapter to illustrate what could be done by responding reactively to a request for service. In this scenario, the production manager said that (1) the communication between the day and night shifts during changeover was poor (performance need); (2) day and night supervisors weren't giving adequate information to those who were coming on shift and there appeared to be hostility between the two shifts (performance need); and (3) the manager wanted to talk about a training program that could increase communication and build more of a team (training need).

Here we have been provided both performance and training needs as the manager perceives them. The highest-level need we have been provided is that of performance. Therefore, we will begin by focusing on those needs. We might consider asking the following questions, which are designed to identify both the performance need and work environment conditions:

1.   You indicated that complete and accurate information is not being communicated at shift turnover. Could you provide me with more specifics regarding:

   ■   What type of information is incomplete?

   ■   What is an example of inaccurate information?

   ■   Is this occurring for all supervisors and production lines or only certain ones?

   ■   Was this always a problem or is it a recent change?

   ■   Why do you think this is happening?

2.   You indicated that there appears to be hostility between the shifts.

- What have you observed people saying or doing that has led to this conclusion?

- Is this occurring for all production lines or only certain ones?

- Is this a recent change or has it been occurring for some time?

- Why do you think this is happening?

3. What is the impact on your operation because information is not completely and accurately reported and because there is some hostility between the lines? How is this situation affecting the ability of your production lines to meet their goals? (*Note:* This question moves you into the business needs box.)

4. You indicated that you could use us to provide a training program in the areas of communication and team building. If we did that and people did learn techniques in these areas, do you feel that would be sufficient to resolve the problem? Or would other actions be required in addition to such a program? (*Note:* This line of questioning is designed to expand the awareness of the manager that training may be insufficient to resolve a performance problem; it moves directly into identification of work environment needs. As Performance Consultants, we want to do all we can to encourage our clients to address *all* the issues that affect performance. Additional techniques for responding reactively to requests for training are provided in Chapter Nine.)

Identifying Business Needs: The Proactive Approach

Figure 2.4 illustrates the proactive approach to business needs. One of the best ways we know of to proactively identify business needs is to make an appointment to meet with someone for the express purpose of discussing his or her business, performance,

Figure 2.4. Proactive Identification of Business Needs.

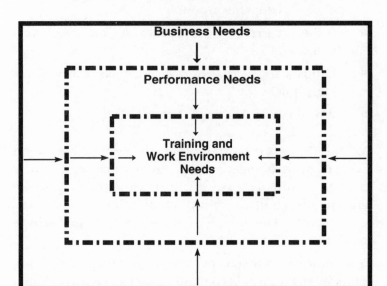

and work environment needs. The purpose is *not* to discuss this individual's training needs; in fact, the word *training* may never be mentioned. Those needs, should they exist, will be identified further into the working partnership. When conducting this type of meeting, you are in the role of Performance Consultant; the Traditional Trainer hat is removed. You are in the meeting to determine what human performance issues may exist that could affect the unit's, department's, or company's ability to achieve business goals. In essence you are "qualifying" this person either into or out of the possibility of working with you in your role as a Performance Consultant.

Performance Consulting Tool 1 is an interview guide that can be used when conducting this type of conversation with managers or others who have business and performance needs. This guide provides questions to ask as well as the reasons why those questions are important. You may need to customize this tool to your specific situation; it is designed only as a guide.

Performance Consulting Tool 1

Sample Interview Guide:
Proactively Identifying Business and Performance Needs

Purposes of the Interview

As a result of information obtained in this interview, you will be able to answer the following questions:

1. What are the major business needs facing this individual now and in the next two to three years?

2. What implications do these business needs have for the performance requirements of key positions within this individual's unit or area of responsibility?

3. What forces and factors, both within and outside the control of the individual, will challenge the accomplishment of business and performance goals?

As a result of this discussion, you and the individual will be able to determine what, if any, assistance you can provide to support the individual in meeting her or his business, performance, and work environment needs.

Prior to the Interview

Make an appointment with the individual. Indicate the following:

1. You want to learn more about the business goals and challenges of various individuals within the organization.

2. You are setting up an appointment with this individual for the purpose of discussing his or her business goals and challenges.

3. The interview will require approximately one hour.

Introductory Comments

Include the following items in the introductory comments:

1. The reason and purposes for the interview

2.   How long the interview will take

3.   How you will be using the information

> Rationale: *It is important for the individual to understand why you are initiating this conversation. A key message to communicate is that you want to ensure that the work you do is directly linked to the business goals and needs of the organization; the individual can provide important information about those business goals. Additionally, indicate that this individual is a (prospective) client for your services and you want to ensure that you are meeting her or his needs.*

Questions Regarding Current Business Goals

Include the following questions:

1.   What are the business goals for (select one) your group, unit, or department in the next year?

2.   What measurements will you use to determine if the goals are achieved?

3.   What are the forces *outside your control* that will make accomplishment of these goals difficult or challenging? (*Note:* You may want to provide an example such as changes in the economy or governmental regulations.)

4.   What forces *outside your control* will help in accomplishing these goals?

5.   What are the forces *within your control* that will make accomplishment of these goals more difficult? (*Note:* You may want to provide examples such as obsolete manufacturing equipment or a reward system that does not encourage people to focus on the business goal that was identified.)

6.   What forces *within your control* will help in accomplishing these goals?

> Rationale: *The most relevant business goals are those that must be achieved and supported right now; therefore, the in-*

terview begins by discussing the most current business needs. Remember, these are the operational goals for the unit, department, or group. It is important to know what should be occurring operationally and how it will be measured. You also want to identify any forces or factors that may challenge the accomplishment of these goals.

Frequently, we are asked why it is important for a Performance Consultant to know what forces exist outside of the organization. After all, no one can do anything to change them. Perhaps the following example will illustrate why this type of information is vital.

Prior to 1984, AT&T was the only long-distance telephone service available in the United States. If people needed this type of service, they telephoned AT&T to request it. The AT&T employee who answered the phone needed to have skills in taking orders to ensure that all information was recorded accurately.

In 1984, AT&T was divested under orders of the U.S. government. This was certainly an external force that AT&T could not control. However, with divestiture came many competitors—MCI and Sprint, just to name a few. Now choices were available to people in the United States who wanted long-distance telephone service. If the AT&T employee who answered the telephone still performed as an order taker instead of as a salesperson, it is unlikely that AT&T could have achieved their business plan. The employee had to demonstrate the skills of asking questions, overcoming objections, and providing benefits.

The point of this example is that forces external to the organization will have implications for the performance requirements of people in the organization. If we are to fulfill our responsibilities as Performance Consultants, we must have knowledge of those forces and work with our clients to identify the implications for employees within the business.

Questions Regarding Future Business Goals

Ask the following questions concerning future business goals:

1. Three years from now, what will have been achieved for your unit, department, or group? What business goals will have been met?

2. What measurements will be used to determine if these goals have been achieved?

3. You have already described several forces, outside of your control, which will challenge or help you to meet your immediate goals. Are there any additional external forces that will have an impact on these longer-term goals?

4. What about any additional factors—either positive or negative—within your control other than those you have already mentioned?

> Rationale: *This individual has been discussing current business goals. Many of the actions needed to achieve these goals may already be defined and under way. This provides limited opportunities to identify a potential need for support. By asking questions about the future (for example, two, three, or four years from now), we are moving into an area where actions may yet need to be defined and taken; this is fertile ground in which to identify potential needs in our role as Performance Consultants. Again, we ask business-based questions that include a focus on what is needed and the forces and factors that will challenge the accomplishment of that goal.*

Questions Regarding
Identification of Performance Implications

Select from the following list (or from your own list) the performer groups that are relevant to the individual who is being interviewed. Choose from among these questions:

1. What type of performance do you believe will be needed

by the people in your unit, department, or group if these business goals are to be realized?

2. What must *supervisors and managers* do differently or better in the future? How prepared do you believe they are to perform in this manner?

3. What must *operators* do differently or better?

4. What must *sales personnel* do differently or better?

5. What must *customer service personnel* do differently or better?

6. What must *professional individual contributors* (like engineers or accountants) do differently or better?

7. What must *staff support groups* (like the human resources or legal departments) do differently or better?

Rationale: *When you begin to ask these questions, you are making the transition into the performance needs box; you will also be potentially identifying training and work environment needs that must be addressed. As a Performance Consultant, your ability to contribute to business goals is dependent upon your ability to identify human performance problems and work with managers and others to resolve them, so these questions are critical in order to potentially identify opportunities where you may be of support.*

Most people with whom you will have this type of discussion will not describe performance requirements in specific or discrete terms. Rather, they will indicate needs by making statements like these:

■ *"We need to move toward more autonomous working teams. Operators must be less dependent upon supervision and management to make all the decisions."*

(Translation: *This manager is seeking an organization in which people are empowered; this has implications for the performance of managers* and *employees.*)

■ *"We need to ensure that our front-line people can take*

actions that will resolve customer problems at that first point of contact."

(Translation: *This individual is identifying the implications for the performance of customer service personnel.*)

■   *"Our engineers must stay current with the latest technology in our area so we can capitalize on it."*

(Translation: *Both access to information and the skill of remaining current become work environment and performance issues for this person.*)

Statements to Make Before Closing the Interview

At this point in the interview, you need to determine if you could provide assistance in any or all of the following areas:

1.   Would it be beneficial to assist the individual in identifying the performance requirements of a particular job group? Perhaps he or she is uncertain what people need to do better or differently now or in the future; this is something you could identify in your role as a Performance Consultant. Chapters Five and Six of this book will assist you in this effort.

2.   Would it be helpful to determine the specific performance gaps for a particular group of employees? Where are they prepared and ready to perform as required so that business needs can be met? Where are they not ready? This is also information that you can obtain and provide as a Performance Consultant. Information in Chapter Seven will be helpful.

3.   Would it be of benefit if you determined the specific training and work environment needs for people in the individual's area and the priority of those needs so that business goals can be achieved? Chapters Seven and Eight will prove helpful.

Summing Up the Information

Next, summarize the conclusions you have drawn. Make the following statements:

1. You have provided me with a great deal of information. It appears that your major business initiatives focus on (*summarize what the individual has indicated*).

2. You have indicated that there are some forces outside your control that will make the accomplishment of these goals more difficult; these are forces such as (*identify two or three forces mentioned by the individual*).

3. You have also indicated that there are conditions within the organization that could become obstacles to the achievement of your business goals, conditions such as (*identify two or three internal obstacles that were identified*).

4. Finally, you have indicated that these goals do have implications for the performance of (*indicate the group or groups of performers who were discussed*).

Option 1:

Ask one or a combination of the following questions if you believe there may be an opportunity to provide assistance:

1. I wonder if there is a way in which I or my staff could be of assistance to you. For example, would it be helpful if we could identify the performance requirements for the position of _____ ? These would be the performance results that people in the position must accomplish if your business goals are to be achieved.

2. Would it be of help if I or my staff could identify the specific performance gaps that exist for people in the position of _____ ? This information would specifically indicate where your people are able to perform as required to meet the business goals and where they are not. It would also provide information on the causes of the performance gaps.

3. Would it be of benefit if I or my staff could determine the specific training and other needs for people in the position of _____ so that you could prioritize the actions

that may be required if these employees are to successfully support your business goals?"

Option: 2

Make the following statement if you believe there is no immediate need for assistance:

I want to thank you for your time and thoughts. This information will be invaluable in assisting me and my staff in ensuring that the programs and services we offer are directly linked to the current and future business goals of the organization.

> Rationale: *This is when you make a judgment about whether or not to qualify this individual as someone with whom you can consult in the area of performance. You must make this judgment at the time, based upon the information provided in the interview. But here are some "messages" to look for; if they occur, then the individual would likely benefit from additional support from you:*
>
> 1. *The individual indicates uncertainty as to what performance is required from certain groups of people. Perhaps she or he responded to your question about performance with the remark, "That is a good question . . . I'm not sure."*
> 2. *The individual indicated frustration with the fact that he or she knows what type of performance is required but doesn't know what to do to make it a reality.*
> 3. *The individual tells you that she or he would like you to provide some training for a particular group of people. Caution: Do not agree to the training need that has been identified but encourage the individual to provide you with some time to gather additional information in order to ensure that the training need is the correct and only action required to change performance. Reflect back on*

questions that were raised but for which information was lacking. Acknowledge the value of obtaining relevant information before moving ahead with any actions.

What is important to remember throughout this interview is that you are identifying business, performance, and work environment needs, not training needs. It has been our experience that if the Performance Consultant meets with several different people, some people will have a need to be addressed and others will not. You only require a couple of needs to stay very busy and to begin moving from traditional training to performance consulting.

Summary

1. Performance Consultants are responsible for identifying four kinds of needs: business, performance, training, and work environment needs.

2. Performance Consultants work with clients—the individuals who own the business, performance, and work environment needs.

3. Business needs can be identified reactively and proactively; Performance Consultants require skills in both approaches.

PART TWO

DESIGNING AND USING PERFORMANCE RELATIONSHIP MAPS

Performance Consultants are continually seeking information. This can be done both formally, through performance assessments, and informally, over lunch with a manager. But information must be obtained within the framework of a plan. Recall the Cheshire-Cat in *Alice's Adventures in Wonderland,* who indicated to Alice that if she didn't care where she wanted to go, it didn't matter which way she went. Performance Consultants need to know where they are headed as they ask questions, targeting each question like a laser beam to help clarify the situation.

The plan used by Performance Consultants should be based upon a model or conceptual framework. For us, this model is the *performance relationship map.* This map is something we have developed and used over the past six years; it serves three purposes:

1. It provides the data gatherer (in our case, the Performance Consultant) with guidance in determining what information is important to obtain (and what information may be unnecessary).

2.   It alerts us when we are missing data in one area—for example, information about what successful performers do.

3.   It acts as a vehicle for displaying information to management. The map specifically illustrates the interrelationship between business, performance, training, and work environment needs. This is critical because managers are most likely to support actions when they understand that these actions will affect the achievement of business goals in a positive manner.

We have been using the map for the past six years; we know it works. It has been adopted by several hundred individuals with whom we have had the opportunity to work. In Chapter Three we explain the map and the various elements in it. Because the focus of this part of the book is on designing and implementing *formal* needs assessments, the remaining chapters in this part provide techniques and tools for that type of assessment.

3

Mapping the Components of Performance

Mark Fenton, a training director, was presenting recommendations for a middle management training program to the executive committee. Mark had surveyed managers and their bosses to find out what training they felt was needed. In addition, he had reviewed the most current literature regarding middle management training.

His recommendation was that middle managers participate in leadership training. The proposed training would provide managers with the skill and knowledge to:

- Develop and communicate vision and mission statements
- Empower direct reports to accept more accountability
- Coach employees in maximizing their potential
- Become a positive model of leadership
- Provide positive and corrective feedback

The executive vice president for operations asked, "Why are you recommending these leadership skills for our organization? In what way will they help us meet our business objectives?"

Mark responded by saying, "The current literature indicates that management needs to move from managing people to leading people using these five principles."

The executive VP asked, "But how do we know it's right for *us*? How do we know it will help us be more effective?"

Mark answered, "My information shows that managers in the more successful organizations use these leadership skills." This did not satisfy the vice president, who still wanted to know, "Is it right for us?"

Training Recommendations Versus Performance Recommendations

Let's examine what Mark did as he developed his training recommendations. At the same time, let's look at what he might have done if he had been in a performance consulting mode.

First, Mark provided the executive committee with a recommendation for middle management training. He was asking them to support training efforts that were based on a review of the literature and on a survey asking what managers wanted to learn. What was lacking in his recommendation was evidence that these leadership behaviors were linked to the business and performance needs of this specific organization. When the executive VP asked how the organization would benefit from this effort, Mark was unable to answer.

If Mark had been using a performance consulting approach, he would first have identified the organization's business needs by interviewing key managers, including members of the executive committee, and would have identified the performance required of middle managers if the organization were to achieve its business goals. The training recommendations for middle managers would then have been based upon the current and future business and performance needs of the organization. The training would have been designed to close the gap between managers' current performance and the performance required of them if business goals were to be met. The training recommendations might have been identical to what Mark proposed. What would have been different was that Mark could have illustrated the linkage between the organization's business needs and his training recommendations.

Second, Mark presented a training recommendation for middle managers but did not involve the executive committee in determining the content of that training. The executive committee appeared to have two choices: to either approve or not approve training.

If Mark had been operating as a Performance Consultant, he would have presented the data on business and performance needs in a manner that would have enabled the executive committee to see the relationship between what they wanted to accomplish—business needs—and the performance of middle managers. They would have seen gaps between what middle managers should be doing in the future and what they were currently doing. Using this information, they could have participated with Mark in making decisions regarding the type of training that was needed. In essence, a more collaborative style would have been used.

Third, Mark presented a training solution, not a performance solution. He did not present data that would show the degree to which the work environment was supportive of the recommended leadership behavior. Mark's plan operated under the assumption that training alone was sufficient to change performance. If Mark had been in the Performance Consultant role, he would have collected work environment data and provided them to the executive committee as well. This information would have enabled the committee to discuss what work environment actions were needed to ensure that the leadership skills learned during the training could be used on the job for an extended period of time.

The Performance Relationship Map

We know that we can best influence management when we can illustrate how actions being proposed will have a positive effect on the business. To do this we must be able to illustrate the interrelationship between business goals, performance requirements, training, and work environment needs. What performance is needed if the business goals are to be realized? What is the current capability of individuals to demonstrate this required performance? And what training and work environment actions will be needed to change performance? These are the types of questions we need to address with management.

For the past several years, we have been using the performance relationship map as a vehicle for helping both Performance Consultants and clients to understand the complex inter-relationships of human performance. This map is illustrated in Figure 3.1 and will be examined in greater detail in this chapter; ways to use the map will be discussed in Chapters Four through Eight.

A specific business need is written at the top of the map (for example, "increase reliability" or "improve profits"). The map then indicates that information is required under box 1 (SHOULD operational results). For this box the specific business goals regarding the business need will be noted—for example, How much waste is acceptable? How much profit is desired?

For box 2, the map requires information regarding the type of performance that people SHOULD demonstrate if the desired operational results are to be realized. If the organization wants to increase profits, what must people do to make that happen? If product reliability is to be increased, how will people have to perform?

For box 3, we identify the current performance (or the IS) of people as compared to the desired performance, or SHOULD, as noted in box 2. What kinds of gaps exist? Of course, it is this performance that yields the current operational results, or IS, in box 4.

Under box 5 we identify the various factors and forces that impact upon the desired performance. EXTERNAL CAUSES are factors that are outside the control of a client team yet affect the achievement of operational results and performance requirements. For example, if the economy is in a recession, it impacts upon an organization's ability to achieve its revenue and profitability goals. Also, corporate headquarters can make a policy decision that affects the performance of a plant; for a plant manager, this would be an external factor.

Figure 3.1. Performance Relationship Map.

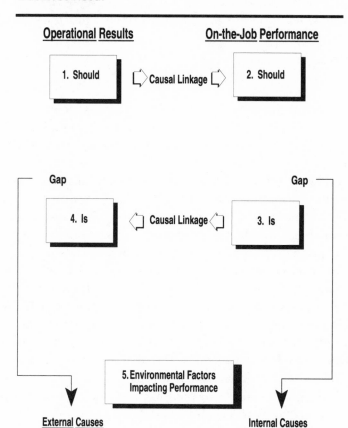

Business Need:

INTERNAL CAUSES are factors that are within the control of a client team and that impact upon achievement of operational and performance goals. If employees lack the skill and knowledge to do what is required of them on the job, this will be a reason for their nonperformance. This cause can be addressed through training and development. If, however, employees lack any incentive or reward to do what is being asked of them, this will also be a reason for their nonperformance. However, it cannot be addressed through training actions; a client team will need to redesign the incentive system.

We have provided a general description of each box in the map. Now let's examine how the performance relationship map was used in a real situation.

Quik-Data Division

We worked with a division of an information systems company that, for the sake of this example, we will call Quik-Data. The company is a global, multidivisional organization; the division with which we worked was based in North America and sold computers and peripheral equipment to North American business and governmental agencies. When we were called in to consult with the training manager, top management had already examined the problem and had made some strategic decisions. The shaded portion of Figure 3.2 shows the amount of analysis that had been completed when we first started to work with Quik-Data.

Examination of the operational results for the past year indicated that Quik-Data was not achieving its goal of $26 million in sales with a 13 percent gross margin. Instead, for the year just completed, sales had been $20 million with a gross margin of 8 percent. The bottom line was that the division was not meeting its goals, and management was concerned.

During the time we worked with this division, the North American economy was healthy, and the computer and information systems market was experiencing moderate growth. However, competition was fierce, and there was heavy downward price pressure on organizations selling business equipment such as computers and photocopiers.

Management's business need was to increase both revenue and gross margin. As top management examined the marketplace, they determined that they needed to replace the current sales strategy of selling computers and other equipment as stand-alone components or "boxes." Research conducted with the organization's customers indicated that the "selling-a-box" approach was not valued. Customers were seeking suppliers who could understand their business needs and information flow

**Figure 3.2. Business Need and Operational Results
for a Quik-Data Division.**

Business Need: Increase Sales and Profits

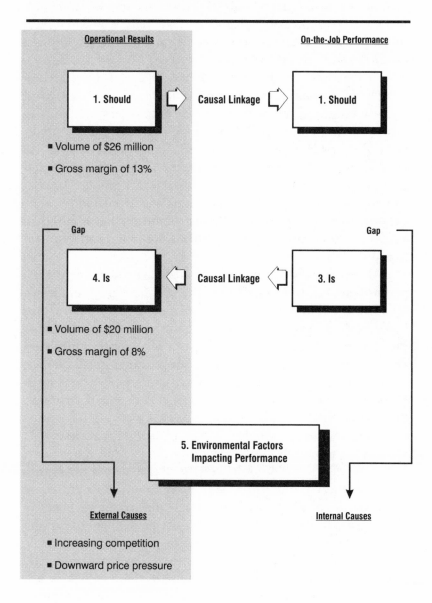

problems. They wanted to work with suppliers who would then resolve these problems and meet future requirements through technology. The customers clearly indicated that they would view a company that could take this business-solutions approach as a supplier of choice. Quik-Data market research indicated that their more successful competitors were moving to a business-solutions sales strategy.

A decision was made to adopt a business-solutions approach. This meant that sales representatives would have to call on customers and prospective customers to determine their information processing problems as well as their future needs. Once the problems were determined, the sales representatives would work with Quik-Data engineers to develop a new and improved system for information flow and processing. This system (the solution) would be presented to the customers. The customers would then be purchasing a solution that would consist not only of components but also of installation and technical support.

We were asked by the training manager to help define the performance and training needs of the sales force in order for this sales strategy to be successful. Certainly, other performers within Quik-Data would need additional training and job restructuring; this marketing strategy would impact upon technical service personnel, buyers, engineering support personnel, marketing personnel, sales managers, and customer service personnel. However, the project that directly involved us focused only on the sales force.

Our first task was to determine what successful salespeople actually *do* when selling business solutions within a high-tech environment. It would not be very helpful to say to a salesperson, "Beginning tomorrow, you need to utilize a business-solutions approach to selling." Also, how could we identify training needs before we identified what people had to do (the performance needs)? This is where we began our work.

Fortunately, the parent organization already had two divisions in other areas that were using a business-solutions approach. Our task was to study what the successful salespeople in those divisions were doing and to determine how their performance related to the situation in Quik-Data. In addition, our research included a review of the current literature to determine what techniques others, outside of Quik-Data, did to successfully use a business-solutions approach. In essence, we were identifying the specific on-the-job behaviors required of sales personnel if they were to demonstrate a business-solutions approach to selling.

Figure 3.3 shows the data we collected in our analysis of the performance of successful salespeople. The major new requirement was that the sales force must move from short-cycle to long-cycle sales techniques.

Another key performance requirement was that sales personnel had to make contact with the various end users within the organization—the people who had the information flow problems or who had identified future requirements. This means that the salesperson would have to make contact and form relationships with the heads of the information systems, marketing, research, and operations departments as well as with the purchasing agent.

Once the sales force had obtained the required information from several managers, they would need to use that information to develop (with their engineers) a solution to the client's situation. This would then lead to a presentation by the salesperson to the key managers within the customer's organization. In this presentation the salesperson would describe the situation and the proposed solutions.

Once we had collected this information about what salespeople should be doing, we met with top management to present our findings, which they accepted with minor adjustments. The next step was to determine what the sales force was currently doing so that we could define the performance gap.

Figure 3.4 shows the performance relationship map with actual (IS) performance highlighted compared to the SHOULD performance. As noted, the sales force was using short-cycle sales techniques. The figure shows that the sales force typically formed relationships only with the manager of information systems and/or the purchasing agent; they did not make contact with any of the end users within the organization. They also

Figure 3.3. On-the-Job Performance Requirements for Sales Personnel for a Quik-Data Division.

Business Need: Increase Sales and Profits

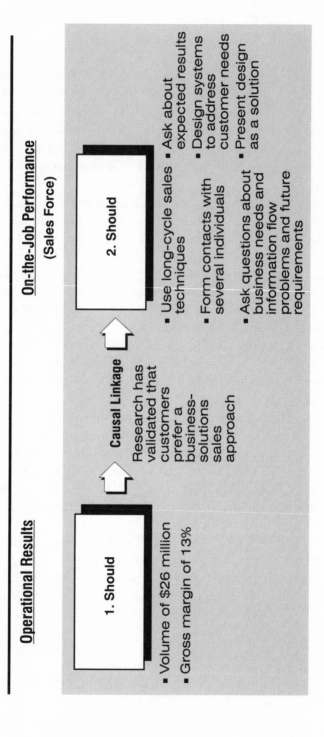

Operational Results

1. Should

- Volume of $26 million
- Gross margin of 13%

Causal Linkage

Research has validated that customers prefer a business-solutions sales approach

On-the-Job Performance

(Sales Force)

2. Should

- Use long-cycle sales techniques
- Form contacts with several individuals
- Ask questions about business needs and information flow problems and future requirements
- Ask about expected results
- Design systems to address customer needs
- Present design as a solution

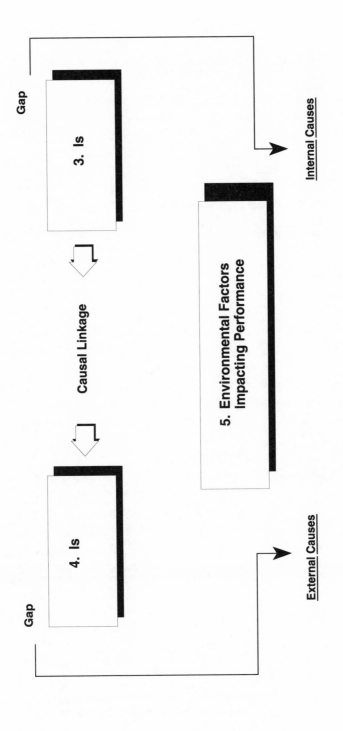

**Figure 3.4. Performance Gap of Sales Personnel
for a Quik-Data Division.**

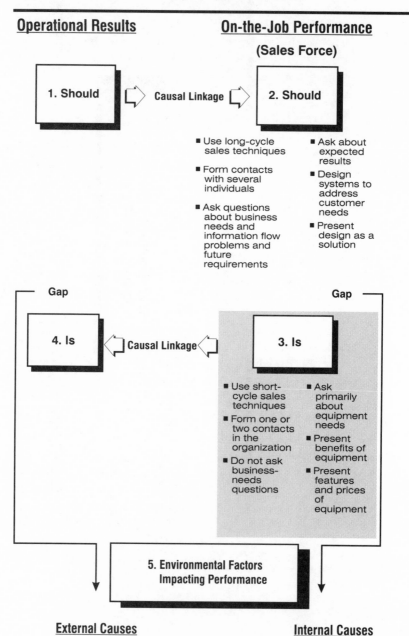

Business Need: Increase Sales and Profits

Operational Results

On-the-Job Performance
(Sales Force)

1. Should   ⇨ Causal Linkage ⇨   2. Should

- Use long-cycle sales techniques
- Form contacts with several individuals
- Ask questions about business needs and information flow problems and future requirements

- Ask about expected results
- Design systems to address customer needs
- Present design as a solution

Gap   Gap

4. Is   ⇦ Causal Linkage ⇦   3. Is

- Use short-cycle sales techniques
- Form one or two contacts in the organization
- Do not ask business-needs questions

- Ask primarily about equipment needs
- Present benefits of equipment
- Present features and prices of equipment

**5. Environmental Factors
Impacting Performance**

External Causes

Internal Causes

primarily asked questions about what equipment the customer required rather than about current information flow problems or future information flow requirements. Frequently, salespeople would also call on a customer to inform him or her about new equipment (the "latest gizmo," as one customer called it); again, absent from the conversation was a focus on the customer's business requirements concerning information flow. Instead, presentations made to the customer focused on equipment capabilities. Clearly, there was a gap between the performance that customers said they wanted and the performance currently in evidence.

We had a good description of the performance gap—the difference between what salespeople should be doing in the future and what they were currently doing. Now the question was "Can the performance gap be closed through training programs alone or will other actions be required?" As you may suspect, we found that there were multiple causes for the performance gap; therefore, multiple actions would be needed.

Figure 3.5 lists causes for the performance gap. Certainly, the sales force did lack skill in long-cycle sales techniques, including the skill to ask business-needs questions that related to the information flow and processing needs within the prospective customer's organization. Training would be needed. But training by itself would be insufficient because several other work environment factors were also identified. First of all, sales personnel were unaware that their current sales strategy was ineffective and would no longer be supported. Their management would need to provide information as to why a change was necessary and what that change would be.

A second factor was that the new sales strategy would require sales personnel to become involved in more technically complex sales. In the past, the salespeople discussed equipment, something with which they were very familiar. Now they needed to learn more about the customers' information flow needs in order to develop a systems solution. The solution might involve equipment sold by other company divisions with which the salesperson was unfamiliar. This type of systems design required the expertise of engineers. Currently, there was no such group

Figure 3.5. Work Environment Factors
Affecting Performance of Sales Personnel for a Quik-Data Division.

Business Need: Increase Sales and Profits

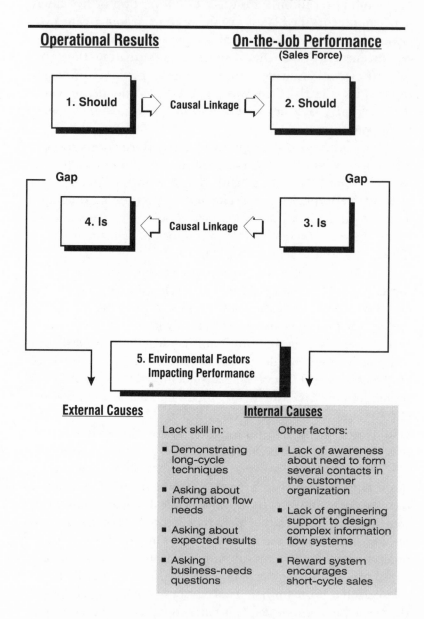

Operational Results

On-the-Job Performance
(Sales Force)

1. Should → Causal Linkage → 2. Should

Gap

4. Is ← Causal Linkage ← 3. Is

Gap

5. Environmental Factors
Impacting Performance

External Causes

Internal Causes

Lack skill in:

- Demonstrating long-cycle techniques
- Asking about information flow needs
- Asking about expected results
- Asking business-needs questions

Other factors:

- Lack of awareness about need to form several contacts in the customer organization
- Lack of engineering support to design complex information flow systems
- Reward system encourages short-cycle sales

to support the sales force. Therefore, the management of the division formed a group to support the sales force by designing the new information systems for the customers.

Finally, the reward system presented a problem. Salespeople were compensated through a base and commission; 40 percent of their total salary consisted of commissions. The new solution-oriented sales approach would require a sales cycle of approximately seven months. The current "sell-a-box" approach had a sales cycle of six to eight weeks. Thus, if the sales force moved aggressively toward the solution-oriented approach, there would be a period of time when their commissions would be reduced, while they were filling their pipeline with solution-oriented prospects. Without any change in the compensation system, the salespeople would be motivated to continue to sell in the traditional manner. When faced with this dilemma, management decided to guarantee, for the next six months, commissions equal to those earned by the salespeople in the previous six months. This would enable the salespeople to develop solution-oriented prospects during the transition period when their actual sales would decrease, without threatening their personal income.

Figure 3.6 illustrates all the information obtained for this Quik-Data division. The performance relationship map not only provided a template on which to collect data but also was a vehicle for displaying to management the interrelationships between business needs, performance requirements, and training and nontraining actions. In this manner, senior managers could clearly determine and support *all* the actions required if profits and revenue were to increase.

Components of Performance Relationship Maps

We have discussed in depth one situation in which we used the performance relationship map. Figure 3.7 provides a general description for each part of the map. Let's discuss each of these components once again, this time providing more information regarding what information is needed and how it is obtained.

Figure 3.6. Performance Relationship Map for a Quik-Data Division.

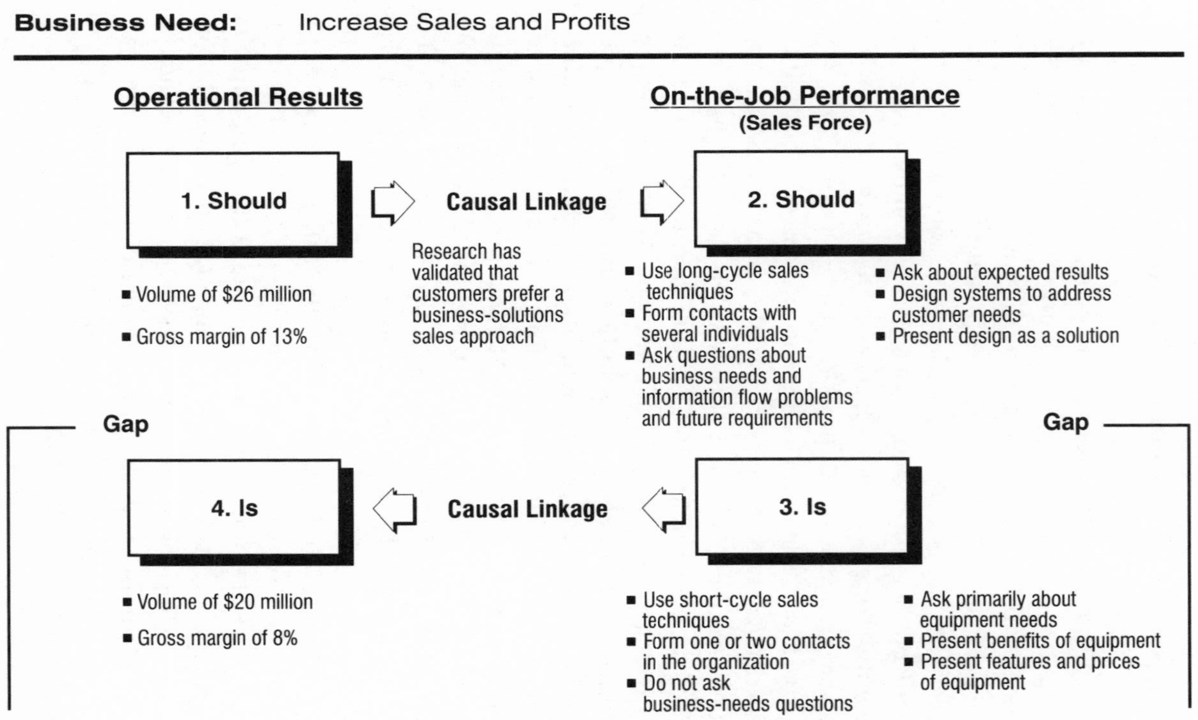

Business Need: Increase Sales and Profits

Operational Results

1. Should

- Volume of $26 million
- Gross margin of 13%

Causal Linkage

Research has validated that customers prefer a business-solutions sales approach

4. Is

- Volume of $20 million
- Gross margin of 8%

Gap

On-the-Job Performance
(Sales Force)

2. Should

- Use long-cycle sales techniques
- Form contacts with several individuals
- Ask questions about business needs and information flow problems and future requirements
- Ask about expected results
- Design systems to address customer needs
- Present design as a solution

Causal Linkage

3. Is

- Use short-cycle sales techniques
- Form one or two contacts in the organization
- Do not ask business-needs questions
- Ask primarily about equipment needs
- Present benefits of equipment
- Present features and prices of equipment

Gap

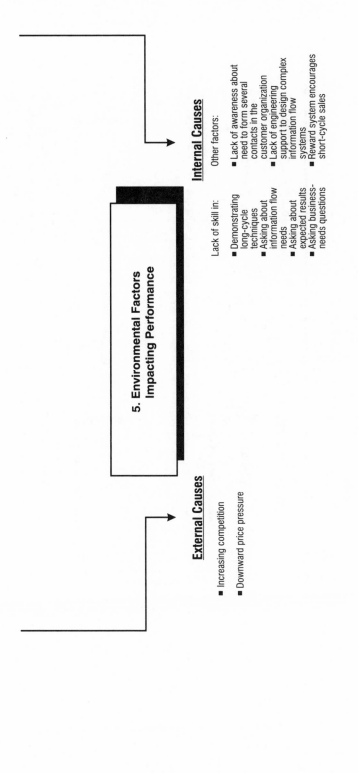

5. Environmental Factors Impacting Performance

External Causes

- Increasing competition
- Downward price pressure

Internal Causes

Lack of skill in:

- Demonstrating long-cycle techniques
- Asking about information flow needs
- Asking about expected results
- Asking business-needs questions

Other factors:

- Lack of awareness about need to form several contacts in the customer organization
- Lack of engineering support to design complex information flow systems
- Reward system encourages short-cycle sales

Figure 3.7. Performance Relationship Map.

Business Need:

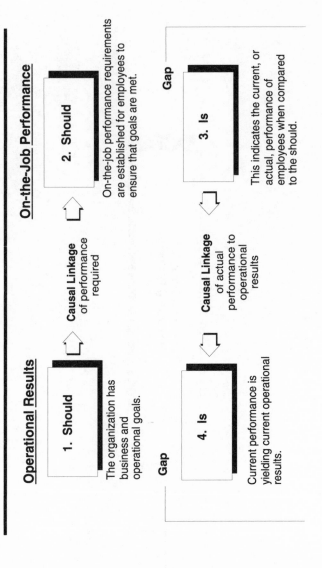

Operational Results

1. Should

The organization has business and operational goals.

Causal Linkage of performance required

On-the-Job Performance

2. Should

On-the-job performance requirements are established for employees to ensure that goals are met.

Causal Linkage of actual performance to operational results

3. Is

This indicates the current, or actual, performance of employees when compared to the should.

Gap

4. Is

Current performance is yielding current operational results.

Gap

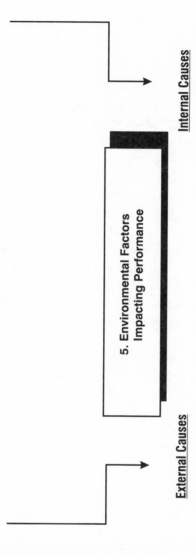

5. Environmental Factors Impacting Performance

External Causes

Causes outside the control of management can contribute to a gap in operational and performance results.
Examples:

- Competition
- Economy
- Governmental regulations

Internal Causes

Causes within the control of management can contribute to a gap in performance and operational results.
Examples:

- Lack of clearly defined accountability
- No incentive or reward to perform as required
- Lack of managerial coaching and reinforcement
- Lack of employee skill or knowledge

Operational Results

At the top of the map we see an area entitled "Business Need." In Quik-Data, the business need was to increase sales and profits. The business strategy for accomplishing this was to move to a solution-oriented sales approach. The identification of a business need and its business strategies comes from information obtained from the client team. The client team is made up of the people who are accountable for the business results. In addition, the team consists of people who can assist in or otherwise impact upon the achievement of those business results.

The next step is to obtain relevant data on operational results. Operational results are the measures the client teams use to track their progress toward achieving their business needs and goals. In Quik-Data, management was tracking both sales revenue and gross margin. Operational results are usually expressed as hard numbers and can include such measures as:

■   Percentage of product meeting quality standards

■   Customer satisfaction index

■   Response time

■   Cost per unit

■   Sales per salesperson

■   On-time deliverables

Initially, the source of these data is a client team. However, as you collect information from successful performers in your own or other organizations, you may find that additional information on operational results is desirable. Techniques for obtaining data on business needs and operational results are provided in Chapter Four.

Performance Results

Once the desired operational results are clear, we move to the identification of SHOULD performance; in other words, what do successful performers do to achieve these results? The best source for this information is successful performers—individuals who are meeting the operational results that we require. In the Quik-Data situation, we were looking for successful performers who met the specific criteria that the client team defined. The criteria that were used to identify successful salespeople were that the individual:

1. Used a business-solutions approach to selling a product to managers within business and governmental organizations

2. Operated in a long sales cycle (greater than six months)

3. Had each sale average in excess of $75,000

4. Was in the top 10 percent of the sales force in terms of sales performance

By using these criteria, we could observe and interview the salespeople who were actually achieving sales results using the strategies we had identified as necessary. In this way we were establishing a causal linkage between the desired operational results and the on-the-job behaviors used by sales personnel who were achieving those results.

SHOULD information is collected through one-on-one interviews, focus group interviews, direct observation, documentation reviews, and literature reviews. As Performance Consultants, we analyze the information, bring it back to our clients, and present it so our clients can visualize not only the performance but its linkage to the operational results. Methods and processes for obtaining SHOULD information are discussed in detail in Chapters Five and Six.

Once the client team has agreed to the desired future SHOULD performance, we then move to the next step of determining what is actually happening with current performers. In this step, we want to obtain a picture of the *typical* performer. This typical performance is the best description of the actual performance within the organization. Our data sources can be the performers, their bosses, their employees (if they have direct reports), and customers (if they have customers). With large

numbers of people, we will typically obtain data by questionnaire. With smaller groups, we may use a combination of questionnaire and interview. In certain situations we may use direct
observation supplemented by documentation review. Once these
data are collected, we are able to determine the performance gap.
In Chapter Seven we discuss methods for obtaining and summarizing this type of information.

Environmental Factors

While we're collecting both the SHOULD and IS performance, we
will concurrently be collecting CAUSE data about the performance gap from the same data sources, using the same data
collection methods. Thus, we are continually obtaining this information in our data collection process. The information is
then analyzed prior to a meeting with the client team. During
our meeting with our clients, we are able to present the data
clearly and talk about options for meeting the business need
originally discussed with our client group. Chapter Eight describes how to obtain and report CAUSE data.

Why Is the Performance
Relationship Map Necessary?

Before providing more detailed information about building performance relationship maps with clients, we would like to step
back for a moment and look at the benefits of using the map.

First, as Performance Consultants, it is imperative that we
have a model or conceptual framework to which we subscribe as
we complete our work. If good consultants must "know how to
ask the right questions right," then the performance relationship map is the tool to use for determining what the "right"
questions are. The right, or necessary, questions are those that
complete the map—no more, no less. We need to have this map
in our mind when we begin to obtain data, whether formally or
informally. What information does it require us to know, in
total? Which information is unknown and therefore must be

obtained? By using this type of tool, we keep a focus to our questions and avoid asking about irrelevant data.

Second, the performance relationship map provides a vehicle for analyzing the information that has been obtained. The Performance Consultant can clearly see the comparison between what performers should be doing and what they actually are doing. The map provides a vehicle for analyzing the various factors affecting the performance gap. When the rigor that this map requires is brought to the data collection process, the Performance Consultant is assured of identifying *all* the reasons for a performance gap, those that can be addressed by training and those that cannot.

Third, the map is a vehicle for displaying information for the client team. It assists the team in understanding the interrelationships between training needs, performance requirements, and business goals. It also helps them to accept difficult information such as work environment factors that are impacting negatively upon the desired results. Recall the situation in the Quik-Data division, where the client team agreed that an engineering support group needed to be formed and the reward system needed to be modified if sales and profits were to increase. Also recall that this was the bind that Mark Fenton found himself in at the start of this chapter. When he was asked how leadership skills (training need) would benefit the organization (business need), he could not respond. The interrelationship was unclear. If he had used the map to both obtain and report information, he could have avoided that problem.

In instances where we have used the performance relationship map with clients (which we do with frequency), many have indicated that it was the first time they fully understood the relationship between training, other work environment factors, and performance. Where previously clients might have recommended only one action (such as training for performers), they now recommend several actions.

The performance relationship map demonstrates that human performance is complex and is affected by a variety of factors; the map also provides clients with the information they require to make sound decisions about modifying and changing human performance. When Performance Consultants provide these services, they are truly acting in a partnership role to clients and are providing value-added services to those clients.

Summary

1. The performance relationship map is used by Performance Consultants to focus a data collection effort; this map identifies what information must be collected when analyzing business, performance, training, and work environment needs.

2. The performance relationship map is also a way to display data so that clients understand the interrelationships between business needs, performance gaps, the causes of those gaps, and any actions that may be necessary to close them.

3. Most performance problems have many causes. Therefore, the Performance Consultant must seek out *all* major causes of performance problems. When this is done, it is highly probable that both training and work environment causes will be identified.

4

Identifying Business Needs
in Operational Terms

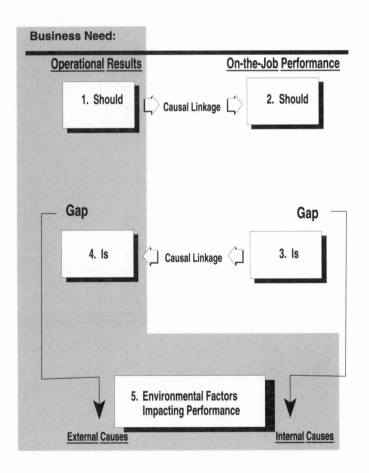

"A critical business need for the next three years is to double the profitability of Retail Marketing." This statement was made by Jake Coleman, vice president of retail marketing for Gaso Petroleum Company, to Janet Waterman, the training manager for this same company. (Gaso Petroleum Company and the employees mentioned here are composites of companies and individuals with whom we have worked.) Gaso has approximately two thousand service stations (referred to as retail stations) throughout the western United States. This company is a "low-end" gasoline business, selling gas for two to three cents less a gallon than most of its competitors. The majority of the stations are company-owned; therefore, the service attendants and station managers are employees of the company. However, some stations are independently owned; their owners are referred to as dealers. The organizational structure for the retail marketing group is illustrated in Figure 4.1.

As shown, there are two regional managers who are each responsible for half of the stations in the company. Reporting to them are nine district managers, who lead and manage territory managers. Territory managers are the individuals who actually visit the stations; they are key in assisting station managers and dealers to sell gasoline and nongas products (like tires). In general, territory managers are each responsible for about twenty stations, of which some are company-owned and others are independently owned.

Unfortunately, Gaso is experiencing several business problems. Senior management knows that changes must be made in the retail marketing organization, the largest part of the company. Jake felt certain that these changes would have implications for the performance of employees within the group. He called Janet to discuss this situation; they have talked on two occasions.

In these conversations, Janet and Jake agreed that it was important to determine exactly what performance would be required of territory managers and others within the organization in order to increase profits. All Jake could do at this time was make an educated guess as to these performance requirements.

Figure 4.1. Gaso Petroleum Company, Retail Marketing Division.

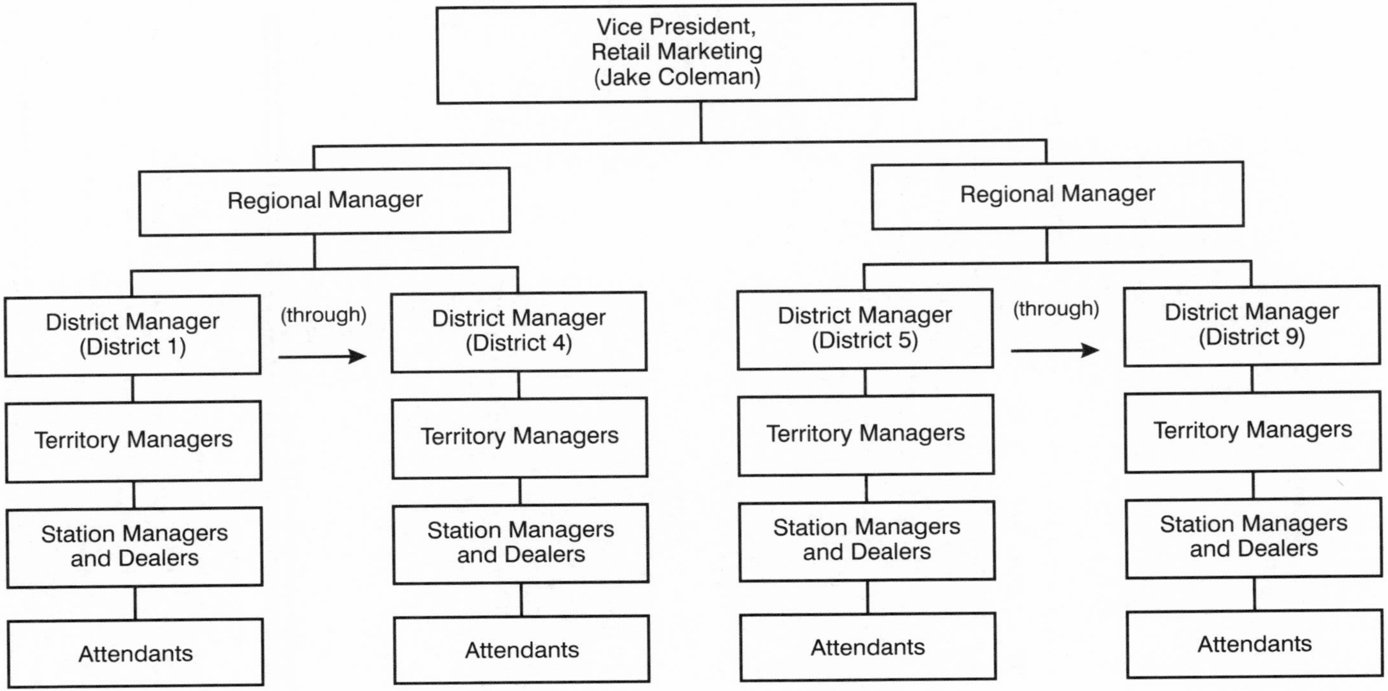

For such an important task, "guesses" were not sufficient, so
Janet will design and conduct a performance assessment with
Jake.

The Three Phases of a Performance Assessment

A performance assessment is a three-phase diagnostic process. As
the performance relationship map (Figure 3.7), indicates, the first
box that requires identification is the SHOULD box for operational
results. Therefore, the first phase of an assessment is to clearly
identify the business needs that are relevant to the project together
with the operational indicators used to measure those needs. The
overall result of this phase is agreement with the client on business goals, initiatives, and challenges and on how they will affect
the performance requirements of the performers.

The second box of the map is the on-the-job performance
SHOULD box; this is the second phase of a performance assessment. In this phase, detailed descriptions of the performance
required to achieve operational SHOULDS are identified. The
overall result of this phase is agreement with the client on the
performance models.

The third box identifies performance actuals or IS information. This is the final and last phase of a performance assessment. In this phase, current performance strengths and gaps are
determined as compared to the desired, or SHOULD, performance.
Throughout the performance assessment, it is important to identify any external and internal environmental factors that challenge both operational goals and required on-the-job performance. Therefore, in each phase of the process, work
environment information is obtained. The overall result of
Phase III is agreement with the client team on actions to be
taken. These include training actions that will provide the performers with needed skills and knowledge. They also include
management actions that remove work environment barriers and
maximize work environment enhancers. Table 4.1 summarizes
the three phases in a performance assessment.

Table 4.1. Three Phases of a Performance Assessment.

Phase I **Identification of Business Goals and Challenges**	Phase II **Identification of Performance Results or SHOULDS**	Phase III **Identification of Current Performance and Organization Obstacles**
Identification of:	*Identification of:*	*Identification of:*
Business goals and initiatives External challenges to goal accomplishment Internal challenges to goal accomplishment Performance implications as viewed by senior management	Key performance results Performance activities (best practices) Quality requirements Work environment factors	Relative importance of all performance results Current skill to perform as required Obstacles to performance Skill gaps (difference between importance of result and current skill)
Agree with client on:	*Agree with client on:*	*Contract with client for:*
Business goals, initiatives, and challenges Performance implications	Required performance ■ Performance models ■ Competency models	Training actions Work environment actions

Identifying Business Needs

Performance assessments must begin with a clear definition of the business goals, objectives, and strategies for a unit, division, department, or entire company. These serve as the stakes in the ground against which all performance requirements will be anchored. For example, the following questions may be asked:

- If an organization must reduce fixed and variable costs, what are the implications for the performance of operators who make the product, technicians who install and maintain the product, or managers of these individuals?

- What if the primary need of an organization is to increase market share? to become more global? What are the implications for sales and marketing personnel? for customer service personnel? What must they do differently or better?

This first phase of a performance assessment generally has the following purposes:

- Defining the business needs in operational or measurable terms, including identification of any gap between actual and desired results

- Determining the driving forces and reasons behind the needs

- Identifying the business strategies that will be used to meet the needs

- Determining the external and internal factors that affect accomplishment of these business goals

- Identifying any implications for performance as envisioned by clients

To obtain this information, interviews are typically conducted with the client team (the individuals who own the business need). If the business needs in question are for a department, then the head of the department would need to be interviewed;

if the needs are for the entire organization, the individuals responsible for that entity will be interviewed. However, additional sources of information are recommended so that various perspectives of the business goals and their implications can be uncovered.

One possible source of information consists of the people who have some aspect of responsibility for the business needs. Generally, these will be key individuals who work with clients and are partially responsible for the business goals. In some instances these individuals will include suppliers and/or customers.

A variety of documents, both internal and external, can also be reviewed. Internally, these are statements of strategic intent, business plans, operating statements, customer demographic information, competitive reports, and so on. Documents that may be relevant from outside the organization are governmental agency reports and studies, industry reports, economic reports and projections, trade journals, and business magazines. The client team is a good resource to work with in identifying which documents are most pertinent and important; this team can also provide access to documents that typically are not available for review.

We may have reached this point because a manager called us with a need and we are reacting to the request for assistance, or we may have formed the need in a proactive manner. For example, we may have conducted an interview such as the one described in Performance Consulting Tool 1 in Chapter Two. In that conversation, we identified a potential opportunity to work with a client. Now we are returning to discuss the business need in a more in-depth way. No matter how we arrived here, our purpose is to gather information about specific business and performance needs.

Performance Consulting Tool 2 is structured for a situation where you and the client team have agreed to move ahead with a performance assessment. This tool differs from Tool 1. With Tool 1, you asked questions to determine if there was a need. With Tool 2, you already know there is a need; now you require more information about it. This information will become the foundation for later stages of the assessment. Tool 2 provides an interview guide for the first part of a performance assessment. We will also demonstrate how Janet Waterman used the interview guide in a discussion with Jake Coleman.

Performance Consulting Tool 2

Interview Guide: Identifying Business Needs

This interview guide is to be used when:

1. A specific performance assessment project has been identified and the client team has agreed to proceed with the project.
2. A client team is to be interviewed to obtain information about the business needs of the unit or group involved in the assessment.

Purposes of the Interview

As a result of information obtained in this interview, you will be able to answer the following questions:

1. What are the major business needs for the unit or group being discussed?
2. What are the driving forces behind these needs?
3. How will these business needs be measured operationally?
4. What factors, external to the organization, will impact upon accomplishment of these goals?
5. What implications for performance does the client believe these needs generate?

Prior to the Interview

Make an appointment with each team member. Indicate the following:

1. You want to learn more about the business goals and needs of the organization to ensure that the performance assessment is focused on these needs.
2. The interview will require up to one hour of time.

Introductory Comments

Mention the following items:

1. Briefly refer to previous discussions about this business need with this person or other client team members.

2. Indicate the purpose of the interview.

3. Confirm the available time.

4. Ask if the person has questions before the start of the interview.

Ask the following background questions if you are not familiar with the individual or with her or his responsibilities:

1. It would be helpful to know more about your responsibilities. What are the primary accountabilities for you in this position?

2. How long have you been in this position?

> Rationale: *While you usually will be interviewing someone with whom you have a working relationship, there can be occasions when the individual you are interviewing is someone with whom you have had limited contact in the past. It is also possible that the individual is new to his or her position (which is why the individual is working with you—to gain assistance in implementing some new ideas or initiatives). In any case, when you lack familiarity with the individual and her or his responsibilities, it is best to spend a few minutes discussing them. This is also a nonthreatening way to get the conversation started. In addition, you will want to overview the purpose and focus of the project if the person is unfamiliar with it.*

Janet and Jake had worked together on previous projects; therefore, Janet omitted this part of the interview.

Future Business Needs, Goal One

Ask the following questions:

1. As you know, in our project we will be identifying performance as it SHOULD be so that current and future business goals can

be achieved. As you look out over the next two to three years, what is one major operational or business goal you want to accomplish?

> Rationale: *This interview begins by asking the client to identify goals or initiatives for the client's organization over the next two to three years. Even if you already know the organization's goals, it is good to ask about them here. This way you can find out which are most urgent and whether there are any changes or additions. It is good to acknowledge that even though you are aware of the goals, you still want to discuss them with your client.*
>
> *In forming performance SHOULDS (the next phase in this process), you want to identify performance as it should be in the future, not performance as it has been. In order to have this future focus, we must know where the unit or organization is headed. What will be the major areas of concentration for this organization? The list of options is endless, and each option brings strong, but differing, implications for employees' performance.*
>
> *Generally, we have found that clients have from three to seven business needs of keen interest to them. If you are working with a client in a small unit of twenty-five people, there may be only one or two areas of concern; when you are working with a client in a large, complex organization, there could be several needs.*

When Janet asked Jake for his primary business needs, he mentioned three: (1) doubling profits in the next three years, (2) bringing all stations into full compliance with environmental regulations and laws, and (3) increasing customer satisfaction with service and price so that Gaso would be the station of choice.

In all three cases, Jake was dealing with business problems. As previously described, a business problem is a situation that is currently causing pain to the managers who are accountable for the results. For Jake, the actual operational performance for each of these areas was below what was desired (the SHOULD), so he was motivated to take action.

2.   Why is this goal an important need at this time? What are the driving forces behind this need?

> Rationale: *To truly understand the business problem or opportunity being discussed, we need to identify the driving forces that make this problem or opportunity of critical importance to the client. Has there been a change in competitive pressures? Is profitability in the company lower? Is there a new CEO who has a different agenda for the organization than that of the previous CEO? Do governmental regulations require a change? Is a new product not meeting its projections? In essence we are discovering why this is a business need now.*

Jake indicated that one of his primary needs is to double profits in the next three years. The major reason for this is that the organization's capital requirements are going to increase dramatically. Many of the retail stations lack the modern features customers value, such as convenience stores where a customer can purchase food items. Additional funds will be needed if the massive modernization effort that is planned is to occur. All divisions within Gaso are being asked to increase their contributions to the capital budget.

3.   What are some of the strategies you or others will be using to ensure that these operational goals are realized?

> Rationale: *The business goal tells us* what *is to be accomplished. Now we need to determine* how *it will be accomplished. The strategies describe who will need to do what. From this information we will be able to determine what performer groups will have the most effect on the goal. Will front-line supervisors, operators, sales personnel, middle managers, or all of the above be the groups whose performance contributes most to the accomplishment of the goal? The strategies will assist us in determining the answer to this question.*

When Janet asked Jake about strategies for doubling profitability, she learned that:

■   *The retail stations will need to increase the quality of their product merchandising (that is, the way in which the products are displayed so that customers will inquire about them).*

■   *Sales of nongas products such as tires and batteries need to increase. These products have high gross margins (profits).*

■   *Both fixed and variable costs will need to be controlled.*

■   *District managers will need to identify retail stations that need to be closed because of operating losses.*

From this information Janet determined, and Jake agreed, that the key positions to be assessed were district managers, territory managers, station managers and dealers, and customer service attendants.

4.   How will you measure this goal operationally? What are the current operational results associated with this goal? What do you want them to be in two or three years' time?

> Rationale: *At this point in the conversation, we have learned of a need or goal of critical importance to our client. We may not, however, have learned how this goal will be measured. These are the hard data measures that our client will use to monitor progress toward the business goal. Most likely, the client is already using these measures to define the business problem or opportunity. If it is a business problem, management has undoubtedly been monitoring certain measures that have identified the existence of a problem. If it is a business opportunity, then management has put together a plan with some measures that are projections (or hopes).*

Once the strategies were identified, Janet inquired about what indicators would be used to measure results. What were the operational goals? What was the current status compared to those goals and what was the operational gap? While it may be important at some point to identify the actuals and goals for various districts within Retail Marketing, in this conversation Janet focused on the measures for Retail Marketing as an entire group.

It was determined that return on investment for Retail Mar-

keting had to double within three years from 7 to 14 percent, and that the percentage of retail stations meeting their return-on-investment goal had to increase from 68 to 96 percent. The number of retail stations was to decline by 300 from 2,000 to 1,700.

5. What forces or factors *outside* of the organization are going to challenge achievement of this goal? Are there any factors *within* the organization that will challenge achievement of the goal?

> Rationale: *As noted in the performance relationship map, both internal and external factors can have a significant impact upon the accomplishment of business goals. External forces are factors that cannot be eliminated. Performers will need to perform successfully despite them (as the AT&T example in Chapter Two indicates). By understanding these forces, the Performance Consultant will have increased insight into the reason for the business strategies. Additionally, this information will provide the Performance Consultant with situations that the performers need to manage and work within.*
>
> *In our experience, the most frequently mentioned external factors that are identified when interviewing a senior manager or executive are governmental regulations, the economy, competition, and shareholder and customer expectations. These factors exist outside of the organization as a whole.*
>
> *There can also be internal factors that negatively impact upon accomplishment of goals. These can be changed if management determines that a change is necessary. Because the person you are interviewing is a senior manager or head of a business unit, it is possible that this person could make a decision to address internal barriers. Therefore, it is important to determine what those barriers might be. Internal factors could include such items as operating and capital budget constraints, availability of resources such as employees, obsolete computer systems, and insufficient investment in research.*

When Janet discussed factors external to Retail Marketing that were affecting the goal of doubling profits, she learned that they included:

■ *Environmental regulations that, while important, are very costly to support, particularly with older stations that were built prior to these requirements. These costs reduce profits.*

■ *Taxation of gasoline. To the customer the price paid per gallon is what is important; it doesn't matter to the customer that forty cents of every gallon goes for taxes. The price of a gallon of gas can increase through taxation and none of that increase will go to the service station. The current bias of the federal government is to use gas taxes as a means of generating federal revenue.*

■ *The economic conditions that limit people's willingness to make long car trips (which require more gasoline).*

■ *Shareholders' expectations of a greater return on their investment.*

When Janet inquired about internal forces, Jake reiterated the fact that many of the stations lack the modern features customers prefer. This places Gaso at a competitive disadvantage; they must work harder to get the customer traffic through their stations.

Future Business Needs, Goal Two

Repeat the process just described for each specific business need or goal deemed critical by the client.

Janet continued her interview with Jake by asking these same questions for the remaining two business needs: complying with environmental regulations and increasing customer satisfaction.

Performance Implications

Ask the following question:

What implications are you aware of for the performance of (*name of performer group*)? What do you think they will need to do better or more or less frequently in the future if these business goals are to be achieved? (Continue with this same question for each performer group to be assessed.)

> Rationale: *Once all business needs have been discussed, we ask the client about the implications these needs have for the performance of the work groups being assessed. It has been our experience that, at times, clients will have identified some of these implications before the interview begins; often, however, these implications begin to form from the discussion itself. It is important to remember that just because a client indicates that a type of performance will be required doesn't mean that it will be found to be important, but knowing what is in the client's mind as you begin your work can be very helpful.*

In this part of the interview, Janet said: "You have provided me with a great deal of information regarding the business requirements for your organization; this information will be helpful to me as I begin the work to identify performance requirements for people within Retail Marketing. What implications are you aware of for the performance of station managers and dealers? What do you think they will need to do better or more or less frequently in the future if these business goals are to be achieved?"

- *Station Managers and Dealers: Jake believed that they would need to become business managers; currently, they were in the role of high-level doers. He wanted them to become more knowledgeable about fixed and variable costs and to be able to manage them more effectively than was currently the case. It was also important for station managers and dealers to become more knowledgeable about the competition and what it was doing.*

Janet also wanted Jake's insight on how the business goals would impact upon each position within Retail Marketing, so she asked about those performer groups:

- *Station Attendants: Jake felt certain that these individuals needed to become more interpersonally skilled in working with customers. It was also important that they become better at merchandising and selling nongasoline products.*

■ *Territory Managers: Jake viewed territory managers as key to the success of Retail Marketing. These individuals had the responsibility of working with all station managers and dealers and attendants to increase their skills to merchandise and sell product; territory managers also provided guidance to station managers and dealers in their management of the business. Jake believed that a lot of change was needed in this group but was uncertain as to exactly what would be required. He looked forward to having Janet help him to figure it out.*

■ *District Managers: These individuals definitely needed to become coaches and developers of territory managers. Currently, district managers were neither held accountable nor rewarded for developing staff. They spent too much time doing paperwork and weren't getting out in the field to work with their territory managers enough. This had to change.*

Closing the Interview

Ask the following questions:

1. Are there any documents you think I should read to further my understanding of your business goals and needs?

> Rationale: *In closing the conversation, it is helpful to ask the client about documents to be reviewed, other individuals to be interviewed, and any other information or suggestions that would be helpful. The project is just* beginning; *clients are very busy people. Now is the opportune moment to gain all the insight and guidance you can from this individual.*

Jake felt that Janet should have a copy of the annual business plan and arranged for her to get a copy.

2. Are there any individuals you believe it is important for me to interview in addition to (*names of individuals to be interviewed*)?

Jake felt that it would be beneficial for Janet to interview the two regional managers and to meet with the president of the company.

*He would set those interviews up, providing her access and legiti-
macy with these individuals.*

3.   Is there anything I have not asked you that would be good for
     me to know as I begin this project with you?

> Rationale: *In our experience this has been one of the highest-
> yield questions. We have learned some amazing pieces of in-
> formation from this one question. There was the time one of
> us was closing an interview with a manager. This manager
> was the first one interviewed in a large project; one of the pur-
> poses of the interview was to field-test the interview guide so
> that edits and modifications could be made. When asked this
> last "anything I should know" question, the manager men-
> tioned that the company had just announced a massive re-
> structuring and that several people were going to be laid off.
> He didn't know if any of them were ones we would be inter-
> viewing, but he felt certain that this situation would affect peo-
> ple's motivation to cooperate. This prompted a quick call to
> our client, who affirmed that this had occurred and that it
> would be a good reason for postponing the interviews until the
> major components of the restructuring had been
> implemented.*

*Jake indicated that doubling the profits in Retail Marketing was
very important to Gaso Petroleum. Therefore, it was essential to
determine what the people within Retail Marketing had to do to
make this happen.*

Thank the individual for his or her time and thoughts.

*Janet thanked Jake for his time and information. She indicated that
the project was off to a good start. When Janet returned to her office,
she began to fill in the performance relationship map for the Retail
Marketing project. Figure 4.2 is the map she developed for the business need of doubling profits. Remember, there would also be a map
for the other two business needs: bringing stations into environmental compliance and increasing customer satisfaction.*

Figure 4.2. Display of Operational Measures for Gaso's Business Goal of Doubling Profits.

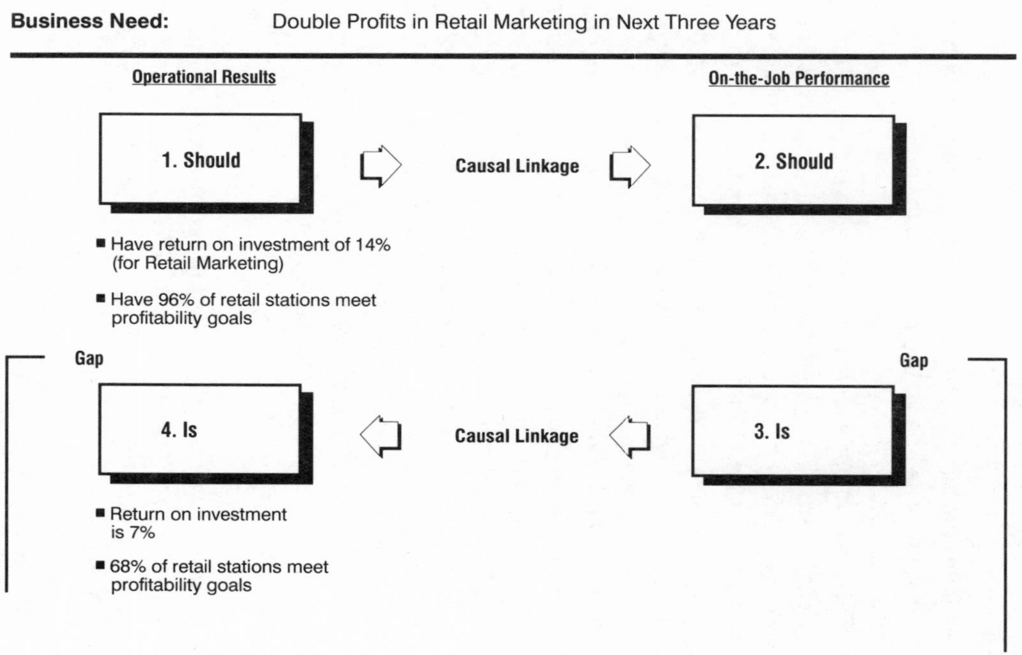

Business Need: Double Profits in Retail Marketing in Next Three Years

<u>Operational Results</u>

<u>On-the-Job Performance</u>

| 1. Should |

| 2. Should |

Causal Linkage

- Have return on investment of 14% (for Retail Marketing)
- Have 96% of retail stations meet profitability goals

| 4. Is |

Gap

| 3. Is |

Gap

Causal Linkage

- Return on investment is 7%
- 68% of retail stations meet profitability goals

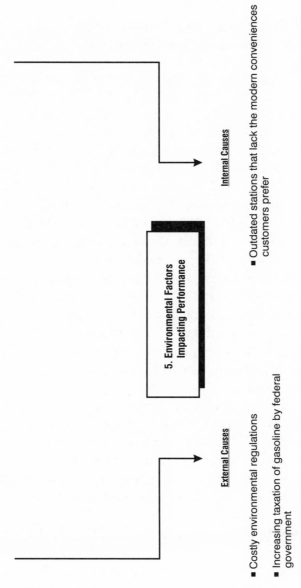

5. Environmental Factors Impacting Performance

External Causes

- Costly environmental regulations
- Increasing taxation of gasoline by federal government
- Reduced interest by customers in making longer trips

Internal Causes

- Outdated stations that lack the modern conveniences customers prefer

Additional Tips About Obtaining
Business Need Information

We want to clarify when to use the two interview guides—Tool
1 and Tool 2. Tool 1, described in Chapter Two, is to be used
when you have *initiated* a conversation with a manager to discuss business needs. There is no stated project as yet; you are
merely exploring possibilities. In the interview described in this
chapter, you and your client have agreed that there is a possible
project. You are truly digging for information that will assist
you in beginning this project. Tool 2 is used for this purpose.

Two primary data collection methods are used to obtain
operational data: ask and read. We have discussed at length the
type of interview (ask) that is conducted for this purpose. A
second method is to review documents (read). Here, the concept
of "asking the right questions right" still pertains, but the emphasis is on "looking at and selecting the right data." In the
interview that Janet conducted, Jake suggested that she review
the annual business plan. Janet will review this document for
information about business goals and their implications for employee performance.

Once all the interviews associated with this phase of the
process have been completed, it is important to summarize your
findings and forward them to the client for review. This is a
short summary in which you list the major business needs you
have identified together with forces, external factors, strategies,
and measures. There are two purposes for this summary:

1.   It ensures that you have accurately understood the information
      provided to you.

2.   It presents you in the role of Performance Consultant and not
      in the role of Traditional Trainer, a representation that it is
      good to reinforce every chance you can.

Things That Can Go Wrong

As with any process, we need to consider Murphy's Law—anything that can go wrong will go wrong. Certain things can make

the process more difficult to follow. Here are a few we have encountered.

You Have No Access to the Clients

The individuals who truly own the business need may not be accessible for some reason. They may be physically unavailable (for example, out of the country) or the organizational norms dictate that you "go through" someone else. Whatever the reason, when lack of access occurs, discuss the issue with your contact (the individual with whom you *are* working) and work toward a resolution. Could you develop an interview guide that would be used by your contact, with the results of the interview being provided to you? Are there source documents that would have the majority of the information you require? Could you interview any other individuals who may not be clients but who do have relevant information? It is important to explore options.

The Contact Feels That He or She Knows All That Is Necessary

In this situation you are working with a contact who is not the "true" client. This individual believes that she or he knows all there is to know about the business and the operational needs. The individual speaks for the client team and blocks your access to the real clients.

We were faced with this situation a few years ago. We did not assertively pursue the situation and accepted our contact (who was a direct report of the client) as the spokesperson. About two months later, the "true" client called, quite distressed. He indicated that we were not doing what he required and said that if we could not do quick changes in our process, the project would be terminated!

How can you get to the true client without alienating the contact?

■ Ask the contact questions that are difficult for him or her to answer. Then ask if (*name of client*) would be able to provide that information. Ask if the *two* of you could meet with the client.

- In a direct but tactful manner, indicate your concern at not having direct access to the client. Ask your contact what could be done to alleviate your concern.

- Gain agreement from your contact that your meetings and interviews will be summarized and that a copy of that summary will be forwarded to the clients. If the clients do read the information and are concerned about what is being done, they will surface.

Summary

1. The first phase of a performance assessment project is to interview clients and others who have information about the critical business needs. These needs will be the "stake in the ground" for all the performance requirements you are about to identify.

2. When obtaining information on business needs, it is important to discuss the driving forces, strategies, operational measures, and factors both outside and within the organization that challenge accomplishment of goals.

3. Clients have opinions regarding the performance required of employees to meet business goals; it is important to discuss these opinions during the interviews.

4. Source documents can also be helpful in identifying and clarifying business needs.

5

Developing Models
of Performance Required
to Achieve Business Goals

Business Need:

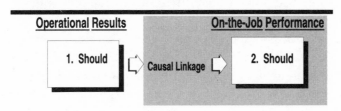

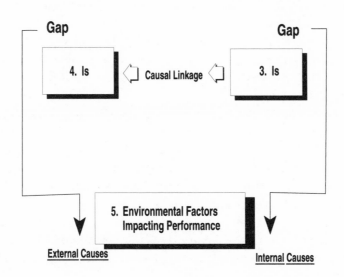

Consider the following observations that are made with frequency in today's business world:

- "Our production people need to work smarter and harder."
- "Everyone needs to become more focused on our customers."
- "Managers need to empower our people."

These are very poignant slogans, but what does each of them actually mean in terms of human performance? What must operators and technicians actually *do* differently in order to work "smarter and harder"? And what about customer service personnel—what must they do with more effectiveness if they are to be "focused on the customers"? What must managers *and* employees do better and differently in the future if people are to be "empowered"?

A model provides answers to these questions. A model is a behavioral description of performance as it SHOULD be for the organization to achieve its current and future business goals. It raises the performance "bar" to the new required level. Joseph Juran, the quality expert, has frequently acknowledged that if people always do what they have always done, they will continue to obtain the same results. In a model we are identifying performance as it SHOULD be so we will be able to achieve what is required for the future; a model challenges the status quo. In our opinion, assisting clients in the formation of models is one of the most valuable services a Performance Consultant provides.

Models have always been a part of the training process, although they may not have been identified as such. By definition, any content provided in a training program is a performance SHOULD, or model. Otherwise, why would it be in the program? If you are conducting a workshop on how to program a computer using the C+ language, then you are undoubtedly providing participants with the best, most effective techniques to use when demonstrating this performance. If your focus is on how to negotiate terms and conditions for agreements, you most likely are instructing people to use the techniques that research has indicated to be the most effective. Each of these is a model for a particular type of performance.

Models have also been formed for people in the HRD profession. For example, the American Society for Training and Development has produced models for the HRD profession. Their publication entitled *Models for HRD Practice* (McLagan, 1989) describes models for eleven roles, including evaluator, needs analyst, program designer, and instructor. The International Board of Standards for Training, Performance, and Instruction also has several publications describing models for our profession: *Instructional Design Competencies: The Standards* (Foshay, Silber, and Westgaard, 1986) and *Instructor Competencies: The Standards* (Hutchison, Shepherd, and Stein, 1993). So the concept of models is not new; what is new is that increasing numbers of training professionals are partnering with client managers to form models that directly support organizational goals.

Components of a Model

A model for any specific position within an organization includes four components:

1. Performance results
2. Best practices or competencies
3. Quality criteria
4. Work environment factors

Performance Results

These are the outcomes a performer must achieve on the job if the organization's business goals are to be attained. For example, a performance result for a sales representative would be to achieve revenue goals; for an employee who operates equipment, it could be to operate equipment in a safe manner. It is our experience that most jobs require between ten and fifteen performance results. Each performance result is both labeled and defined to ensure shared understanding as to what is being described.

Best Practices or Competencies

The second component of a model is a description of the best practices or competencies required if the performer is to successfully accomplish the performance results. As we indicate later in this chapter, this component is a decision point for Performance Consultants and their clients. Is there a preference for describing best practices or for describing competencies? If the decision is to use *best practices,* then performance models are being formed. Best practices are what the very best performers (people we will refer to as exemplary performers) actually do on the job to achieve each of the performance results for a specific position. Sometimes these practices are identified through benchmarking efforts or a review of the literature; often they are identified by observing and interviewing exemplary performers.

Perhaps we have been asked to assess the position of shift supervisor in a manufacturing facility. It is probable that such an individual must demonstrate many performance results including a result we will title "managing shift compliance to health and safety requirements," defined as "ensuring that health and safety policies, procedures, and processes are followed day to day by all shift employees." In order to determine what practices are required to accomplish this result, we could interview and/or observe shift supervisors who consistently meet or exceed safety goals. In doing so we might learn that successful shift supervisors perform practices such as the following:

■   They continually reinforce the need to avoid shortcuts and the value of following procedures.

■   They evidence through words and actions that safety is *the* priority even when it conflicts with other requirements.

■   They conduct formal and informal safety audits and provide feedback to operators as necessary.

- They train and develop operators to perform in support of safety procedures and conduct safety "what if" drills.

Because these practices are known to contribute to positive safety results, they should become a part of the performance model, or expectation, for all shift supervisors. As you can see, the practices are written in a behavioral language that provides clarity as to what performers should do on the job.

If the decision is to describe the skills and knowledge required to produce results, then a *competency* model is formed. If we use the same position of shift supervisor but describe the performance result of managing shift compliance to health and safety requirements in terms of competencies, we might list the following:

- *Safety knowledge:* Knowledge of all company safety policies, procedures, and guidelines and their implication for the operation of a unit

- *Judgment:* Making timely and responsible decisions based upon assessment of a situation

- *Developing others:* Building the current and future capabilities of others in the organization

- *Feedback skill:* Communicating observations regarding performance so that the observations are understood and accepted

These become the competencies to develop and evaluate as shift supervisors work toward accomplishing the performance result.

We will describe the differences between these two approaches more completely later in this chapter, but it is important to remember that the second component of any model is a listing of the best practices and/or competencies required to complete each performance result in the position.

Quality Criteria

The criteria are listed that will be used to measure the quality with which the performance result or output is achieved. Criteria are formed for *each* performance result. Again, if we return to the shift supervisor who must manage shift compliance to health and safety requirements, then the quality criteria used to measure success could include:

- "Zero" lost-time injuries

- A shift-safety compliance rate of 100 percent

- No incidents recorded by the Occupational Safety and Health Administration for the shift

- Operators who actively participate and offer ideas in safety meetings

Work Environment Factors

Finally, a model includes a list of the forces, within and outside the control of the organization, that will either encourage or inhibit the accomplishment of each performance result. As described in Chapter Three, if the forces are outside the organization, performers must learn techniques and skills for optimizing positive factors and overcoming negative factors. If the factors are within the organization, it is hoped that clients will begin to take actions to address them. In our example, shift supervisors who are to manage shift compliance to health and safety requirements must do so despite the following barriers:

- Production rates that place pressure on operators who, in working quickly, may use safety shortcuts

- Equipment inspections that do not occur consistently within the time period indicated, allowing a safety problem to begin and go unnoticed until a safety incident occurs

- The need for all operators to know and function in support of the changing and varied requirements in a unit that produces different products requiring different safety considerations

On the other hand, the following factors will encourage shift supervisors to manage shift compliance to health and safety requirements:

- Monthly compliance inspections that identify specific noncompliances

- Safety training that is conducted monthly

- A leadership team that continually reinforces the message that safety is an important issue and is everyone's responsibility

The components for the two types of models we've discussed are as follows:

Performance Model:	*Competency Model:*
1. *Performance results:* The outcomes a performer must achieve on the job if the organization's business goals are to be attained (these are both labeled and defined)	1. *Performance results:* The outcomes a performer must achieve on the job if the organization's business goals are to be attained (these are both labeled and defined)
2. *Best practices:* What exemplary performers actually do on the job to achieve a performance result	2. *Competencies:* The skill and knowledge required to perform the result, together with examples of the best practices for each competency
3. *Quality criteria:* The criteria used to measure the result	3. *Quality criteria:* The criteria used to measure the result
4. *Work environment factors:* The forces, within and outside of the organization, that encourage or inhibit accomplishment of the result	4. *Work environment factors:* The forces, within and outside of the organization, that encourage or inhibit accomplishment of the result

It is important to remember that models describe performance as it should be *in order for the organization's business goals to be achieved.* In other words, these models define performance that is causally linked to accomplishment of the business goals. The business goals of the client team are the stake in the ground to which these models are attached. That is why it is critical to have a full understanding of these business goals; without that understanding, you risk identifying inaccurate or incomplete models.

Two Types of Models

As noted earlier in this chapter, performance can be described in two ways: as best practices and as competencies. When using a performance language, the model for a specific position is described in terms of the actual techniques and behaviors (that is, best practices) that exemplary performers use to accomplish a result. These people, who consistently do a superior job of accomplishing a result, tell you what they do step by step. By obtaining this information from several people, you build a pattern as to which techniques, practices, and approaches will achieve the desired result in an excellent manner.

Let's look at the position of a field services supervisor in a telecommunications organization. People in this position manage service technicians who install and maintain the telecommunications equipment and transmission capability for a wide range of customers. One of the performance results required of someone in this position is to "provide excellent service to all customers." This result is defined as to "continually seek information about customer requirements and implement actions to meet those requirements."

Models Described in Performance Language

Table 5.1 illustrates the components for this result when it is defined in performance terms. This type of description can become a road map for a new supervisor because it describes the best practices to successfully accomplish this result. It also identifies for the supervisor the criteria against which performance will be measured and the work environment factors that may be encountered. For people who are currently in the position, it

Table 5.1. Result Described in Performance Terms.

Performance Model: Field Services Supervisor

Performance Result (what must be accomplished)	Best Practices[a] (how the result can be accomplished)	Quality Criteria (how to know the result has been accomplished in an excellent manner)
Provide Excellent Service to All Customers Definition: Continually seek information about customer requirements and implement actions to meet them.	1. Ensure that parameters within which technicians can make decisions independently to satisfy customers are clearly understood and utilized.	✓ The customer satisfaction index is at acceptable ratings.
	2. Set up and facilitate meetings with customers and technicians to hear customers state their requirements.	✓ Service has been restored within the target time.
	3. Develop one-on-one relationship with customers in which the customers know that they can reach the supervisor.	✓ The number of service interruptions has been reduced by X%.
	4. Consistently model excellent customer service (lead by example).	✓ The number of customer commendations increases.
	5. Regularly coach technicians on ways to provide excellent customer service and put customers first.	✓ The number of customer complaints is reduced.
	6. Discuss the causes of complaints with technicians; work as a team to determine root causes and appropriate solutions.	
	7. Gather and discuss information about competitors and how they service customers.	
	8. Delegate to technicians the responsibility of managing customer calls and determining the needs of customers.	
	9. Network with other departments within the organization to share information and provide assistance.	
	10. Use creative problem-solving techniques in team meetings to develop new ways to provide customers with excellent service.	

[a]This is a partial list of best practices.

provides insight into some practices that they may not be doing at this time. Remember, only the individuals who are outstanding performers in this position are interviewed and observed. Those who are more "typical" in their performance may be unaware of some of these practices and can now begin to incorporate them into their day-to-day performance.

Models Described in Competency Language

When a competency language is used, the model is described in terms of the skills, knowledge, and attributes required to accomplish the result. Again, exemplary performers form the primary source of information, but the type of information that is obtained and reported is different from that used for a performance approach. Table 5.2 illustrates how the performance result of providing excellent service to all customers could be defined when using a competency approach.

In both the results format and the competency format, work environment factors are identified. These are expressed as enhancers and barriers to the desired performance. The work environment factors for the field services supervisor position are as follows:

Enhancers:	*Barriers:*
Most supervisors are personally committed to totally satisfying the customer.	Supervisors' lack of technical knowledge often results in their inability to understand what customers are asking.
Identifying customer requirements leads to more business, which results in technicians feeling appreciated and challenged.	Some supervisors lack the leadership skills to lead a team in this kind of effort.
Identifying and meeting customer requirements leads to more revenue and job security.	Some technicians do not understand how their individual performance affects customer satisfaction and retention.

Top management provides a strong message that providing outstanding customer service is required for the organization to be successful.

A larger span of control requires that supervisors empower all technicians to provide outstanding customer service.

The customer information system often lacks current and accurate information.

A low head count means that more results must be accomplished by fewer technicians.

Some technicians do not think that they should ask customers about their wants and needs.

In determining which of these two approaches would be best for a given situation, you should look at the benefits of each. Which set of benefits most closely aligns itself with what you and your clients wish to achieve?

Benefits of Using Performance Language

Following are some of the benefits of using a performance language:

- Best practices are specific activities; they list what people can actually do. Therefore, they become a guide or road map for people who are new to the position by describing the best practices to accomplish the required results.

- Best practices provide specific activities that can be reviewed by others to determine if they are, in fact, what should be done. They provide an opportunity to redesign the position if it is appropriate.

- Performance models described in terms of best practices are a "language of the line" in the sense that managers can relate to and understand what is being described. If the job is technical in nature, then the practices will also be technical; if the position is managerial, then the practices will be described in that language.

Table 5.2. Result Described in Competency Terms.

Performance Model: Field Services Supervisor

Performance Result (*what must be accomplished*)	Required Competencies and Definition	Best Practices for Competencies[a]	Quality Criteria (*how to know the result has been accomplished in an excellent manner*)
Provide Excellent Service to All Customers Definition: Continually seek information about customer requirements and implement actions to meet them.	1. Customer Orientation: Anticipating and responding to the needs of customers (both internal and external); making customer orientation a high priority.	■ Set up and facilitate meetings with customers and technicians to hear customers state their requirements. ■ Develop a one-on-one relationship with customers in which the customers know that they can reach the supervisor. ■ Gather and discuss information about competitors and how they service customers.	√ The customer satisfaction index is at acceptable ratings. √ Service has been restored within the target time. √ The number of service interruptions has been reduced by X percent. √ The number of customer commendations increases. √ The number of customer complaints is reduced.
	2. Empowering Others: Creating a sense of ownership of the job or projects by providing clear expectations, control of resources, responsibility, and coaching.	■ Ensure that parameters within which technicians can make decisions independently to satisfy customers are clearly understood and utilized. ■ Regularly coach technicians on how to provide excellent	

customer service and put customers first.

- ■ Delegate to technicians the responsibility of managing customer calls and determining the needs of customers.

3. Leadership: Using appropriate interpersonal styles and methods to inspire and guide individuals toward goal achievement.

- ■ Consistently model excellent customer service (lead by example).
- ■ Network with other departments within the organization to share information and provide assistance.

4. Problem Solving: Identifying problems and developing effective means to resolve them, settle issues, and give direction.

- ■ Discuss the causes of complaints with technicians; work as a team to determine root causes and appropriate solutions.
- ■ Use creative problem-solving techniques in team meetings to develop new ways to provide customers with excellent service.

[a]This is a partial list of practices.

■   Describing results in this manner provides a strong frame-work for training programs and curriculum design. Each practice can become a training objective in a learning experience that is designed to build the skill and knowledge needed to perform a particular result. For example, the practice of setting up and facilitating meetings with customers and technicians to hear customers state their requirements could be converted into the following learning objective: "As a result of attending this training, participants will be able to set up and facilitate meetings with customers and technicians to hear customers state their requirements."

■   Models defined in a performance language are a very good option when a *specific* job is being assessed, for example, the job of field services supervisor.

Benefits of Using Competency Language

The following list describes some of the benefits of competency-based performance models:

■   Competencies form a common language across positions within an organization. Whereas in performance models, the best practices required to produce a result will be unique and specific to a particular position, the competencies required to accomplish those results will be similar across positions. For example, operators who manufacture products require judgment skills; so do sales representatives, customer service representatives, and managers. Therefore, the need for judgment skills is a shared need across positions.

■   Competencies are the best approach when the purpose is to form models to develop a performance management system. By *performance management system*, we refer to an integrated set of systems in the human resources area, such as selection, development, and succession planning. In one major corporation with which we worked, the goal was to form an integrated performance development system in which managers would use competencies to select individuals into positions, establish performance goals, develop employees, and assess performance. Considering the fact that this organization had several hundred jobs and tens of thousands of employees, competencies became the way to describe performance in a common manner. Performance models do not provide this option.

■ With competencies, an organization has the option to identify *core competencies,* which are defined as the competencies required of any employee in any position across the entire organization. Typically, when this is done, it is for the purpose of drawing attention to the critical needs of the organization and/or culture. For example, if the organization is committed to being more collaborative internally, rewarding team performance and not just individual performance, then a core competency could be "team performance," defined as "building and maintaining constructive partnerships with others in the organization." The focus and attention given to this competency through its inclusion as a core competency will go a long way toward institutionalizing both the value of demonstrating teamwork and the required skills. Because performance models identify practices, which will be unique from job to job, they do not lend themselves to this application.

■ Competencies can also be easily translated into training curricula. If skill in the competency of negotiating is limited in an organization, a negotiating workshop can be offered.

■ Competency language is the best option when a job family or job cluster is being assessed. For example, if the need is to form a model for the position of manager—a position title that encompasses many different managers—then a competency approach would be preferred.

Performance Model or Competency Model?

In summary, we prefer to develop a performance model when we are describing SHOULD performance for a specific position—for example, maintenance supervisor. The performance model describes the best practices—what a maintenance supervisor must do to achieve the performance results for that job.

We prefer to develop a competency model when we are describing SHOULD performance for a job family—for example, all supervisors within the organization. The competency model describes the skills and knowledge that all supervisors must have to be successful. These are more generic because supervisors work in many different functions, such as the operations, maintenance, engineering, or administration areas. In competency models we will use best practices for a cross-section of the jobs as examples of how the skill and knowledge can be applied.

Causal Linkage

Whether a performance or competency approach is utilized, the purpose of a model is to define the performance needed for the organization's business goals to be achieved. In other words, if employees actually *do* what is noted in the model, they will contribute to business results. Performance and business goals must be causally linked if the model is to be credible and valued.

Suppose that an organization is experiencing very high turnover in the position of computer programmer; historically, employee turnover has been 6 percent, but in the past year it has risen to 15 percent and is increasing. Let's also suppose that the manager of the unit calls and asks you to deliver a workshop to her managers on the subject of empowerment. She believes that people are primarily leaving the organization because they are dissatisfied with the amount of autonomy and accountability they are being given. If managers in the department were to begin delegating more responsibility, then programmers would remain. What do you think? Do you believe that the performance of empowering people and the operational result of turnover are causally linked? How would you go about determining if they are?

Or perhaps you get a request to conduct a workshop on teamwork for a design team made up of engineering and manufacturing people. Once a basic product concept has been formed and supported by management, this team is to form the specifications and processes required to bring the product to market. Currently, the cycle time (the interval between the time when the team is chartered to begin work and the time when the product is actually produced) is too long. Your client believes that a large part of the reason is a lack of cooperation and collaboration between the team members, who come from various parts of the organization. If they are better team players, according to the logic, the cycle time will certainly be reduced. What is your opinion? Will it be reduced? How could you find out?

These are the types of questions that are answered when you identify the causal linkage between performance and operational results. For a model to be valid, it must identify the on-the-job behaviors and skills that, if used, *will* affect a change in the operational results. Note that we use the term *causal linkage* and not *cause and effect*. This is because the SHOULD performance will yield the desired operational results only if it is supported on the job. Often, the desired operational results can be achieved only through the SHOULD performance of several functions, such as Engineering, Purchasing, Manufacturing, and Distribution. This performance must be reinforced and supported by management for the desired operational results to occur; skills and knowledge by themselves are insufficient to yield the desired performance.

How do we identify causal linkage? We do this by determining the specific operational results we seek and then interviewing individuals (people we refer to as exemplary performers) who are achieving this level of results. Let's look more closely at the sources of information we can use to form models and build causal linkages.

Sources of Information and Data Collection Methods

Several sources of information can be used to identify causal linkages and to form models. The sources that are primarily used include:

1. Exemplary performers
2. Managers of exemplary performers

3. The literature

4. Customers

5. Subject matter experts

Exemplary performers are individuals within the organization who are already performing in a quality manner and are yielding the desired operational results. If you are focusing on sales personnel, these are the individuals who are consistently meeting or exceeding their sales goals. If you are focusing on operators, these are the individuals who produce product at both desired yields and qualities. The rationale is that if these individuals are able to perform so successfully, others can also be developed and encouraged to do so. This source is vital to the Performance Consultant; we will provide additional information on it later in this chapter

Although exemplary performers are very important sources of information, it is also true that sometimes they cannot describe what they do that results in their success. They are performing in an unconsciously competent manner. However, someone who manages these individuals is in a position to describe what sets them apart. *Managers of exemplary performers* can indicate what the exemplary performers are doing differently from the more typical performer.

Our experience indicates that exemplary performers and their managers are the two best sources of information, but there are other options to consider as well. Much of the performance we require in organizations has already been researched by others and is available in the literature. For example, if you want to describe the model for an empowering manager, you can locate the behaviors in several books such as *The Leadership Challenge* (Kouzes and Posner, 1987) or *Empowerment in Organizations: How to Spark Exceptional Performance* (Vogt and Murrell, 1990). If you are interested in knowing the model for the performance of a sales representative who must sell within a long cycle (that is, one that takes several months or more before an agreement is reached), then a good reference is Neil Rackham's book, *Account Strategy for Major Sales* (1988). The literature is filled with quality research you can draw on as a Performance Consultant; use it.

If you are developing a model for a position that has *customers* (either internal or external), seek their input as to what type of performance would be of benefit. We had the experience once of forming performance models for sales positions. We used exemplary performers and their managers as our primary sources. When our interviews were completed, we formed a draft of the performance models so our clients could get a preview of what we were learning. Then we interviewed external customers of these sales professionals and identified twelve additional practices the customers wanted that had not been mentioned! These were integrated into the models, increasing the probability that the sales representative who used the practices would be viewed as a supplier of choice by the customer.

Subject matter experts become a very important source of information when you are forming models for a technical position. What is the most effective and efficient way to operate a piece of equipment? to program a computer? to engineer a solution to a problem? This is also an important source if there are no exemplary performers to interview in your organization. Perhaps the operational result is new, so no one has ever had to perform in support of it before. A few years ago, one of our clients wanted to form a performance model for a new engineering position; it became necessary to go to universities that were specializing in this field to obtain information for the model.

Criteria for Selecting Exemplary Performers

We have indicated that the exemplary performers and their managers are the two best sources of information when obtaining data for models. In identifying exemplary performers, it is critical to form criteria to use in selecting the individuals who will be interviewed. This ensures that those who are interviewed are obtaining the desired performance results, which, in turn, are causally linked to operational results. The following types of criteria are typically used:

1. *Length of time in position:* As good as people may be, unless they have been in the position for a reasonable amount of time, it would be difficult to refer to them as exemplary. We typically suggest that a minimum of one year be used; however, this time requirement can be modified depending on the situation. We once had a contract to form competency models for a position where people typically stayed only one year before moving on to another position; the time requirement for inclusion in the interviews was reduced to six months.

2. *Rating on appraisal:* If the organization's performance appraisal has credibility, it should be used as one of the criteria. Typically, we suggest that the client select people who have rated in the top 10 to 20 percent in their last two appraisals.

3. *Achievement of operational results:* We seek people who have demonstrated an ability to achieve the operational (quantifiable) results identified as important to the client. This is where you will truly be focusing on causal linkage; after all, these individuals are achieving business results by using a specific set of behaviors or practices. What are they? Could other people be developed to use them?

4. *Achievement of qualitative results:* Rarely are exemplary performers superior only because of *what* they achieve; we also need to look at *how* they do it. If someone achieves results but alienates people in the process, it is unlikely that this would form the basis for a model. Select the qualitative results and processes that are important to the position and ask the client to consider them in selecting people to be interviewed.

It has been our experience that only 5 to 10 percent of the people in a given position qualify as exemplary. Therefore, out of 100 people in the entire population, there may only be 5 to 10 who should be interviewed. It is our suggestion that when you are forming models, you interview the few exemplary people in-depth to obtain the best information.

Methods of Obtaining Information

You may have noted our reference to interviews. This is because the primary method of obtaining information for the purpose of forming a competency or performance model is the interview. Interviews can be conducted one on one (over the telephone or face to face) or in a focus group format. Remember that when you are forming a model for a position, you are essentially starting with a blank sheet of paper. You are attempting to identify performance as it SHOULD be and not as it IS. With so many unknowns, it becomes important to interview those who are in the best position to provide relevant information, looking for patterns and trends. In this manner you begin to fill in the blank sheet.

In Chapter Six we will describe this interview process more completely. But here are a few pointers regarding methods of obtaining information:

■ Typically, interviews with exemplary performers and their managers require two hours of time. These are in-depth interviews designed to find out as much as possible about what these people do that makes them so successful. Interviews with other sources, such as customers, will be shorter.

■ You ask questions about what the person actually *does*, not what he or she knows.

■ In a focus group format, this interview requires three to four hours. We recommend that exemplary performers be placed in one group and their managers in another. When they are in the same group, the responses of the managers will often influence the responses of the performers.

■ The best two sources of information for models are exemplary performers and their managers. If you can use no other source, we encourage you to use these two.

■ Organize the interview around the business goals and initiatives that have been identified. For example, if safety performance is a key business focus, ask about the actions and techniques the performers use to achieve safety goals; if another business goal focuses on quality service to customers, find out what the performers do to provide service that is seen as excellent by customers. In this way you are continually reinforcing the fact that performance is causally linked to operational results.

In addition to the interview, a documentation review can be a method of gathering information when building models. Procedural manuals and research done by others and documented in books and articles all qualify as documentation. But this documentation cannot stand alone; it must be supported by interviews with some relevant sources of information.

Summary

1. Models describe the performance of people as it must be if the organization's goals are to be achieved. The components of a model include identification of the performance results, best practices or competencies, the quality criteria used to measure performance, and the obstacles that are encountered in accomplishing performance results.

2. The Performance Consultant, in collaboration with the client team, needs to decide if the models will be described as performance or competency models. The process for obtaining data for each is the same; the way the information is analyzed and reported is different.

3. Models identify the causal linkage between performance and operational results. This ensures that the best practices or competencies are linked to business and organizational goals.

4. The best two sources of information for building models are exemplary performers and their managers. It is important to form criteria for identifying exemplary performers.

6

Creating Performance Models: A Case Example

Business Need:

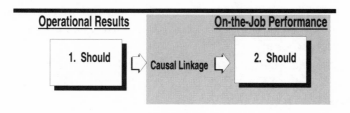

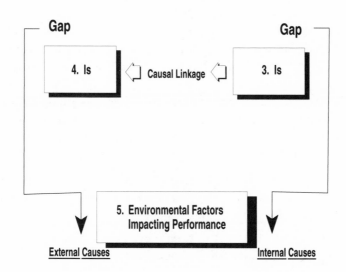

Let's return to Gaso Petroleum Company and the work that Janet Waterman is doing with Jake Coleman of Retail Marketing. As you may recall, Jake has three primary business goals that must be achieved:

1. Doubling profits in the next three years

2. Bringing all stations into full compliance with environmental regulations and laws

3. Increasing customer satisfaction with service and price so that Gaso will be the customer's station of choice.

It was agreed that Janet would assist Jake in forming performance models for several positions within Retail Marketing. Jake asked Janet to begin with the position of territory manager, which is critical to the company's future success. Because people in this position have direct contact with station managers and dealers, the position has the greatest opportunity to contribute to business success.

Gaso has 100 territory managers and 9 district managers. Jake and Janet agreed that Janet should interview exemplary territory managers and all district managers. Although it was not necessary to interview all 9 district managers in order to form models, Jake wanted to avoid alienating any managers who might feel left out of the process.

Jake and Janet first agreed upon the criteria to use in identifying exemplary territory managers. For territory managers to be interviewed, they had to have the following characteristics:

■   They had been in the position of territory manager for a minimum of two years. Territory managers tend to remain in their position for five years or more, so a minimum of two years seemed appropriate.

■   They had received a rating of "exceeds" (or higher) on their appraisal for the last two years. The "exceeds" rating is the second highest in the Gaso system.

■   They had obtained at least 95 percent of their gas *and* non-gas revenue goals for the past two years. Because of the problems Gaso had been having, an insufficient number of territory managers had met their goals; therefore, the criteria needed to be reduced to 95 percent.

■ They had received high evaluation ratings by the district manager for bringing stations into environmental compliance and for increasing customer satisfaction. These measures are key to the future business goals of Gaso; therefore, efforts were made to identify territory managers who already evidenced strong performance in these two areas.

■ They had strong verbal communication skills. Territory managers would be interviewed in depth and would be asked questions regarding their performance. It was important for them to skillfully articulate responses to the interviewer's questions.

These criteria were reviewed with the district managers, who submitted the names of territory managers within their districts who met the criteria. When all names were submitted, Janet and Jake reviewed the list to ensure that it represented the various markets and geographic locations within Gaso as a whole. Some adjustments were made to the list, and when it was completed, a total of ten territory managers were identified for interviews. As noted, all district managers would also be interviewed; therefore, a total of nineteen interviews were to be conducted. Because each interview would require two hours, thirty-eight hours of interviews were to be completed. While some of the interviews would occur face to face, the majority would be conducted over the telephone to keep from incurring travel costs.

In addition to the time required to conduct the interviews, Janet needed time to perform content analysis of the information and to form a draft of the models. She and Jake agreed that the first draft would be provided to Jake in six weeks. Janet would work with a member of her staff to complete the interviews.

Interview Guides and Process

The process begins with prework that is sent to those who will be interviewed. The quality of the interview is enhanced when people have taken time to prepare for it.

Prework

The next step for Janet was to prepare the interview guides and the prework. Prework actually has two major purposes:

1. To introduce the term *performance result* or *output* so that the individual has an understanding of what is being focused upon

2. To provide the individual with time to thoughtfully identify the major performance results expected of him or her

Performance Consulting Tool 3 is an example of the prework that Janet sent to the territory managers who were to be interviewed. In reviewing this prework you will notice that in the first section of the worksheet, the individual is asked to identify the three major performance results expected of him or her, and in the second section, the individual will list other performance results that directly support the specific business goals that were identified in the first phase of the analysis. By categorizing the performance results according to the business goals, you are assured of obtaining information on performance that is *causally linked* to these goals.

It is unlikely that you will be able to discuss in depth each of the performance results identified in the prework. Therefore, at the close of your interview, you should collect the prework and review it during the content analysis phase.

Performance Consulting Tool 3

Sample Prework: Sent to
Exemplary Territory Managers Prior to Interview

TO: (*Name of Territory Manager*)

FROM: Janet Waterman

Shortly, I will interview you to discuss your job. The purpose of this interview is to identify the major performance results expected of you in your position of territory manager. Also, I want to learn what you do to accomplish those results.

The term *performance result* means a key objective or goal that must be accomplished by someone who is in a particular position if that individual is to be successful. Generally, the major performance results of a job are required each year; they do not vary much from year to year.

Example

A physician with a private practice would be expected to:

1.   Diagnose patients

2.   Prescribe medications

3.   Invoice patients and insurance carriers for provided services

These performance results would need to occur each year, in a skillful and effective manner, if the physician is to be successful. In developing other physicians it would be beneficial to show them how successful doctors perform each of these results. What steps do they take to accurately diagnose patients? to ensure that invoicing is done promptly and correctly? That is the type of information we wish to obtain from you regarding your position.

Worksheet

Jot down your thoughts in response to each question on this worksheet. In the interview I will ask you about the type of information noted here; this advance preparation will expedite the interview process.

1. What are the *three* most important performance results expected of you in your position? These are results you *must* accomplish each year if you are to be successful.

    Result 1: _____

    _____

    Result 2: _____

    _____

    Result 3: _____

    _____

2. Listed below are specific areas of performance that may or may not be relevant to your position. Consider each area and its applicability to your job. If an area is one where you must accomplish results, list two major performance results expected of you. If you have already identified the performance results for this area in response to question I, then skip the item.

    Business Goal Area 1: *Double profits in the next three years.*

    Performance Result 1: _____

    _____

    Performance Result 2: _____

    _____

    Business Goal Area 2: *Bring all stations into full compliance with environmental regulations and laws.*

    Performance Result 1: _____

    _____

    Performance Result 2: _____

    _____

Business Goal Area 3: *Increase customer satisfaction with service and price so that Gaso will be a customer's station of choice.*

Performance Result 1: _____

_____

Performance Result 2: _____

_____

You have completed this worksheet. Please bring it with you to our interview.

The Interview Guide for Exemplary Performers

When collecting data, it is crucial "to ask the right questions right." To ensure that you do ask the right questions, it is essential to develop an interview guide, one that is customized for the specific purposes of the interview and tailored to those being interviewed. Performance Consulting Tool 4 is a sample interview guide for obtaining SHOULD information from exemplary performers. Included here are the questions, their rationale, and information Janet learned from interviewing the territory managers.

Performance Consulting Tool 4

Sample Interview Guide:
Interviewing Exemplary Performers for SHOULD Information

Introductory Comments

Follow the procedure described here:

1. Introduce yourself; confirm the time required for the interview.
2. Describe the purposes of the entire assessment.
3. Present an overview of the purposes of this interview.
4. Clarify how the information is being obtained and reported.

Rationale: *When an interview begins, the context and big picture of what is being done must be explained to the individual. Therefore, introductory comments must be prepared, which typically include this type of information. The importance of each introductory comment is as follows (each point here refers to its corresponding number on the preceding page):*

1. *It is important to introduce yourself, if necessary, and to reaffirm the amount of time the interview will require to ensure that it is still convenient for the individual.*

2. *This provides the interviewee with the big picture of the project. It is also an opportunity to affirm the business goals you have identified.*

3. *The overview of the interview's purposes includes the information that the interviewees will be asked to provide.*

4. *Here, describe how the interviews are being used with the performers and their managers to obtain performance information. Most people want to know how many people will be interviewed, how (and to whom) information will be reported, and whether they will receive any of the findings. Clarify that all information will be confidential. All data will be analyzed, and a summary of the findings will be reported. While the names of those interviewed will be known, no specific statements will be attributed to a specific person. People also want to know why they were selected to be interviewed. This can be a delicate situation; you do not want to offend others who were not selected, nor do you want to communicate that the individual selected is headed for a promotion in the organization! We typically say that the individual was selected because he or she is experienced in the position and has been successful in it; this seems to be sufficient for most people.*

Before launching into the interview, it is a good idea to ask the individual if she or he has any questions to ask of you. Sometimes there is an item for which clarity is required; it is wise to discuss any questions before proceeding.

Demographic Information

Typical demographic information includes:

1. Name
2. Title
3. Geographic area and/or organizational unit
4. Length of time in position
5. Phone number (in case you need to recontact the individual)

> Rationale: *The demographic information will vary greatly with each situation. This information is obtained for two purposes. The first is to provide those reviewing the information with a profile of the people who were interviewed. What characteristics will be of interest to your clients? There are times when the criteria used to identify people can also become the demographic information that is reported. For example, if years of experience is a criterion, you could obtain this information and summarize it to indicate the average years of experience for those interviewed.*
>
> *The second purpose is to sort the results by a particular quality. Perhaps you are interviewing managers for the purpose of forming a model. It is possible that you and your client have determined that there will actually be two models: manager of exempt personnel and manager of nonexempt employees. If this is the case, you only need one interview guide, because the questions will be identical; however, you must indicate in the demographic information how this information should be sorted.*
>
> *One caution with demographic information: obtain only what is required. There is a tendency to obtain too much information and then do nothing with it. Our advice is to make this interview process as efficient as possible; one of the ways to do this is to avoid obtaining information you will not use.*

Janet and Jake discussed what demographic information was of greatest importance to them. Janet's interview guide asked about the following areas:

1.   *Name of individual: Jake wanted a list of the people who were actually interviewed.*

2.   *Title of individual: Territory managers had different grades as part of their title, ranging from Territory Manager 1 (largest districts) to Territory Manager 3 (smallest districts). Again, Jake wanted to know how many of each grade were interviewed.*

3.   *District: Territory managers could work in any of nine districts; Jake was interested in knowing how many from each district were actually interviewed.*

4.   *Length of time in position: Experience was one of the criteria used. It was important to Jake to know the actual length of time in the job for these exemplary performers.*

5.   *Phone number: Some of the interviews would be conducted over the phone, so this information was required. However, it was also possible that Janet would need to recontact interviewees during the analysis phase. Sometimes, for example, a piece of information collected during the interview cannot be interpreted later; therefore, Janet wanted to ensure that she had accurate phone numbers for all territory managers.*

Primary Focus

Ask the following questions:

1.   Before we begin discussing the specifics of your position, it would be helpful if you could step back and indicate what you see as the major focus for your job. Why does it exist?

2.   How, if at all, will that be changing in the next few years?

Rationale: *Prior to getting information on the performance results, it is helpful to step back and obtain the big picture for the position and its ultimate purpose as the performer views it to be. In essence, the first question is asking the individual to describe the mission for the job. When you obtain this type of information from a variety of people, some interesting patterns emerge:*

- *There can be widespread agreement, which is good. Those in the position share a similar view as to why they are there and what they must accomplish.*

- *There can be widespread disagreement, which is a problem. In this instance there is lack of clarity and uniformity as to the reason for the position.*

- *There could be two primary purposes that are somewhat different, resulting in individuals feeling as if they are being pulled in different directions. For example, customer service representatives who take calls from customers over the telephone could indicate that the primary purposes for their position are to provide quality service to customers and to handle a specified number of calls each day. It is possible for these two focuses to be in conflict because providing quality service could require taking time with customers on the phone; this, in turn, would reduce the number of calls actually managed in a day.*

The second question determines whether the individual believes that the focus of the position will be changing. Your client team has provided input about the future; now you have an opportunity to determine what the people actually doing the job perceive as the future needs. Future needs are the reason to form models; we want to obtain this information from all perspectives.

Janet asked the territory managers to describe in two or three sentences what they saw as the focus for their position. She obtained responses such as the following:

- *"To be the link between the station managers and dealers and Gaso."*

- *"To be a point of contact for the station managers and dealers."*

■   *"To work with the station managers and dealers to make them
     as successful as they can be."*

*When Janet did her analysis, she determined that there was a
fairly consistent view of the purpose of the territory manager's position, which she summarized as: "To operate as a link between the
station managers and dealers and the company, working with these
managers so that they fully achieve the business potential for their
respective stations."*

*When Janet asked the second part of this question, "How, if
at all, will that [focus] be changing in the next few years?" The
territory managers were consistent in their opinion that the focus
would not change; what would be changing would be the methods
and approaches used to accomplish this mission.*

Performance Results

Ask the following questions:

1.   Prior to this interview you received some information that de-
     scribed the term *performance result* and provided you with
     some examples. Do you have any questions about the term
     before we begin?

2.   I would like to discuss the three performance results that you
     identified as most important for your position. What are the
     three that you listed in your prework?

Write down each result on the following pages but obtain no additional information. Then return to the results to obtain more specific
data.

> Rationale: *The next step in the interview process is to identify
> the performance results that the individual believes are impor-
> tant to accomplish. We have found that the process that
> works best is to have the individual begin by identifying the
> three most important results and then return to each one for
> an in-depth discussion. In essence, we have provided the in-
> dividual with a blank sheet on which to write down the most*

important outputs. Later, we will categorize these responses into the appropriate business goals; for now we want to provide the individual with the freedom to answer with whatever he or she views as most critical.

One problem that can occur is that the individual may list something as a performance result that does not meet our criteria for a result. For example, a shift supervisor could list "resolving conflicts between workers" as a result; we would view that as part of a larger performance area such as "fostering teamwork among workers." Sometimes people provide several results in one statement: "To manage all operations so that quality product is produced in a safe and environmentally sound manner." We would then split this apart and ask the individual to tell us what she or he does to:

- *Produce quality product*
- *Meet safety goals*
- *Meet environmental goals*

By first asking the individual to describe the three most important results, you have an opportunity to understand the scope of the individual's job and can then determine which results you will probe and in what order.

Performance Result 1: _____

_____

Ask the following questions regarding this result:

1. When you accomplish this result, what specifically do you do? Please walk me through the steps and actions you take to accomplish this result.

    Rationale: *Once the three most important performance results are identified, you will want to begin discussing each of them in depth. In response to the first question, the individual will provide you with specific actions, steps, decisions, analyses, and so forth that are done to accomplish the result. You want to ensure that these are as specific and behavioral as possible. If the individual indicates that he or she "communicates the information to people," find out what information is communicated, in what manner, and to what people. If the person claims to "gain consensus before moving ahead," find out what she or he does to gain this consensus. While this process may seem tedious, it is the most critical information you will obtain. During the analysis phase you will use these data to form best practices (if you are forming a performance model) or to identify competencies (if you are forming competency models).*

2. (When all steps have been described) Are there any other steps or actions you believe you should be taking in support of this result that you are not currently taking?

   Rationale: *With some frequency, exemplary performers know what actions should be taken; they are not doing so for a variety of reasons that could include lack of accountability, lack of reinforcement, or an actual policy that prevents them from doing so. This question helps to push the edges of the envelope of the position so that a model, of performance as it* SHOULD *be, can truly be formed.*

3. How do you know that you have accomplished this result in an excellent manner? What criteria do you use to determine that the result was a success? (*Note:* Obtain quantitative *and* qualitative criteria.)

   Rationale: *Here, you encourage the individual to identify both quantitative (numerically based) and qualitative (behaviorally based) criteria. What criteria are used to know whether a manager is developing employees effectively? It helps to ask the individual for a description of the criteria his or her manager uses to measure this performance. There are times when you will find that no criteria can be articulated; this is certainly an issue to bring to the attention of your client.*

4. What work environment factors do you encounter as you attempt to accomplish this result? What makes it difficult for you to accomplish this result in a successful manner?

5. What helps you to accomplish this result?

> Rationale: *Finally, we want to identify any work environment barriers or enhancers the individual encounters in accomplishing the result. We want to address obstacles and leverage enhancers, so both are important. We know from our performance relationship map that these could be either external or internal to the organization. We have found that the majority of work environment factors identified by a performer will be internal. Typically, barriers include such things as lack of time, lack of authority, or role conflict with another position regarding whose responsibility it is to perform the result. Often the enhancers include coaching by the direct manager, accessibility of information, or sufficient authority. Usually, performers identify two or three work environment factors for each performance result. Occasionally, a person does not identify any.*
>
> *Once you have discussed the first performance result in this manner, you move on to the second result. This process will continue through the remainder of the interview. A typical interview for the purpose of forming models requires two hours to complete. In that time you will be able to discuss, in depth, between five and eight performance results. It is probable that the individual has noted more than that on the prework; therefore, it is important to take the prework with you to analyze later.*

Now let's look at how Janet used these questions as she interviewed the territory manager. She made the transition into the questions about performance results by asking if the individual had any questions about the prework or the term performance result. *She then asked to see the three results listed as most important. She found that the territory managers consistently mentioned three of the following:*

- *To meet gasoline sales goals*

- *To meet nongas sales goals*

- *To ensure compliance with health, safety, and environmental regulations*

- *To identify locations for future stations*

- *To maintain a high station image*

For each performance result, Janet asked the following questions:

1. *When you accomplish this result, what specifically do you do? Please walk me through the steps and actions you take to accomplish this result.*

The territory managers provided many techniques, decisions, and actions (best practices) that they take in support of each performance result. For example, regarding the performance result "To meet gasoline sales goals," they mentioned the following:

- *Gathering information on competitors in the market area and communicating that information to the station managers and dealers*

- *Determining the purpose of a sales call prior to meeting with a station manager or dealer*

- *Developing station attendants so that they evidence strong customer service skills to customers when they come into the station*

- *Reviewing gasoline sales results monthly for each station; providing this information to the station managers and dealers and to all attendants so they know their actual sales compared to the goal and how they compare to other stations in the territory*

2. *(When all steps have been described) Are there any other steps or actions you believe you should be taking in support of this result that you are not currently taking?*

One person said that territory managers have twenty or more stations in their territory. As a result they are in a position to learn about what each station manager or dealer is doing to achieve results; these are ideas that could be shared with other station managers and dealers. Currently, no system was in place to transfer this information to the station managers and dealers; transfer was dependent upon the territory managers' own recall of what was learned and commitment to sharing it. However, if these ideas could be routinely shared across the territory—and across the district—everyone would benefit

3.   *How do you know that you have accomplished this result in an excellent manner? What criteria do you use to determine that the result was a success?*

The territory managers described many quality criteria that could be used to measure excellent performance. The overwhelming majority of these criteria were quantitative (for example, meeting or exceeding sales goals, ending the year at but not over the operating budget set for the territory, avoiding penalties or fines for nonenvironmental compliance). A few qualitative criteria were identified, such as having a customer praise the station's appearance either verbally or in written comments or having station managers and dealers indicate that they were pleased with the support of the territory manager. These types of criteria were also used to measure performance.

4.   *What work environment factors do you encounter as you attempt to accomplish this result? What makes it difficult for you to accomplish this result in a successful manner?*

The territory managers indicated that lack of operating revenues was a real problem in accomplishing the business goal of being the station of choice to customers. Increasing customer satisfaction required improvement of station image and services, the very types of capital improvements envisioned for Gaso. But until those improvements could be made, the stations were viewed as old by cus-

tomers; unfortunately, old sometimes translated into "dirty" for a customer even though that was not the case.

A second major obstacle seemed to be the lack of support the territory managers felt they had from their district managers. Jake had identified this as a concern. If exemplary performers felt that they were not being provided with adequate guidance, feedback, and reinforcement, how did the more typical territory manager feel?

5.   What helps you to accomplish this result?

In response to this question, the exemplary territory managers mentioned that it was helpful to work with the district manager to form a territory business plan, because the process clarified the goals for the territory. It also gave them an opportunity to discuss strategies for achieving those goals with their district manager. It is important to find out if this performance enhancer is occurring for all performers, not just the exemplary ones.

Other Results

At this time, you may want to ask the respondent if you can review the prework in order to identify areas to discuss. Open discussion of these areas by saying:

> We have discussed the major results expected of you in your job. Now I would like to ask you about certain aspects of your job that may or may not be important. It would be helpful to know of any performance results that are expected of you in any of the following categories.

Business Goal, Area 1: *(Fill in before the interview.)*

Performance Result: _____

_____

Ask the following questions regarding this result:

1.   When you accomplish this result, what specifically do you do?

Please walk me through the steps and actions you take to accomplish this result.

2. Are there any other steps or actions you believe you should be taking in support of this result that you are not currently taking?

3. How do you know that you have accomplished this result in an excellent manner? What criteria do you use to determine that the result was a success? (*Note:* Obtain quantitative and qualitative criteria.)

4. What work environment factors do you encounter as you attempt to accomplish this result? What makes it difficult for you to accomplish this result in a successful manner?

5. What helps you to accomplish this result?

Rationale: *Once you have explored in depth the three most important performance results, you need to inquire about specific business goals and what the individual must do to support these goals. From the data you collected earlier in the project, you know the primary business goals that must be achieved. If these goals are to be realized, people must accomplish certain performance results. What are they? How do exemplary performers accomplish them?*

In "Other Results," you write in the business goals that were mentioned in the prework you sent to the interviewee.

During the interview, you probe to determine what this particular individual does to support that goal. If the performance results for a specific business goal were adequately discussed previously during the interview, pass by that goal for now. There is plenty to discuss!

Ideally, you want to discuss in depth at least one performance result for each business goal you've identified. Therefore, if there are four business goals, you would hope to discuss at least four performance results.

In the prework, Janet asked territory managers to identify the performance results expected of them in each of the following business areas:

■   *Increasing the profitability of stations in the territory*

■   *Ensuring station compliance with environmental regulations and laws*

■   *Increasing customer satisfaction so customers would view the station in their area as the station of choice*

Often, when Janet asked territory managers to identify the performance results completed in support of the profitability goal, they again mentioned their need to meet sales goals for gasoline and nongas products. Obviously, one of the ways in which they affect profits is by producing a revenue stream into the organization. If territory managers mentioned these results in response to the question about the three most important results, Janet did not discuss them again. Instead, she probed to find out what else is done that has an impact on the profitability picture. In doing this, she found such performance results as "To provide financial and business counseling to station managers and dealers." Included in this result was guidance provided to station managers and dealers who were experiencing financial difficulties. The territory manager would review a station's fixed and variable costs, identifying ways to reduce these costs. The territory manager also provided guidance in ways to increase traffic through the station, thus increasing revenue. Janet was very excited when this performance result began to form because she knew it was something that was now being done inconsistently; she was certain that by developing all territory managers so they could do this and by providing the necessary work environment support so they would do it, the business goal of doubling profits would be positively affected.

Closing the Interview

Ask the following questions:

1.   Is there any performance result you are expected to perform in addition to those we have discussed?

2.   Is there anything else that was not already covered that it would be important to know?

3.   Do you have any questions to ask of me?

In addition, either collect the prework (if you are in a face-to-face interview) or ensure that you have noted all the performance results identified by the interviewee even though they may not have been discussed in depth. If you are conducting a telephone interview, ask the individual to fax the prework to you.

Thank the individual for his or her time.

> Rationale: *By the time you get to this section of the interview, there will be approximately ten minutes left in the two hours. You will have at least reviewed the results listed on the prework and will have discussed several of them in depth. Now you want to provide the individual with an opportunity to identify any other performance result that did not happen to fit into the structure you established for the interview. When we ask this question, we typically do not learn anything new; occasionally, however, we have identified new results. Often they are in the administrative area—for example, completing paperwork or organizing the workday or work week.*

Janet found that when she asked about performance results that had not been discussed, she usually received information about managing time and the territory. She probed to find out what a territory manager, who typically works in an independent manner from his or her home, does to organize a workday or a work week, and she asked how a territory manager ensures adequate coverage to all station managers and dealers? She also learned that a great deal of paperwork is involved in the sales process, such as expense reports and sales call reports that must be completed. She took down this information, uncertain how she would organize it into the model. However, it was important to obtain it; she would determine its placement later.

Interview Guide for
Managers of Exemplary Performers

As has been noted previously, the two best sources of information in forming models are exemplary performers and their managers. You will typically send prework to the manager prior to the interview. And, of course, you will develop an interview guide to use when interviewing the manager. Both the prework and the interview guide for managers are virtually identical to those for exemplary performers. The primary difference is that during the interview, the manager is asked to think of the *best* performer the individual has ever managed in this position and to describe what that person did to accomplish a result. Once you have obtained this information, it is important to determine what sets this exemplary performer apart from typical performers. You specifically ask the manager, "What sets this strong performer apart from those who are more typical?" With those exceptions, the interview process is identical to the one described for the exemplary performer.

In the interview process for Gaso Petroleum Company, Janet and Jake agreed that all nine district managers were to be interviewed. When these interviews were conducted, Janet found that there was a high degree of similarity between what the district managers described in terms of results, activities, and criteria and what the territory managers had noted. A very interesting pattern began to emerge when she asked what set apart the very strong territory manager from a more typical one. She repeatedly heard such things as "The exceptional territory manager becomes a business partner to the station manager and dealer" and "The territory manager is sincerely interested in the station manager and dealer being a success—not just Gaso." Janet was able to probe district managers to obtain the specific behaviors used by territory managers to evidence this sense of partnership. She felt that Jake would be pleased when he saw this type of information.

Forming the Models

Once all the information has been obtained, content analysis of the information and formation of a draft of a model begins. This is when the decision about whether to form a performance model or a competency model is critical. If you are forming a performance model, the process of analysis requires that you:

1. Identify the performance results that are critical to the job and business goals.

2. List the activities you have identified under each result.

If you are forming a competency model, then you will:

1. Identify the performance results that are critical to the job and business goals.

2. List the competencies required to accomplish each result. This step requires that you deduce the competencies that are being described from the behaviors you have been provided. For example, if someone indicated that a required step was to "review documents pertinent to the situation," you may code this as "fact finding." If someone told you they needed to "gain support of others for a proposed plan of action," you may code that as "building consensus."

If you are using a competency model approach, it is helpful to have a list of probable competencies with definitions as you begin your work. You also should use activities as behavioral descriptions of how a competency is demonstrated by people in this specific job. For example, we don't want to simply report that fact finding is a critical competency; we want to illustrate how that competency is demonstrated.

With both performance and competency models, it is often useful to identify the attributes that are needed for success in the job. An attribute is a personal characteristic or trait that should be incorporated into the selection criteria for the job, such as integrity or flexibility. Although you can create environments that encourage integrity, the individual must bring this characteristic with her or him to the job. If people are basically rigid in their approach, it is improbable that any amount of training will make them flexible. What attributes are required for success

in the position you are assessing? Are these attributes being selected for at this time? If not, could the people who interview and
recruit people into the position be developed to obtain information on these attributes? These are the types of questions that can
be addressed through the model process; they add value to the
entire effort.

One technique we have found very helpful when forming
models is to rewrite the information that has been obtained from
the interviews onto Post-it Notes. We use one color of notes for
information obtained from performers and a second color for
information obtained from managers. Using a very large wall,
we move the notes around and recategorize them with ease.
Often information received during an interview will be placed
into a different performance result from the one in which it was
discussed; Post-it Notes provide this type of flexibility. They also
allow you to stand back and look at the big picture of the model
as it is forming.

It is helpful to work with a subject matter expert when
organizing data into a model. We have found this to be particularly helpful in forming models for positions that are technical
in nature (such as programmer, technician, or engineer). A subject matter expert has in-depth knowledge of the concepts, terms,
and processes that can be most helpful as you organize your
information into a model. What is important is that the individual not only know the job but lacks biases as to what the model
should be. Typically, therefore, subject matter experts are individuals who once worked in the position but no longer do so.
Remember, you will be forming a model of how the job SHOULD
be, not how it IS; the individuals working with you need to be
free of any vested interest that biases their judgment in favor of
a status quo result.

In the Gaso Petroleum Company, Janet transferred information from her interview guides onto Post-it Notes and worked
with a colleague (who had also conducted some interviews) to
code the information into a model. Some results were obvious
("To meet gasoline sales goals"); others required more time because they were less clear. When she was done, Janet had formed

a draft of a performance model for the territory manager that she could take to Jake for review.

The following list shows the big picture of all the results that were identified for the three business goals discussed for the position of territory manager. Each business goal now defines a performance cluster or a set of performance results that are causally linked to accomplishment of the business goal:

Performance Cluster for Profitability

1. *Meet gasoline volume goals:* Manage the territory to ensure that annual gas volume goals are met or exceeded.

2. *Meet nongas product volume goals:* Manage the territory to ensure that annual nongas product volume goals are met or exceeded.

3. *Maximize participation in, and return from, station promotions:* Work to ensure full support of promotions by all Gaso station managers and dealers.

4. *Maximize profitability of stations:* Provide guidance to station managers and dealers on the effectiveness and profitable management of their businesses.

Performance Cluster for Health, Safety, and Environmental Requirements

5. *Ensure compliance with safety and environmental requirements:* Take actions to ensure that all station managers and dealers in the territory are in full compliance with local, state, and federal safety and environmental regulations and requirements.

Performance Cluster for Service Quality

6. *Maintain high image and service standards:* Work with station managers and dealers to maintain consistently high image standards throughout the territory.

7. *Establish positive relationships with customers:* Form and maintain strong partnerships with station managers and dealers and their regular customers within the territory.

Performance Cluster for Planning and Administration

8. *Manage time and territory:* Organize and ensure coverage of all stations within the territory.

9. *Develop a territory market plan:* Work with the district manager to develop annual territory budgets and revenue strategies.

Table 6.1 is a matrix that illustrates which business goal is supported by each performance result. Once again, we are reinforcing the principle that performance is directly linked to business goals. As you will note, sometimes a performance result like "Manage time and territory" supports several business goals. Occasionally, a business goal may have only one performance result, or possibly none, in support of it. It may be a business goal that is suffering from lack of attention even by the exemplary performers. It is also possible that the goal is being supported effectively by another position and requires little support from the position being analyzed.

Table 6.2 illustrates a complete description for one performance result for the position of territory manager. You will note the best practices that were identified together with quality criteria and obstacles. A page of information like this would be developed for each of the nine performance results identified for the job of territory manager. Note the practices in italics; they are the ones that surfaced from the question, "Are there any other steps or actions you believe you should be taking in support of this result that you are not currently taking?" You want to bring them to the attention of your client as practices that should be considered for inclusion in the model.

At Gaso, Janet continued to compile a list of work environment factors—both barriers and enhancers. This was an initial list, but it was important for Jake and other members to have an opportunity to review them. The client team often adds to the factors or provides more details about factors that are ambiguous. The impact of the work environment factors upon perfor-

Table 6.1. Business Goals for Gaso Retail Division.

Performance Results	Double Profits in Next Three Years	Ensure That All Stations Are in Environmental Compliance	Be Station of Choice to Customers
Profitability Cluster			
1. Meet gasoline volume goals	✓		
2. Meet nongas product volume goals	✓		
3. Maximize participation in, and return from, station promotions	✓		
4. Maximize profitability of stations	✓		
Health, Safety, and Environmental Cluster			
5. Ensure compliance with safety and environmental requirements		✓	
Service Quality Cluster			
6. Maintain high image and service standards	✓		✓
7. Establish positive relationships with customers	✓		✓
Planning and Administration Cluster			
8. Manage time and territory	✓	✓	
9. Develop territory market plan	✓		✓

Table 6.2. Description of a Performance Result.

Performance Model: Territory Manager
Performance Cluster: Profitability

Performance Result (what must be accomplished)	Best Practices[a] (how the result is accomplished)	Quality Criteria (how to know the result has been accomplished in an excellent manner)
Maximize Profitability of Stations Definition: Provide guidance to station managers and dealers on the effective and profitable management of their businesses.	√ Determine the level of knowledge and skill the station manager or dealer has for the financial aspects of the business. This includes knowledge of computing cash flow, projections, net profit, and accounts receivable and payable.	√ Station managers and dealers seek out and use the advice and counsel of the territory manager.
	√ Review the monthly profit-and-loss statement with the station manager or dealer.	√ Station managers and dealers are financially viable.
	√ Seek opportunities to acknowledge the positive aspects of the financial management of the business.	√ A business plan is developed annually and is available for review.
	√ Identify ways in which the station manager or dealer can reduce the cost of supplies and materials.	√ The return-on-asset goal is achieved for all stations in the territory.
	√ Work with the station manager or dealer to form a business plan on an annual basis. Monitor actuals against the plan on a monthly and quarterly basis.	

√ Counsel the station manager or dealer on ways to deal effectively with personnel problems, such as an employee who is frequently tardy or absent.

√ Counsel the station manager or dealer on ways to manage his or her time.

√ Determine reasons for line-item accounts that are running over budget; identify ways to bring these items in line with the budget.

√ Ensure that inventory control sheets are being used; seek the ideas of the station manager or dealer about ways to control losses from inventory.

√ Teach the station manager or dealer how to compute margins on a daily and weekly basis.

√ *Counsel the station manager or dealer on strategies to use and issues to consider when pricing gasoline and nongas products.*

---

[a]The activities on this page are not listed in sequence or order of importance.

mance will be quantified during the cause analysis, which we discuss in Chapter Eight.

Finally, Table 6.3 displays the attributes required for the success of a territory manager. Janet knew that no system was in place to ensure that they were, in fact, used in the selection process of a territory manager; she was hopeful that Jake would want to work with her to change that situation. Because of the difficulty of developing these attributes, it is strongly advised that they be included in the selection criteria for territory managers.

Janet will be taking this draft to a meeting with Jake and the regional managers. She has also suggested that one territory manager and one district manager be present in the meeting. The draft is therefore viewed from multiple perspectives: that of someone in the position, someone who manages the position, and senior managers.

Summary

1. Interviews that are conducted with exemplary performers and their managers are more productive if these individuals receive prework to complete prior to the interview.

2. Performance results are obtained by specifically asking what an individual does in support of each business goal. This ensures a causal linkage between the business goals and employee performance.

3. The manner in which the interview data are analyzed will determine whether results are displayed as *performance* or *competency* models.

4. Attributes are characteristics required for success in a position that are difficult to develop. To the degree possible, it is helpful to identify the attributes for a specific position. These attributes can then be incorporated into selection criteria for the position.

Table 6.3. Attributes Required for Success as a Territory Manager.

Attribute	Definition	Examples of Ways Attribute Is Displayed by Territory Manager
Resilience	Handling disappointment and/or rejection while maintaining effectiveness	Keeps personal frustrations from interfering with work Sustains positive relations with others despite past conflict or disagreements Handles disappointments while maintaining business and professional effectiveness
Self-Confidence	Demonstrating self-assurance in unfamiliar or stressful situations	Exercises independent judgment about what is right or best Demonstrates self-assurance in the presence of senior management
Flexibility	Adaptive and receptive to the changing priorities of the business and the varying personalities of individuals	Switches to different approaches as conditions change Quickly reorganizes own schedule or activities in response to business needs Adjusts quickly to new procedures or ways of doing things
Initiative	Actively attempting to influence events and take action without request to do so	Makes the extra call, putting in the added effort to get the job done Makes significant decisions without always having to check with manager
Stress Tolerance	Stability of performance under pressure and/or opposition	Handles difficult problems with others openly and directly Manages the balance between conflicting demands from different people

7

Performance Assessments: Identifying Actual Performance

Business Need:

<u>Operational Results</u>   <u>On-the-Job Performance</u>

| 1. Should | ⇨ Causal Linkage ⇨ | 2. Should |

Gap   Gap

| 4. Is | ⇦ Causal Linkage ⇦ | 3. Is |

| 5. Environmental Factors Impacting Performance |

<u>External Causes</u>   <u>Internal Causes</u>

Now that a performance model has been constructed and approved by the client team, how do we identify the actual performance of individuals who are in the position? If we have developed a competency model, how do we identify the gaps between the SHOULD competencies and the actual or IS competencies?

Up to this point we have identified the performance results required for the position being examined. We have also described the best practices required to accomplish those performance results. Now our task is to determine any gaps between what the performers as a group are doing and what they should be doing. We also want to determine their skill level for each of the best practices. Finally, we want to determine which external and internal factors (CAUSES) are making it difficult for the performers to demonstrate best practices. Once we have this information, we will be able to make recommendations to management about the actions that should be taken to close any gaps that exist between IS and SHOULD performance. While you would typically obtain information on IS performance and CAUSES at the same time, we will be discussing them separately. In this chapter we will provide techniques and tools for obtaining information on current performance and skill; in Chapter Eight we will provide specific how-to's for identifying causes, other than lack of skill, for nonperformance.

Designing an Is Assessment

In creating an assessment that will define performance gaps there are many decisions to be made. Let's look more closely at what must be considered when designing an IS assessment.

What Do We Need To Know?

We need to identify skill gaps so that we can work with management to arrive at appropriate actions to close those gaps. Because it may not be possible to implement all actions at one time, we also want to know the relative importance of the skill gaps so that we can set priorities. In other words, we need to know which gaps should be addressed first so that recommended actions can have the greatest impact in the shortest period of time.

We have determined that two types of data will provide the required information regarding actual performance. These two types of data are relatively easy to collect, tabulate, and interpret. The information required consists of:

1. The relative importance of job practices or competencies to achieving performance results (importance is defined as low, basic, or key)

2. The current skill level of the incumbent performers (skill levels are defined as minimal, adequate, or proficient)

As shown in Figure 7.1, we are able to plot the relative importance of each job practice or competency along the X axis and the current skill level of performers on the Y axis. This creates a three-by-three matrix. The areas within heavy lines indicate the top training needs. The rationale behind this selection is as follows:

■   *Key requirements:* Key requirements are the practices that are so critical to success in a job that someone who could not perform them would most likely fail. Therefore, it is essential for performers to be proficient in these requirements.

■   *Basic requirements:* These requirements are important but not "make-or-break." Therefore, a lesser skill level can be tolerated. Training will be considered a priority only when the actual skill level is low for these requirements. When the skill level is either moderate or high, there is reason to question whether allocation of training resources is appropriate.

■   *Low requirements:* Any job requirement or competency that has been assessed as a low requirement is something for which training would rarely be considered. Therefore, an IS assessment can result in identification of the things for which no training resources will be allocated.

Figure 7.1. Three-by-Three Training Needs Matrix.

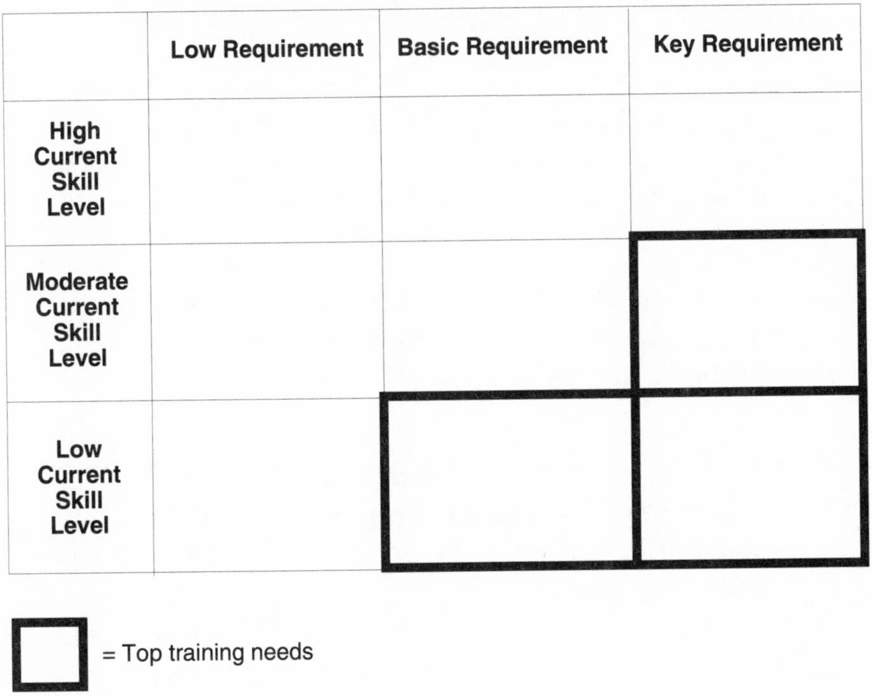

	Low Requirement	Basic Requirement	Key Requirement
High Current Skill Level			
Moderate Current Skill Level			
Low Current Skill Level			

□ = Top training needs

This approach has several advantages. Conceptually, it is not complex and is easily understood; logically, it makes sense. These characteristics make it highly credible with managers.

Where Do We Get the Data?

When considering sources of data, we must go to the people who know the most about the relative importance of practices and competencies and the skill level of performers. Of course, performers know more about their own jobs than anyone else. They know what practices enable them to achieve performance results. They know which competencies are critical to job success. Therefore, they become a key source of information.

The dilemma is that if the organization is large, many people may be included in the category called performers. We may not have the time, money, or need to go to all of the performers. How do we decide which performers to use in our data collection process?

To answer this question, we need to review what we want to identify. In this phase of our assessment we want to clarify what the skill of typical performers is in a given position when compared to the SHOULD performance for that position. Skill gaps will result in recommendations for ways to increase skill (often through training programs or other structured learning experiences). By viewing Figure 7.2, you can see that we can identify three categories of performers. Which of the following is most important for us?

- To identify the performance gaps of exemplary performers

- To identify the performance gaps of individuals who are new to the job or who are on probation because of performance problems

- To identify the performance gaps of the majority of people who are performing the job in a satisfactory manner but who could improve, directly affecting the results of the business or organization

The most cost-effective and potentially important approach is to identify areas of improvement for the large number of people who are in the middle of the bell curve (the typical performer).

If we collect data from the entire population of performers, we become able to accurately describe what the typical performers are doing because they are included in this universal population. For example, if the manufacturing facility had forty shift supervisors, we could send a questionnaire to each shift supervisor. After tabulation of the questionnaires, we could determine the relative importance of the four job practices within the health and safety performance result and the skill levels required, as reported by the forty supervisors. Tabulation of the questionnaires would give us information about both categories. Utilizing

Figure 7.2. Three Performance Categories.

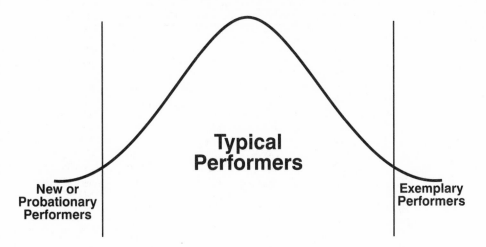

the three-by-three grid in Figure 7.1, we would be able to identify the practices where action is most immediately required.

Sending a questionnaire out to 40 shift supervisors is an easy process. But let's suppose that our population consisted of 1,000 shift supervisors; then, sending out questionnaires would be quite costly. However, we could sample the population. To do this, we would want a random sample with responses from 277 shift supervisors according to the sample size table in Table 7.1. When the total population is 300 or more, random sampling can reduce costs, because the number of questionnaires sent out, retrieved, and tabulated can be reduced. It is important to re-member that the table indicates the number of people from whom questionnaires are *returned*. Therefore, if you expect a return rate of 80 percent, you need to increase the number shown in the table by 25 percent. For a population of 500, you would need to send out 272 questionnaires to expect an 80 percent return rate. For a population of 5,000, you would need to send out 445 questionnaires for an 80 percent return rate. In this manner, you will have a 95 percent certainty that whatever re-sults you obtain are, in fact, true for the whole population.

Another possible data source is the direct manager of the

Table 7.1. Sample Size Table.

Population	Sample	Population	Sample	Population	Sample
10	9	230	144	1,400	301
15	14	240	147	1,500	305
20	19	250	151	1,600	309
25	23	260	155	1,700	313
30	27	270	158	1,800	316
35	32	280	162	1,900	319
40	36	290	165	2,000	322
45	40	300	168	2,200	327
50	44	320	174	2,400	331
55	48	340	180	2,600	334
60	52	360	186	2,800	337
65	55	380	191	3,000	340
70	59	400	196	3,500	346
75	62	420	200	4,000	350
80	66	440	205	4,500	354
85	69	460	209	5,000	356
90	73	480	213	6,000	361
95	76	500	217	7,000	364
100	79	550	226	8,000	366
110	85	600	234	9,000	368
120	91	650	241	10,000	369
130	97	700	248	15,000	374
140	102	750	254	20,000	376
150	108	800	259	30,000	379
160	113	850	264	40,000	380
170	118	900	269	50,000	381
180	122	950	273	60,000	381
190	127	1,000	277	70,000	382
200	131	1,100	284	120,000	382
210	136	1,200	291	160,000	383
220	140	1,300	296	1,000,000	383

Note: This table indicates the number of people who must respond to obtain a representation of the population under study. The information obtained should be representative of the population at the 95% confidence level, where the degree of possible error is ±5%.

performer. Direct managers have valuable insight regarding the importance of the job practices and skill levels of the performers. They have often been in the position of the performers themselves. In addition, they have a big picture perspective that helps when assessing the relative importance of the job practices or competencies.

Other possible data sources include people who have an

opportunity to observe the performers on the job. For many performers, internal or external customers are a valuable data source. It is important to remember that customers can report only on the part of the job they observe. In other words, customers could not reliably report on the importance and the skill with which customer service representatives (CSRs) update customer and inventory files if they do not observe the CSRs doing this. Likewise, airline passengers could not report on the skill with which flight attendants handle emergency situations if they do not observe the flight attendants in emergency situations.

Other data sources could be peers or direct reports of other performers. Again, these people can report only on the parts of the performers' jobs they can observe.

When we collect performance data, we want our information to be reliable—in other words, to reflect the real on-the-job situation. One way to increase reliability is to collect data from multiple sources. When you are collecting is performance data, we recommend a minimum of two data sources for each practice or competency being assessed. This may require you to use three or four data sources, because the various data sources may have the opportunity to observe only parts of the performers' job. Table 7.2 demonstrates this for a flight attendant's position.

Table 7.2. Data Sources for Is Data
for a Flight Attendant's Position.

	Sources of Data		
Performance Result	*Flight Attendant*	*Direct Manager*	*Passenger*
Preparing the cabin for the flight	√	√	
Greeting passengers	√		√
Making required announcements	√	√	√
Securing the cabin for the flight	√	√	
Directing the evacuation of the aircraft	√	√	
Completing administrative reports	√	√	

Many times, documents produced during the course of business are used as data sources. For example, audiotapes of CSRs as they converse with customers provide a reliable source of information about what is really happening on the job on a day-to-day basis. In some instances videotapes are available, for example, in banks, hotels, or convenience stores. In other situations employees and supervisors are required to maintain handwritten or computerized incident logs. All these may be valuable sources of is data and should be considered when deciding upon data sources.

What Data Collection Methods Should Be Used?

In deciding upon a data collection method, we consider the following five criteria:

1. The type of data desired. Do we and our clients want descriptive data that describe the performance in narrative terms or quantified data that provide numerical information?
2. The size and location of the groups from whom data will be collected.
3. The resources available for data collection, including how many people are available to collect the data.
4. The cost and available funds for collecting the data.
5. The amount of time available to collect the data.

Five types of data collection methods are used when collecting data for performance or competency assessments. These include:

1. The one-on-one interview (either face to face or on the phone)
2. The focus group interview
3. The questionnaire or survey
4. Direct observation
5. Documentation review—the review of business documents

The one-on-one interview, focus group interview, and direct observation are most frequently used to collect descriptive data, such as the information used to describe SHOULD performance. This type of narrative information, however, is difficult to analyze when we want to determine the performance gaps for a population of employees or managers. Our experience has been that client teams readily understand the data on importance and skill when they are presented in a numerical (quantified) manner. Therefore, questionnaires are our method of choice when assessing IS performance, because they

- Are well suited for collecting quantifiable data
- Allow easy computer tabulation of quantifiable data
- Can reach small or large numbers of people
- Can reach people in a variety of geographic locations
- Ensure the confidentiality of the respondent
- Are familiar to respondents, who will tend to respond candidly
- Present all questions in a consistent manner to respondents
- Cost less than other data collection methods

However, direct observation and documentation review are also used at times. As we discussed earlier in this chapter, documentation review is the best data collection method to use when the sources of data consist of business documents, including paper documents, computer data, audiotapes, and videotapes. Direct observation is appropriate to use when the population or the random sample is relatively small and it is important to note deviations from required procedures. Both documentation review and direct observation are used, for example, with commercial airline pilots. All communication between pilots and air traffic controllers is audiotaped. The "black box" in each commercial aircraft records the conversations of the crew members on the flight deck. In addition, Federal Aviation Administration inspectors and check pilots ride with pilots and observe them on a periodic basis. It goes without saying that direct observation is a costly data collection method. Observers must be highly qualified to observe and rate another person's performance. In addition, direct observation is labor-intensive in that it requires an enormous number of hours compared to the other types of data collection.

Because the questionnaire is well adapted for the collection of is performance data, the remainder of this chapter, including the case study, will focus on its use.

Designing a Questionnaire

When you are designing a questionnaire to provide importance and skill-level data, we recommend the following procedures:

1. Clarify the purpose of the data collection

2. Determine the rating scales to be used

3. Create a list of behavioral items for a questionnaire

4. Design and pilot the questionnaires

5. Revise the questionnaire

6. Design companion questionnaires

7. Distribute the questionnaires to data sources

Clarifying the Purpose of the Data Collection

Although in most cases the purpose is to identify the importance of the job activity and the current skill level of the performers, in some instances the purposes may vary. For example, if the importance of the job activities has already been identified, the purpose may be to determine the frequency with which the job activities are occurring rather than their importance. In any case, the purposes of the questionnaire should be clearly identified.

Determining the Rating Scales to Be Used

We often use the following importance scale. Note that the scale goes from "not required" to "key" and that the description of each of the five scale points is unique:

1 =   *Not required for this result or job:* The activity is not required to achieve the expected job results and/or is not necessary for the job.

2 =   *Nice to have:* The activity may be helpful but is not always needed to achieve expected job results.

3 =   *Basic requirement:* The activity is required to achieve expected job results, but other activities are more important.

4 =   *Important:* The activity is among the most important for achieving expected job results.

5 =   *Key:* There is no way a person could achieve expected job results without skillfully demonstrating this activity.

An example of a current skill-level scale follows. The scale allows us to rate people who have minimum ability (in the area being rated) as well as those who are so effective that others come to them for help and coaching. Note that there is a unique description for each of the scale points:

1 =   *Little or no skill:* I demonstrate little or no skill in performing the activity.

2 =   *Minimal skill:* I demonstrate skill in performing the activity in routine situations but need help to do so.

3 =   *Adequate skill:* I demonstrate skill in performing the activity in routine situations without help, but in unusual or nonroutine situations I need help.

4 =   *Proficient skill:* I consistently demonstrate skill in performing the activity even in unusual and nonroutine situations.

5 =   *Expert skill:* I am among the very best at performing the activity; others come to me for assistance and coaching in how to do this activity.

Creating a List of Behavioral Items for a Questionnaire

In a performance assessment, this requires extracting from the performance model the specific activities (best practices) that should be used by the performers. In a competency assessment, it requires extracting from the competency model the specific practices used to demonstrate the required competencies. We will not get reliable data if we ask performers to rate their "judgment skill"; this is too broad and open to interpretation. Instead, we form three to four behavioral statements that demonstrate judgment skill and ask the individual to rate her or his skill to demonstrate each of these behaviors. Examples of this type of behavioral statement are "I make an exception to standard ways of doing things when circumstances require it" and "I make a decision based upon experience and intuition when time is an issue."

Designing and Piloting the Questionnaire

Once we have determined the questionnaire items and the scales, we can design the questionnaire. (A sample questionnaire is shown later in this chapter.) We will first design the questionnaire for the performers. Once it has been designed and piloted, we can revise it to create companion questionnaires for direct managers, customers, and others.

We pilot questionnaires to make sure that they are providing reliable information. The instructions should be understandable to the population receiving the questionnaire. We also want to make sure that each item on the questionnaire is correctly understood by the respondent. Jargon or trade terms may not be correctly interpreted. In addition, we want to ensure that respondents correctly understand each point on the rating scales. A checklist for piloting questionnaires is shown in Performance Consulting Tool 5.

Piloting of the questionnaire is essential. No matter how experienced we may be in questionnaire design, it is not possible to know all the characteristics of the population or the situations these individuals encounter. We remember a situation where we were designing a questionnaire for a governmental agency. This questionnaire was to go to several hundred employees and their managers. When we piloted the questionnaire, we found that we had not included a response option that, in reality, was an ap-

Performance Consulting Tool 5

Checklist for Piloting Questionnaires

_____ 1. Select a sample from each group that will be receiving a questionnaire. For example, if you are sending questionnaires to performers in three different positions, then a sample of each of those three groups will be required.

_____ 2. Arrange for each of the groups to meet with you in a room where you might observe them completing this questionnaire. (*Note:* If geography prohibits you from conducting the pilot, coach an on-site individual to do it for you.)

_____ 3. Distribute the questionnaire, with its instruction sheet, to the participants. Do not answer any questions unless the people are totally unable to complete the questionnaire. (This will certainly affirm that the instruction sheet needs to be rewritten!)

_____ 4. Note the time when each person begins to complete the questionnaire and the time when each person has concluded it.

_____ 5. As the questionnaire is being completed, observe any particular questions or pages that appear to cause difficulty. By the way, it is helpful to ask people to make a checkmark next to any question they found unclear; this helps them to locate those questions during the debriefing.

_____ 6. Once all of the individuals have completed the questionnaire, go through it page by page. Ask people to indicate any questions they found confusing or difficult to answer. Look for patterns of feedback from the people who are present. When someone indicates a difficulty, ask whether anyone else ex-

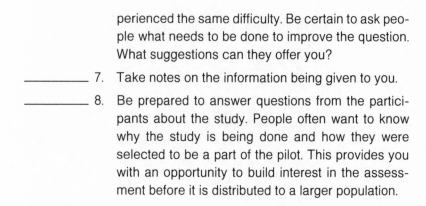

perienced the same difficulty. Be certain to ask people what needs to be done to improve the question.
What suggestions can they offer you?

_____ 7. Take notes on the information being given to you.

_____ 8. Be prepared to answer questions from the participants about the study. People often want to know
why the study is being done and how they were
selected to be a part of the pilot. This provides you
with an opportunity to build interest in the assessment before it is distributed to a larger population.

propriate response about 15 percent of the time. The option was
unique to this particular agency. Without piloting the questionnaire, we would have collected data that were of dubious value.

Revising the Questionnaire

Based upon the results of the pilot, the questionnaire is revised.
If major revisions are required, it is wise to pilot the questionnaire again. If small revisions are required, then the questionnaire is ready to be distributed.

Designing Companion Questionnaires

Now that the questionnaire for performers has been developed,
companion questionnaires can be drafted for additional data
sources, such as direct managers, customers, and colleagues. Because the performer questionnaire has been pilot-tested and revised, there is no need to pilot-test a companion questionnaire
that is being developed for others who work in the same environment, such as direct managers or direct reports. However, if
the companion questionnaire is being distributed to customers
or other people who are not intimately familiar with the job of
the performer, pilot-testing of the companion questionnaires is
recommended.

Distributing the Questionnaires to Data Sources

Once all the questionnaires are complete, they are ready to be sent out to the data sources. To ensure a good response, a cover letter describing the following is required:

1. The purposes of the questionnaire and of the project

2. The sponsors of the project (the client team)

3. Why it is important for this person to complete the questionnaire and the benefits to the individual for doing so

4. How long it takes to complete the questionnaire

5. Where and how to return the questionnaire

6. What information the respondent will receive about the results of the study

The cover letter should be signed by a member of the client team, someone who has high credibility with those responding. The questionnaire sent to performers and their direct managers may be signed by someone different from the person who signs the questionnaires sent to customers.

Data Tabulation and Reporting

The personal computer has made tabulation of questionnaires relatively easy and inexpensive. The current generation of personal computers can easily support the software required for input and tabulation of questionnaire data. Because computer hardware and software are changing at such a rapid rate, we will not describe either the hardware or software required for data tabulation. Instead, we will focus on the data required for the output report and suggest that you utilize a local resource for more information about computer hardware and software.

Once they are tabulated, the data are displayed in the training needs matrix for each performance result or competency. As shown in Figure 7.3, the columns represent the different levels

Figure 7.3. Training Needs Matrix.

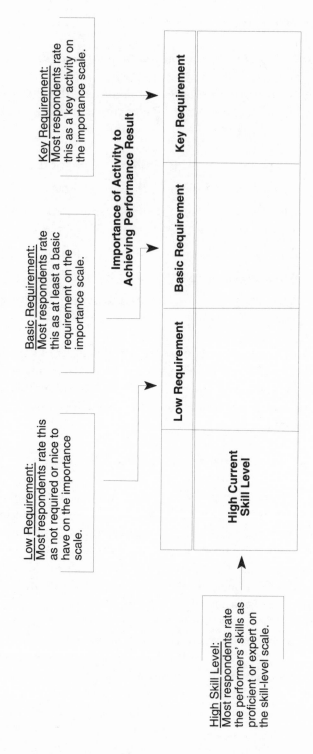

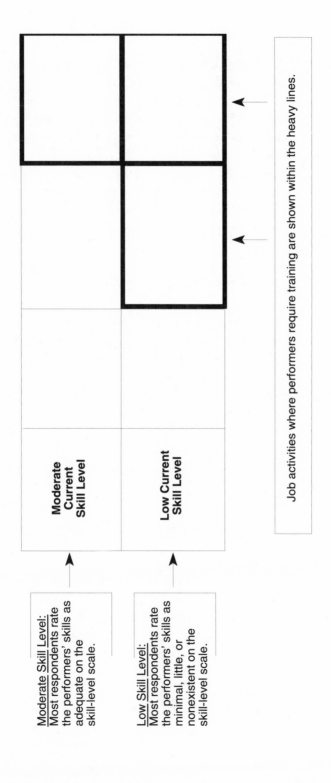

Moderate Current Skill Level

Low Current Skill Level

Moderate Skill Level:
Most respondents rate the performers' skills as adequate on the skill-level scale.

Low Skill Level:
Most respondents rate the performers' skills as minimal, little, or nonexistent on the skill-level scale.

Job activities where performers require training are shown within the heavy lines.

of importance of the job activities (best practices). The rows identify the current skill level of the performers.

Figure 7.4 shows training needs that were identified for shift supervisors for the performance result "Ensure compliance with safety and environmental requirements." As you will note, two job activities (numbers 2 and 3) were identified as requiring training, even though the current skill is moderate. This is because these activities are viewed as key to job success; it is important for supervisors to manage these activities effectively in both routine and nonroutine situations (the definition for a proficient skill level).

Gaso Petroleum Case Study

Now let's return to Gaso Petroleum Company and see how Janet Waterman and Jake Coleman determined the actual performance of the territory managers. In Chapter Six we learned that nine performance results were required of territory managers if the three primary business goals were to be achieved (Table 6.1). Also, Table 6.2 provided an example of the best practices required to accomplish the performance result "Maximize profitability of stations." Now the issue is to determine the actual skill strengths and developmental needs of the 100 territory managers who work in Gaso. (In Chapter Eight we will discuss how Janet and Jake determined the impact of work environment factors upon the performance of the territory managers.)

What Do We Need to Know?

Janet and Jake needed to know two things to be able to identify the gap between SHOULD performance and IS performance. For each of the nine performance results, they needed to know: (1) the relative importance of the job activities to the achievement of the performance results and (2) the current skill level of the 100 territory managers in performing these activities. Activities identified as being of high importance and low skill would represent the training needs of the territory managers.

Figure 7.4. Training Needs Matrix: Shift Supervisors.

Performance Result: Ensure Compliance with Safety and Environmental Requirements
Position: Shift Supervisor

Importance to Achieving This Result

	Low Requirement	Basic Requirement	Key Requirement
High Current Skill Level			1. Set an example by following all safety policies and procedures established by the unit. 4. Conduct formal and informal safety audits; provide feedback to operators.
Moderate Current Skill Level			2. Conduct safety meetings with operators. 3. Monitor safety performance by reviewing safety statistics each week; provide information to the operators.
Low Current Skill Level			

Job activities where performers require training are shown within the heavy lines.

Where Do We Get the Data?

Three groups of people could provide first-hand information regarding the territory manager's job: the territory managers, the district managers, and the station managers and dealers. To make sure that there were two data sources for each of the nine performance results, Janet and Jake developed the data source matrix shown in Table 7.3. This matrix acknowledges that the territory managers would have data regarding their own behavior in all nine areas. However, the district managers and station managers and dealers would not have first-hand information for every performance result. They could only provide reliable data for the performance results that they could personally observe.

Next, they looked at the number of people within each of the three positions. There were 9 district managers, 100 territory managers, and approximately 1,200 station managers and dealers. (Many managers and dealers had responsibility for more than one station, which is why there were 1,200 of them for 2,000 stations.) After consulting the sample size table (Table 7.1), it was decided that it would be expedient to gather data from all the district managers and territory managers. However, because there were 1,200 station managers and dealers, it would be more cost-

Table 7.3. Data Sources for Is Data
in Territory Manager Position.

| | Sources of Data | | |
Performance Result	Territory Manager	District Manager	Station Manager or Dealer
1. Meet gasoline volume goals	√	√	√
2. Meet nongas product volume goals	√	√	√
3. Maximize participation in, and return from, station promotions	√	√	√
4. Maximize profitability of stations	√	√	√
5. Ensure compliance with safety and environmental requirements	√	√	√
6. Maintain high image and service standards	√		√
7. Establish positive relationships with station managers and dealers	√		√
8. Manage time and territory	√	√	
9. Develop a territory market plan	√	√	

effective to sample that population. A random sample would require 291 responses to provide data at the 95 percent confidence level. Based upon previous experience, it was expected that a response rate of 67 percent could be obtained. Therefore, Janet and Jake decided to send questionnaires to a random sample of 450 station managers and dealers.

What Data Collection Methods Should Be Used?

Janet and Jake examined the five methods of data collection and decided to use questionnaires. Their reasoning was that questionnaires:

■ Would provide the type of quantifiable data that was desired

■ Would provide data in a form that could be tabulated by computer

■ Could be used with both the small populations (district managers and territory managers) and large populations (station managers and dealers)

■ Could reach people in a variety of geographic locations throughout North America

■ Would ensure the confidentiality of the respondent

■ Would allow all questions to be presented in a consistent manner

■ Cost less than other data collection methods

Designing and Piloting the Questionnaire

Once the decisions regarding purpose, data sources, and data collection methods had been made, Janet was able to move ahead and design three questionnaires, one for each of the three populations. Because the purpose was to identify the importance of job activities and the current skill level of the territory managers, Janet selected the importance and skill-level scales shown earlier in this chapter. Next, she went to the best practices listed for each of the nine performance results. She made sure that each of the activities was listed as a specific on-the-job behavior. She then integrated the list of on-the-job activities with the scales to develop a questionnaire for the territory managers. The instructions for the survey are shown in Exhibit 7.1. A sample of this questionnaire is shown in Exhibit 7.2. This sample displays the portion of the questionnaire designed to assess the skills and the importance of activities associated with the performance result "Maximize profitability of stations."

Janet decided to create the territory manager questionnaire first because it included all of the on-the-job behaviors. She would then pilot the questionnaire. Once the questionnaire had been piloted and revised, she would be able to create companion questionnaires for the district managers and the station managers and dealers.

Janet followed the piloting procedure as outlined in Performance Consulting Tool 5 in this chapter. She asked four territory managers to participate in the pilot. These territory managers were selected because they came from varied backgrounds and represented different levels of experience. Fortunately, they were attending a health and safety meeting, so she was able to conduct the pilot just before the start of the meeting.

With the information from the pilot, Janet revised the questionnaire and then designed the companion questionnaires. She felt that the pilot information was sufficient for the design of the district manager questionnaire. In other words, district managers and territory managers were very similar in background and experience; therefore, if the questionnaire was understandable by one group, it would be understandable by the other. However, for the station managers and dealers, she did conduct a second pilot. She sent questionnaires to four station managers or dealers. She then set up telephone time to debrief each of them regarding the questionnaire. This provided her with the information needed to revise the questionnaire.

Now that the questionnaires were complete, they were ready to be sent out to the data sources. Janet had created and piloted a cover letter for each of the questionnaires. The cover letter for the territory managers is shown in Exhibit 7.3.

You will note that the cover letter was from both Jake Cole-

Exhibit 7.1. Gaso Petroleum Company
Needs Assessment Survey Instructions.

Position Being Analyzed: Territory Manager
Position of Person Filling Out Survey: Territory Manager

Instructions:

This survey is designed to gather information about development needs for the territory manager position. As a person currently performing as a territory manager, you can provide valuable information about your job and your current skill level in specific areas. This information will be used to review the effectiveness of the current job structure as well as to identify any areas for further training and development. Your time in completing this survey is important and is very much appreciated.

In this survey you will be asked to evaluate the things you must do on the job to achieve expected results. You will be asked to rate the *importance* of specific job activities to doing your job, as well as the *skill you currently demonstrate* in these job activities. Since important decisions will be made from the data provided by you and others, we ask that you be as honest as possible in assessing your own level of skill. *Your answers will be treated confidentially.* They will be combined with input from other territory managers to determine overall priorities for future initiatives.

Listed in the survey are job activities that have been identified for the territory manager position. It is possible that some of these activities may not be required for your specific job; in this case you will select a "1" on the importance scale.

Step 1: Rate Importance Related to Expected Job Results

First, classify the activities on each page according to their *importance* to achieving expected job results. Circle the response category that best describes your assessment, using the following scale:

1 = *Not required for this result or job:* The activity is not required to achieve expected job results and/or is not necessary for the job.
2 = *Nice to have:* The activity may be helpful but is not always needed to achieve expected job results.
3 = *Basic requirement:* The activity is required to achieve expected job results, but other activities are more important.
4 = *Important:* The activity is among the most important for achieving expected job results.
5 = *Key:* There is no way a person could achieve expected job results without skillfully demonstrating this activity.

Step 2: Rate Current Skill Level

Next, *after you have completed Step 1,* rate the *level of skill* that you currently demonstrate in performing each job activity. Circle the number on the scale that best describes your level of skill:

1 = *Little or no skill:* You demonstrate little or no skill in performing the activity.
2 = *Minimum skill:* You demonstrate skill in performing the activity in routine situations, but need help to do so.

**Exhibit 7.1. Gaso Petroleum Company
Needs Assessment Survey Instructions, Cont'd.**

---

3 =   *Adequate skill:* You demonstrate skill in performing the activity in
      routine situations without help, but in unusual or nonroutine situa-
      tions you need help.
4 =   *Proficient skill:* You consistently demonstrate skill in performing
      the activity even in unusual and nonroutine situations.
5 =   *Expert skill:* You are among the very best at performing the activity;
      others come to you for assistance and coaching in how to do this
      activity.

Note: Be sure to rate your skill on all activities, including ones that are *not
required* in your job.

**Exhibit 7.2. Gaso Petroleum Needs Assessment Survey
for Performance Result of "Maximize Profitability of Stations."**

Importance	On-the-Job Activities	Skill Level
	When providing guidance to station managers and dealers regarding the effective and profitable management of their businesses, I . . .	
1 2 3 4 5	1. Ask questions to determine the level of knowledge and skill the station managers and dealers have for the financial aspects of the business	1 2 3 4 5
1 2 3 4 5	2. Review the monthly profit-and-loss statement with the station managers and dealers	1 2 3 4 5
1 2 3 4 5	3. Seek opportunities to acknowledge the positive aspects of the financial management of the business	1 2 3 4 5
1 2 3 4 5	4. Discuss ways by which the station managers and dealers can reduce the cost of supplies and materials	1 2 3 4 5
1 2 3 4 5	5. Work with the station managers and dealers to form a business plan on an annual basis	1 2 3 4 5
1 2 3 4 5	6. Monitor actuals against the plan on a monthly and quarterly basis	1 2 3 4 5
1 2 3 4 5	7. Counsel the station managers and dealers on how to deal effectively with personnel problems (such as an employee who is frequently tardy or absent)	1 2 3 4 5
1 2 3 4 5	8. Counsel the station managers and dealers on how they can manage their time	1 2 3 4 5

**Exhibit 7.2. Gaso Petroleum Needs Assessment Survey
for Performance Result of "Maximize Profitability of Stations," Cont'd.**

Importance	On-the-Job Activities	Skill Level
1 2 3 4 5	9. Determine the reasons for line-item accounts that are running in excess of the budget	1 2 3 4 5
1 2 3 4 5	10. Identify ways to bring the line items in line with the budget	1 2 3 4 5
1 2 3 4 5	11. Ensure that inventory control sheets are being used	1 2 3 4 5
1 2 3 4 5	12. Seek the station managers' and dealers' ideas on controlling losses from inventory	1 2 3 4 5
1 2 3 4 5	13. Teach the station managers and dealers to compute margins on a daily and weekly basis	1 2 3 4 5
1 2 3 4 5	14. Counsel the station managers and dealers on strategies to use and issues to consider when pricing gasoline and nongas products	1 2 3 4 5

Exhibit 7.3. Cover Letter to Territory Managers.

TO: Territory Managers
FROM: Jake Coleman and Janet Waterman
SUBJECT: Needs Assessment Questionnaire

Our organization faces many challenges today if we are to remain profitable and an industry leader. Those challenges will be met successfully only if each of us is developed and prepared to perform in our jobs. In order to identify what will be required for territory managers to be successful now and in the future, we are undertaking a needs assessment, and we need your help.

Attached is a questionnaire for you to complete. You will be assessing the importance of a variety of on-the-job activities and your current skill at performing them. Your responses will be entered into a computer and tabulated with the responses of all the other individuals who complete this survey. Therefore, your identity is protected; we encourage your honest and candid information.

It is important that you complete and return this questionnaire no later than March 15 if your responses are to be included in the report of findings. It will require approximately twenty minutes of your time to complete. The benefit to you and others in taking the time to complete this survey is an accurate assessment of the most critical needs in our company—needs we will be responding to over the next year. You will receive a summary of our major findings once they are completed.

If you have any questions or want further information, please call Janet Waterman. Once you have completed the questionnaire, place it in the attached envelope and mail it to Janet. Thank you for your participation in this project.

man and Janet Waterman. They wanted to demonstrate that they were working as a team on this project. They also wanted the respondents to realize that Jake was very involved in the project.

Data Tabulation

As the questionnaires were returned, they were entered into the computer. Using data relationship software, Janet was able to sort each on-the-job activity by importance and skill level.

Data Output Report

Janet printed out a training needs matrix for each of the nine performance results expected of a territory manager. Figure 7.5 shows the matrix for the fourteen job activities first displayed in "Maximize profitability of stations." This matrix shows six on-the-job activities that are identified as training needs. It also shows the importance of the fourteen job activities, with seven activities identified as key requirements, six activities identified as basic requirements, and one activity identified as a low requirement.

Thus, Janet and Jake were able to clearly identify both the relative importance of each of the on-the-job activities and the on-the-job activities where territory managers as a group had training needs.

Of course, Janet and Jake also needed information about the impact of the work environment. What about the environment encourages the desired performance of territory managers? What discourages this performance? Chapter Eight describes ways to obtain information about work environment obstacles and enhancers and also indicates what Janet and Jake learned at Gaso.

Figure 7.5. Training Needs Matrix for Territory Managers.

Performance Result: Maximize Profitability of Stations
Position: Territory Manager

Importance to Achieving This Result

	Low Requirement	Basic Requirement	Key Requirement
High Current Skill Level		9. Determine the reasons for line-item accounts that are running over budget. 13. Teach the station managers and dealers how to compute margins on a daily and weekly basis.	2. Review the monthly profit- and-loss statement with the station manager or dealer. 4. Discuss ways in which the station manager or dealer can reduce the cost of supplies and materials.
Moderate Current Skill Level	11. Ensure that inventory control sheets are being used.	3. Seek opportunities to acknowledge the positive aspects of financial management of the business. 10. Identify ways to bring the line items in line with the budget. 12. Seek the station managers' and dealers' ideas about ways to control losses from inventory.	1. Ask questions to determine the level of knowledge and skill the station manager or dealer has for the financial aspects of the business. 5. Work with the station manager or dealer to form a business plan on an annual basis. 6. Monitor actuals against the plan on a monthly and quarterly basis.
Low Current Skill Level		8. Counsel the station managers and dealers on ways to manage their time.	7. Counsel the station manager or dealer on ways to deal effectively with personnel problems. 14. Counsel the station managers and dealers on strategies to use and issues to consider when pricing gasoline and non-gas products.

Job activities where territory managers require training are shown within the heavy lines.

Summary

1. Once the performance or competency model is determined and signed off on by the client team, the gap between IS performance and SHOULD performance can be identified.

2. Priority training needs can be identified by gathering data from multiple sources about the importance of each job activity and the current skill level of the performers.

3. Because questionnaires provide for quantification of results and are adaptable to a variety of populations, they are often used to collect performance gap data.

4. When the relative importance of the job activity and the skill level of the performer are in a training needs matrix, the top training needs quickly become apparent.

5. This system has high credibility with management because of the logic of comparing the importance of the job activity to the skill level of the performers and because the data can be quantified.

8

Identifying Factors Impacting Performance

Business Need:

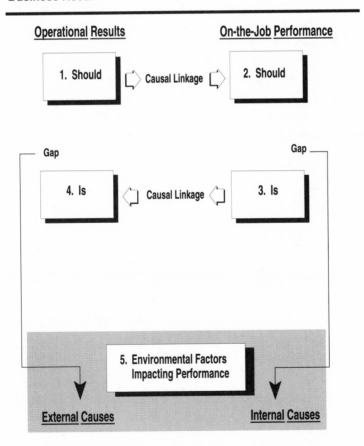

Geary Rummler says, "Pit a good employee against a bad system and the system will win most every time" (Rummler, 1983, p. 75). Employees who have been trained in a set of skills but who work in an environment that does not support those skills will eventually stop using them. The work environment governs whether or not they will utilize the skills they have learned during training.

We have expressed this concept as:

$$\text{Learning Experience} \times \text{Work Environment} = \text{Performance Results}$$

This formula indicates that to achieve performance results, employees must develop the appropriate skills *and* work in a supportive work environment. Learning experiences must focus on the skills required for job success, and the work environment must be free of obstacles that hinder performance. The multiplication symbol indicates that a deficiency in either factor has a direct impact on performance results. For example, if people learn 100 percent of what is required but the work environment is only 25 percent supportive, the improvement in on-the-job performance will be only 25 percent of what is possible. In our Preface we noted research findings that indicate that only 10 to 20 percent of what is learned actually transfers to the job. Certainly, work environment barriers contribute greatly to this problem.

By examining performance problems in a variety of organizations, we have determined there are *multiple* causes for the performance deficiency in over 90 percent of the situations. Thus, resolving just one cause will not correct the problem. All significant causes of performance deficiency must be resolved if performance improvement is to be achieved.

In one organization with which we worked, customer service representatives were identified as requiring training in customer service skills. However, further analysis indicated that work environment factors were obstacles to skill transfer. These factors included:

- Lack of a data base that provided accurate and timely information about products and services

- Too many administrative tasks, which reduced the amount of time the CSRs spent working directly with customers

- The organization's lack of a reliable method to determine customer satisfaction

- Failure of the managers to establish clear objectives with each representative

- Lack of positive feedback from managers when CSRs handled difficult customer situations well

- Lack of skills by managers to effectively conduct coaching discussions with CSRs

Thus, if customer service skill training had been provided without actions taken to improve the work environment, there would have been little change in on-the-job performance.

Cause Analysis: Work Environment Factors

We are actually conducting a cause analysis whenever we gather data about the reasons (CAUSES) for the gap between SHOULD and IS performance. In Chapter Seven we discussed how to obtain reliable data about the specific skill and knowledge deficiencies that would cause a performance gap. In this chapter we will focus on ways to obtain information about the work environment factors that can cause a performance gap. These two analyses (skill and knowledge deficiencies and work environment factors) are both examples of cause analysis. Both need sufficient data to make sound decisions regarding training and work environment needs.

   In conducting a cause analysis, the Performance Consultant and the clients need to identify the factors that affect desired performance. Specifically, for work environment factors they must identify (1) the external and internal factors that discourage the desired performance, (2) the external and internal factors that encourage the desired performance, and (3) the relative impact of each of those factors upon performance.

The external factors are the encouragers (enhancers) and discouragers (obstacles) that are external to the business unit for which the clients are responsible. So if the client team consists of the general manager and staff of a manufacturing plant, the external factors are those external to that plant. Such factors could include the economy, the competition, and governmental regulations. They could also include any actions taken by the corporation that either inhibit or encourage the SHOULD performance of people who work within the plant.

The internal factors are the enhancers and obstacles that are within the control of the clients. They can include such things as the amount of coaching and reinforcement by the direct managers of performers, the reward system, and the amount and usefulness of the information that is available to the performers.

When we are asked, "When do you obtain work environment data?" we often respond, "Every chance we get!" What we really mean is that CAUSE data are collected through every stage of the performance assessment. You will recall that when Janet Waterman interviewed Jake Coleman, she asked about the external factors affecting Retail Marketing within Gaso Petroleum. She learned of several external factors that impact negatively upon the goal of doubling profits. These included:

- Environmental regulations, which are important but also very costly

- A tax on every gallon of gas sold, which increases the price of a gallon of gas to the consumer

- A slow economy, which reduces consumers' consumption of gas

She also learned that one external factor encouraged the doubling of profits. This was the shareholders' expectations for a greater return on their investment.

You will also recall that when Janet obtained information for the performance models, she asked about work environment factors that would help territory managers perform as they should or inhibit them from doing so. She obtained this information through interviews with the nine district managers and the exemplary territory managers.

Janet had still another opportunity to collect information regarding work environment factors when she sent questionnaires to the 100 territory managers. As we described in Chapter Seven, these questionnaires were designed to determine the importance of job activities and the skill level of the territory managers. But Janet could, and did, elect to collect work environment data at the same time that she was collecting importance and skill data. For the purposes of this book, we have separated collection of work environment data from collection of is data; in reality the information for both is obtained concurrently.

Direct observation provides another opportunity to collect work environment data. Observation can be either informal or formal. While we are observing the performers on the job, we can make notes about the factors that enhance their performance, such as easy access to information, and those that inhibit their performance, such as excessive noise or numerous interruptions.

Reviewing documents available within organizations can also be a rich source of CAUSE data. The organization's vision, mission, and strategic plan often provide information regarding both internal and external factors that affect performance. In addition, annual reports, marketing plans, sales reports, and employee surveys will provide valuable information.

However, the most reliable data about work environment factors are obtained from the typical performers. They represent the largest data base and are the people whose performance we ultimately wish to affect. Therefore, in Gaso Petroleum, the questionnaires that were sent to the 100 territory managers will give us the most powerful data regarding the obstacles and enhancers impacting upon them. A major reason for this is that the performers themselves are the best people to indicate how a work environment factor actually affects their performance. The same work environment factor may be perceived by one group of performers as an enhancer and by another group of performers as an obstacle to performance.

An example of this would be highly structured job procedures. Airline pilots see checklists as enhancers; they enable them to follow specific procedures that ensure the safe operation of an aircraft. On the other hand, marketing and sales representatives often find detailed procedures to be obstacles to meeting the needs of their customers. In particular, sales representatives who are negotiating long-term contracts with relatively large customers often feel that they need the flexibility to write each contract in a way that meets the unique needs of the customer.

So, in summary, our sources of CAUSE data are everyone we come in contact with: our clients, the exemplary performers, the typical performers, their immediate managers, and their employees. Specifically, it is expedient to collect work environment data whenever we are collecting other information.

Designing a Work Environment Questionnaire

The key to collecting useful data is to ask the right questions right. This is particularly true with the work environment questionnaire. The challenge is to ask questions about the specific work environment factors that are affecting the performance of the group being studied. As we indicated, the Performance Consultant collects data regarding work environment obstacles and enhancers throughout the entire performance analysis process, including the initial discussions with the client team. This list of work environment obstacles and enhancers becomes a starter list for statements that may be used on the work environment questionnaire.

However, the list should be supplemented with other information regarding work environment obstacles and enhancers. Often, a review of the literature will indicate obstacles or enhancers that are inherent in the type of performance being assessed. For example, in continuous operations involving three shifts each day, communication between shifts often breaks down. If you are unsure whether this is a problem in your specific situation, it would be wise to ask about intershift communication in order to find out.

A great deal has been written about obstacles to skill

transfer. Familiarity with this literature will enable you to construct a better work environment questionnaire. In 1989, we published a list of obstacles to skill transfer based upon earlier research (Robinson and Robinson, p. 117). This list consisted of the following items:

1. Conditions of the performers:

   - *They do not see a payoff for using the skills:* The performers feel that the disadvantages outweigh the advantages of using the SHOULD skills.

   - *They do not have sufficient confidence to use the skills:* The performers feel a lack of confidence to use the SHOULD skills successfully on the job.

   - *They do not know when they are effectively using the skills:* The performers do not have sufficient guidelines to determine if their use of the SHOULD skills is effective.

   - *They fail when using the skills:* The performers tried to use the SHOULD skills on the job but were unable to achieve the success that they felt they should achieve.

   - *They disagree with the values and concepts of the program:* The performers feel that the values and concepts being taught during training are contrary to their personal values and their concepts of people and organizations.

   - *They do not have an immediate application for the skills:* The performers do not see immediate on-the-job applications of the SHOULD skills.

2. Conditions of the immediate managers:

   - *They do not reinforce learners' use of the skills:* Managers do not provide reinforcement to learners when there is evidence that they have used the SHOULD skills.

   - *They are not positive models:* Managers are perceived as not using or supporting the SHOULD skills.

- *They do not coach learners in using the skills:* Managers do not coach learners in handling specific on-the-job situations, even when the performers solicit their advice.

The research we did to form this list of obstacles indicated that the managers must provide reinforcement and coaching, but this may be changing. In today's organizations, many people work in autonomous work teams or have limited contact with their manager. The requirement is that some people must coach, reinforce, and model the desired performance, although some or all of these activities may be handled by a peer or team member rather than the manager.

3.   Conditions of the organization:

- *Task interference:* Many obstacles, including lack of time, a poor physical environment, conflicting procedures and policies, and lack of authority, inhibit learners as they attempt to use the SHOULD skills.

- *Lack of feedback to the learner:* The learners receive little or no feedback about the organizational impact of their use of the SHOULD skills.

- *Negative balance of consequences:* The use of the SHOULD skills by learners results in a punishing effect. (Today, we would also add lack of rewards or incentives as a common obstacle. It is not only that it is "punishing" to perform, but that there is no reward for doing so.)

In 1992, Mary Broad and John Newstrom published a list of obstacles to transfer as reported by trainers (p. 19). This list consisted of the following items:

1.   Lack of reinforcement on the job

2.   Interference from the immediate (work) environment

3.   A nonsupportive organizational culture

4.   Trainees' perception of impractical training programs

5. Trainees' perception of irrelevant training content

6. Trainees' discomfort with change and the associated effort

7. Separation from the inspiration or support of the trainer

8. Trainees' perception of poorly designed or delivered training

9. Pressure from peers to resist changes

A major supplier of training programs has identified six areas that its research indicates have an impact upon service providers' use of customer contact skills. These areas are:

1. Top management leadership

2. Systems policies and procedures

3. Hiring practices

4. Rewards and recognition

5. Measurement of customer satisfaction

6. Support by the direct manager

Reviewing the data from *all* sources, the Performance Consultant selects the work environment factors that seem to be applicable to the performers being assessed. Our experience has been that the typical work environment questionnaire contains ten to fifteen specific factors. The client team, with the Performance Consultant, should review the factors to make sure that (1) no important factors have been omitted and (2) no factors are included that are irrelevant to the situation.

Once the factors have been selected, they need to be incorporated into a questionnaire. An effective way of doing this is to write the factors as statements and ask the respondents whether or not they agree or disagree with each statement. Exhibit 8.1 provides an example of work environment factors as they might appear in a questionnaire with a five-point agree-disagree scale.

All factors are given as positive statements (enhancers). Generally, we list work environment factors by developing posi-

**Exhibit 8.1. Work Environment Questionnaire Statements
for Customer Service Representatives.**

Instructions:

Circle the number that corresponds to the extent you agree or disagree with
each statement using the following scale:

1 = Strongly disagree
2 = Somewhat disagree
3 = Neutral
4 = Somewhat agree
5 = Strongly agree

Work Environment Factors	Strongly Disagree		Neutral		Strongly Agree
1. Management provides strong leadership regarding the importance of identifying and meeting the needs of customers.	1	2	3	4	5
2. Policies and procedures rarely get in the way of meeting the needs of customers.	1	2	3	4	5
3. Lack of time rarely prevents me from meeting customers' needs.	1	2	3	4	5
4. Our organization has a reliable method for determining customer satisfaction.	1	2	3	4	5
5. I have sufficient information about our products and services.	1	2	3	4	5
6. I have sufficient information about our competitors' products and services.	1	2	3	4	5
7. My manager coaches me on handling new customer situations that I encounter.	1	2	3	4	5
8. My manager regularly provides me with feedback on how well I handle customer situations.	1	2	3	4	5

tive statements. For example, the statement "My manager coaches
me on how to handle new situations that I encounter" is a positive
statement. Agreement with this statement indicates that coaching
is occurring (an enhancer); disagreement indicates that coaching
is not occurring (an obstacle). We avoid writing work environment factors as negative statements because of the confusion that
can be caused when we try to respond in the negative to a negative
statement. Consider this statement: "My manager does not coach
me on how to handle new situations that I encounter." If my

manager is a good coach, I would need to *disagree* with that statement in order to convert it to an enhancer!

The statements in Exhibit 8.1 are first written for the performers' questionnaire (Exhibit 7.2). The job activity questions and the work environment factors are piloted with typical performers as described in Chapter Seven. Once they have been piloted, the factors are revised and the questionnaire can be distributed to the performers.

As we indicated earlier, typical performers are the best source of data for work environment information. Each performer knows in what way the factors impact upon him or her, but it is desirable to have a second source of data. Our experience has been that the direct managers are a good second data source. The direct managers are familiar with the work environment; in fact, they are part of it. By having direct managers answer the same questions as performers, we are able to compare and contrast the similarities and differences in their perceptions. For example, it would not be unusual for direct managers to agree with the statement, "Management provides strong leadership about the importance of identifying and meeting the needs of the customer." At the same time, customer contact personnel may disagree with that statement. They may feel that they are pretty much on their own when it comes to identifying and meeting customer needs. These types of data are very useful for the Performance Consultant and the clients. They provide a framework for taking action that will ensure that the management leadership in this area extends down to the customer contact personnel.

Reporting Work Environment Data

The key concept in reporting data is to let the information speak for itself. As Performance Consultants we do not go to a meeting and tell management what we found and what it means. Rather, we bring information to the meeting in a clear and understandable manner. Then we engage our clients in a dialogue to interpret the findings together. This process helps to ensure that the clients own the findings and will be committed to take action in response to them.

A method of reporting work environment information that has proved effective for us is to present the findings in bar chart format. Figure 8.1 is an example of this format. We have found that sorting the factors into three categories assists clients in forming conclusions about the impact of each factor on performance. We often present work environment factors in the three categories shown below:

1. *Enhancers to performance:* When 56 percent or more of the performers agree with the statement, it is considered to be a factor that encourages desired performance.

2. *Minimal impact on performance:* When 45 to 55 percent of performers agree with a statement, it is reported as having minimal impact. In essence, it neither enhances nor obstructs desired performance.

2. *Obstacles to performance:* When 44 percent or less of the performers agree with a statement, it is considered to be an obstacle. In essence, less than half of the people believe the statement to be an accurate one.

The categories are sorted by the responses of performers because they generally are the best source of information to indicate what impact processes and systems are having on their performance. However, both sources of information (performers and their managers) are reported, so that the level of agreement or disagreement between these sources is evident.

External and Internal Causes

We would like to say a few words about the interrelationship between external and internal causes. If you turn to the performance relationship map at the beginning of this chapter, you will see that environmental factors affecting performance come in two flavors: external causes and internal causes. We have indicated earlier in this chapter that external causes are causes that are outside the control of client management, and internal causes are causes that are within the control of client management.

Figure 8.1. Work Environment Data for Customer Service Representatives.

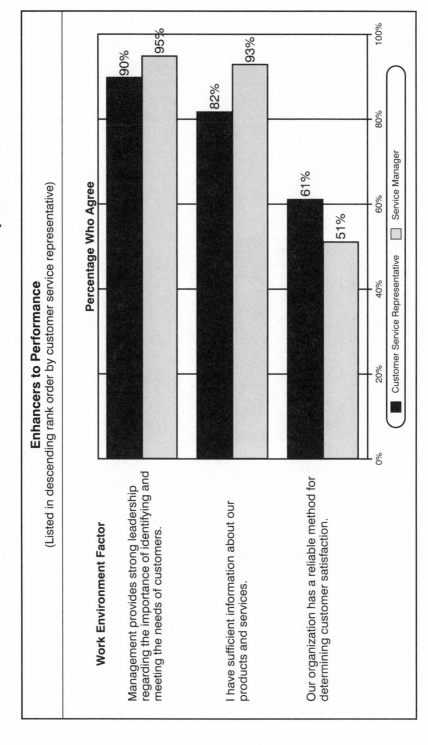

Figure 8.1. Work Environment Data for Customer Service Representatives, Cont'd.

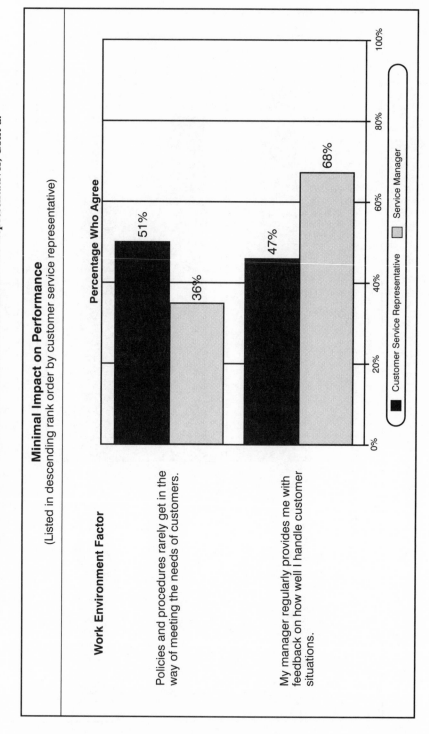

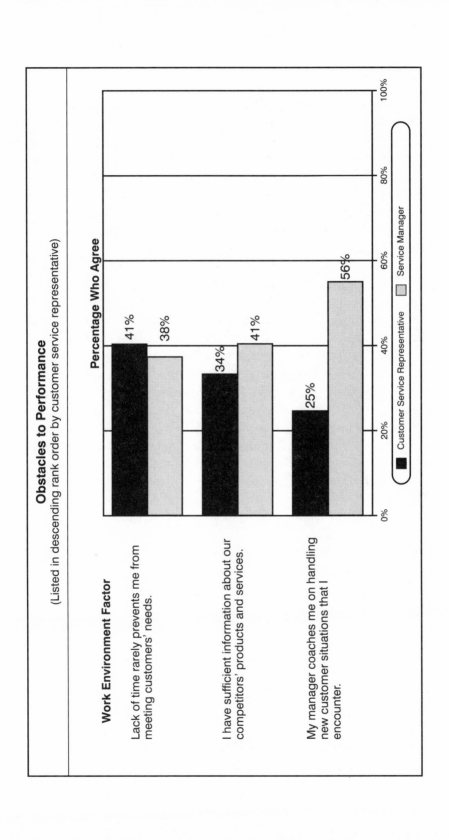

Obstacles to Performance

(Listed in descending rank order by customer service representative)

Work Environment Factor

Lack of time rarely prevents me from meeting customers' needs.

I have sufficient information about our competitors' products and services.

My manager coaches me on handling new customer situations that I encounter.

Percentage Who Agree

41%
38%
34%
41%
25%
56%

0%   20%   40%   60%   80%   100%

■ Customer Service Representative   ☐ Service Manager

The key words are "outside the control" and "within the control." Therefore, if we are dealing with a CEO of an organization, external causes are those outside the control of the organization. On the other hand, if we are dealing with a plant manager, external factors are factors outside the plant. In other words, some factors (such as corporate policy) could be inside the organization but outside the plant.

The manager has very little control—in most cases, no control—over external causes. The issue here is how well management develops a strategy to deal with those external causes. If an external cause is stronger competition in the marketplace, then management must develop strategies to effectively combat that competition. One strategy may be to position the business in a particular niche within the market. Another may be to provide extraordinary service, beyond that offered by the competition.

Information regarding external causes and business strategies is obtained during the business-needs interviews with top managers. In addition, organizational documents such as annual reports, marketing studies, and business plans provide information regarding external causes and the strategies with which management elects to deal with them.

Internal causes are factors within the control of management that impact upon performance. These factors deal with such items as:

- The clarity with which accountabilities and objectives are defined
- The incentive and reward system
- The amount and type of information available to performers
- The effectiveness of managerial coaching and feedback

As we discussed earlier in this chapter, all of these factors can have a dramatic effect on the performance of employees. Therefore, it is crucial that management have information regarding internal factors in order to take appropriate actions.

What is the relationship between external and internal

causes? The external causes are outside the control of the client team with whom the Performance Consultant is working. However, they have an impact upon the total environment within which the client's organization is operating. Therefore, it is crucial for clients to develop strategies that will enable the organization to be successful within this external environment.

Internal causes are those within the control of the client team. They have directly affected the performance of employees within various functions of the client team's unit or department. It is important for the client team to have excellent data regarding the internal factors so that they can take actions that will eliminate the obstacles and maximize the enhancers.

The performance relationship map is an excellent vehicle for highlighting both external and internal causes for the clients. It gives the clients an opportunity to reexamine the external causes and to assess the appropriateness of their business strategies. In fact, the Performance Consultant should facilitate this type of discussion with the client team. This can be done when the business needs are being reviewed and again when the performance model is being discussed.

The internal causes are discussed with the client when the IS data are reported. At this time, the gap between IS and SHOULD performance can be clearly shown; the internal causes creating that gap can be highlighted. It is during this meeting that actions—both training and management—are agreed upon so that the performance gap can be closed.

The key concept here is that the Performance Consultant collects data regarding external and internal causes throughout the performance analysis process. The Performance Consultant provides this CAUSE data at appropriate times, when the client team is examining what should be happening and what actually is happening. One key role of the Performance Consultant is to make sure that the client team examines all causes rather than just one or two of the most visible causes affecting business and performance needs.

Now let's take a look at how CAUSE data were obtained in Gaso Petroleum Company.

Gaso Petroleum Case Study

In the Gaso case study in Chapter Seven, Janet Waterman obtained information about the on-the-job activities that were most
critical to the achievement of performance results for the territory manager position. In addition, she obtained information
regarding the skill level of the typical territory manager in each
of those job activities. This is important information to review
when making decisions regarding the training required by territory managers. However, in the case study in Chapter Seven,
no information was obtained about other causes of performance
gaps. Let us look now at how Janet and Jake obtained work
environment data regarding the territory managers.

Obtaining Work Environment Data

As we discussed earlier in this chapter, CAUSE data are gathered
on several occasions, concurrently with determining the business
needs, SHOULD data, and IS data. So when Janet was interviewing
Jake to obtain business-needs information, she also asked about
factors that would have an impact on the achievement of Retail
Marketing's goals. She discovered that for the goal of doubling
profits within three years, three obstacles existed:

1.   Environmental regulations, while important, are very
     costly to support, and those costs will reduce profits.

2.   Taxes raise the price of gasoline but do not increase the
     profit to the service station.

3.   Poor economic conditions limit consumers' willingness to
     make long car trips.

Certainly, in her conversations with Jake, she uncovered
other factors affecting the territory managers' performance.
However, for the purposes of this case, we will focus on only
those that affect the profitability performance result.

When she interviewed the exemplary territory managers
and the district managers, Janet asked about work environment

factors. She was particularly interested in the factors that would impact upon territory managers in their use of on-the-job activities that led to the achievement of performance results. When a work environment factor was mentioned by three or more people, she added it to a list of factors she was compiling. By the time she had completed her interviews, she had developed the following list:

1. Decreases in facility improvement budgets put stations at a competitive disadvantage.

2. The cost of maintaining older stations is high and therefore decreases their profitability.

3. Territory managers may not have sufficient time to visit station managers and dealers with the desired frequency.

4. Inexperienced territory managers lack the credibility to discuss the financial aspects of the business with station managers and dealers.

5. Several station managers and dealers are reluctant to open their books to territory managers; they distrust how the information will be used.

6. District managers may not be modeling, coaching, or providing feedback to territory managers regarding ways to profitably manage the business of station managers and dealers.

7. It is uncertain how many district managers actually meet with territory managers to form and review progress against territory business plans.

It is important to keep in mind that these factors are there because they were mentioned three times or more during the interview process. What was unknown at this point was the degree to which each factor was an obstacle to a majority of territory managers. A work environment questionnaire was sent to both territory managers and district managers to obtain this information.

Before actually including these items in the questionnaire, Janet reviewed the list with Jake Coleman. Again, she empha-

sized that this was a tentative list; more information was required to determine which factors were causing the greatest concern. Jake had questions about a few of the factors but agreed
to include all of them in the survey. He also wanted to add the
following two factors:

1.   Has the Retail Marketing goal of doubling the profitability
     of the stations been clearly communicated to the territory
     managers? Are they aware of this initiative?

2.   Do the territory managers receive information about the
     profitability of company-owned stations on a timely basis?
     If this information is not being communicated, territory
     managers will have difficulty holding meaningful discus-
     sions with station managers and dealers.

     Now that she had Jake's approval, Janet moved ahead with
the development of the work environment questionnaire. Because the work environment factors were one part of the skill and
importance assessment, they were piloted at the same time as
that questionnaire. The work environment portion of the questionnaire is shown in Exhibit 8.2.

     Janet knew that a second data source would increase the
reliability of the information regarding work environment factors. She knew that customers could provide very little reliable
data about the work environment of the territory managers. District managers were intimately familiar with the work environment, even though they might see some of the factors differently
from the territory managers. Therefore, Janet developed a companion work environment questionnaire for district managers.
The factors were the same; however, she reworded them for district managers. For example, item 6 was revised to read, "I coach
my territory managers on ways to provide guidance to station
managers and dealers regarding effective, profitable management of their businesses."

     As mentioned in Chapter Seven, Janet did not feel a need
to pilot the district manager's questionnaire, primarily because
the factors were the same as those on the territory manager's

Exhibit 8.2. Work Environment Questionnaire.

Instructions:

Listed below are work environment factors that may or may not be affecting you and your performance. Please read each statement and indicate your level of agreement or disagreement with it. Circle the number that corresponds to the extent you agree or disagree with each statement using the following scale:

1 = Strongly disagree
2 = Somewhat disagree
3 = Neutral
4 = Somewhat agree
5 = Strongly agree

	Work Environment Obstacles and Enhancers to Performance	**Strongly Disagree**		**Neutral**		**Strongly Agree**
1.	Decreases in facility improvement budgets are having a limited impact on a station's ability to compete.	1	2	3	4	5
2.	While the cost of maintaining older stations is high, this situation has limited impact upon station profitability.	1	2	3	4	5
3.	Territory managers have sufficient time to visit with station managers and dealers at a desired frequency.	1	2	3	4	5
4.	Territory managers have the credibility to discuss the financial aspects of the business with station managers and dealers.	1	2	3	4	5
5.	District managers are positive models in counseling station managers and dealers regarding profitable management of their businesses.	1	2	3	4	5
6.	District managers coach territory managers on ways to provide guidance to station managers and dealers regarding effective, profitable management of their businesses.	1	2	3	4	5
7.	District managers give feedback to territory managers regarding how they counsel station managers and dealers about effective, profitable management of their businesses.	1	2	3	4	5
8.	District managers form territory business plans with territory managers.	1	2	3	4	5

Exhibit 8.2. Work Environment Questionnaire, Cont'd.

	Work Environment Obstacles and Enhancers to Performance	Strongly Disagree		Neutral		Strongly Agree
9.	District managers discuss progress toward territory business plans with territory managers.	1	2	3	4	5
10.	Station managers are receptive to opening their books to territory managers.	1	2	3	4	5
11.	Retail Marketing's goal to double the profitability of stations has been clearly communicated to territory managers.	1	2	3	4	5
12.	Territory managers receive information about the profitability of company-owned stations each month on a timely basis.	1	2	3	4	5

questionnaire. When the questionnaires were returned, they were tabulated by computer. The results of the work environment data appear in Figure 8.2.

Conclusions from the Work Environment Data

When Janet and Jake examined the work environment data, they found that some factors encouraged use of the desired on-the-job activities and others discouraged it. Enhancers to performance included the following:

- District Managers did form and discuss progress toward territory business plans with territory managers.

- The Retail Marketing goal of doubling the profitability of stations was clearly communicated to territory managers.

- District managers did give feedback to territory managers regarding how they counsel station managers and dealers.

The factors having a minimal impact upon territory managers' performance included the following:

- The cost of maintaining older stations

Figure 8.2. Work Environment Factors: Territory Managers.

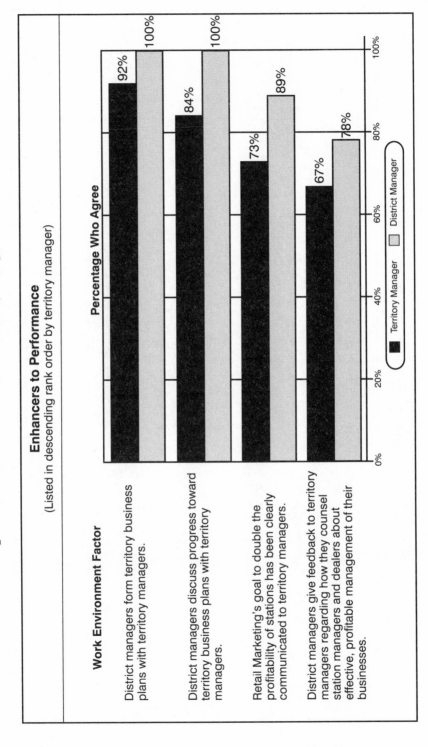

Enhancers to Performance
(Listed in descending rank order by territory manager)

Percentage Who Agree

Work Environment Factor	Territory Manager	District Manager
District managers form territory business plans with territory managers.	92%	100%
District managers discuss progress toward territory business plans with territory managers.	84%	100%
Retail Marketing's goal to double the profitability of stations has been clearly communicated to territory managers.	73%	89%
District managers give feedback to territory managers regarding how they counsel station managers and dealers about effective, profitable management of their businesses.	67%	78%

■ Territory Manager ☐ District Manager

Figure 8.2. Work Environment Factors: Territory Managers, Cont'd.

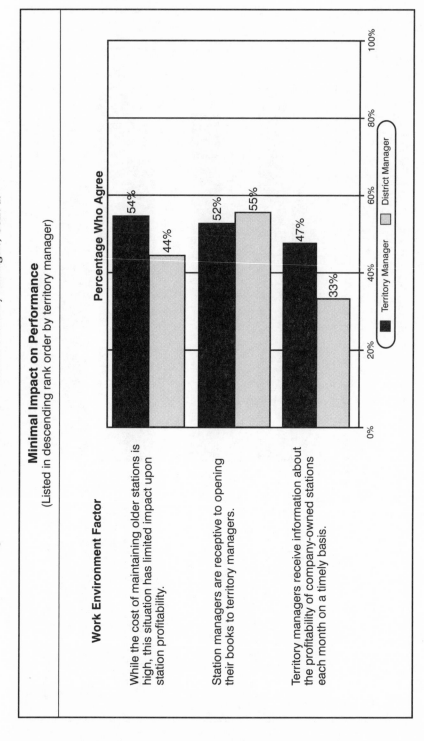

Obstacles to Performance

(Listed in descending rank order by territory manager)

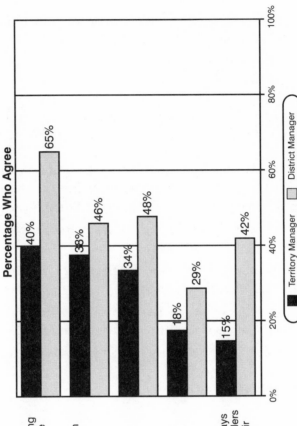

Percentage Who Agree

Work Environment Factor

District managers are positive models in counseling station managers and dealers regarding profitable management of their business. — 40% / 65%

Territory managers have sufficient time to visit with station managers and dealers at a desired frequency. — 38% / 46%

Territory managers have the credibility to discuss the financial aspects of the business with station managers and dealers. — 34% / 48%

Decreases in facility improvement budgets are having a limited impact on a station's ability to compete. — 18% / 29%

District managers coach territory managers on ways to provide guidance to station managers and dealers regarding effective, profitable management of their businesses. — 15% / 42%

■ Territory Manager   □ District Manager

0%   20%   40%   60%   80%   100%

- Station owners' receptivity to opening their books to territory managers

- The difficulty of obtaining information on station profitability

The factors that were inhibiting use of the successful on-the-job activities by territory managers included the following:

- District managers were not positive models in providing guidance to station managers and dealers regarding effective and profitable management of their businesses.

- Decreases in facility improvement budgets put stations at a competitive disadvantage.

- Territory managers did not have sufficient time to conduct frequent visits to stations.

- Territory managers lacked the credibility to discuss financial matters with station managers and dealers.

- There was a lack of coaching by district managers.

Putting It All Together

Now, Janet and Jake could review *all* the findings, both the results from the skill assessment (Figure 7.5) and the findings from the work environment assessment just discussed. They determined that if the performance result "Maximize profitability of stations" was to be successfully implemented throughout Gaso, the following actions were needed:

1. *Skills:* Territory managers required additional development in several skills associated with this result. They needed to develop their competence in counseling on both financial and personnel matters.

2. *District manager skills:* District managers needed to increase the frequency with which they coached territory managers and acted as a positive model for them in counseling situations. Jake wanted each district manager to

counsel one station manager or dealer for each territory manager; in this manner the territory managers could observe the interaction and discuss it with their district manager. This "modeling" experience was to occur after district managers received training in both coaching and counseling skills. While Jake could clearly indicate that coaching was a part of a district manager's accountability, he knew that it was the regional managers who would need to actually ensure that this coaching occurred. Therefore, he planned to meet with the regional managers to discuss what additional actions could be taken to ensure that the district managers did fulfill this accountability. Jake believed that if all of these actions were taken, resulting in increased skills by territory managers in discussing financial matters, the issue of credibility would begin to disappear.

3. *Managing time:* Territory managers felt that they lacked the time to meet with station managers and dealers with the frequency needed to improve profitability. Jake established a task force of three successful territory managers and two district managers to identify techniques for managing time. He also encouraged this task force to identify the administrative and other tasks currently being completed by territory managers that added little value. If these tasks could be eliminated from the work requirements, additional time would be "found." Jake asked this task force to report their recommendations to him within two months.

4. *Limited facility improvement budgets:* Jake did not believe that this would change, but he was hopeful that the results that could be achieved from the actions noted above would overcome this problem.

Janet and Jake discussed the findings with the regional and district managers, describing the actions that needed to be taken. Jake reinforced the need for the district managers to continue to form and discuss territory business plans with territory managers. At this meeting it was decided that district managers would review the findings from the assessment with their territory managers. In this manner all results would be shared, and the territory managers would know that action was being taken based upon their input.

Summary

1. Most performance problems result from multiple causes. For individuals to perform successfully, they must have the required skills and knowledge along with a supportive work environment.

2. CAUSE data should be obtained continuously throughout the performance assessment process.

3. A reliable source for work environment data is the performers themselves. However, data obtained from direct managers of performers can result in a more complete picture of the work environment.

4. When reporting work environment data, let the information speak for itself, but present it graphically so that clients can understand its impact on performance.

PART THREE

CONTRACTING FOR PERFORMANCE CONSULTING SERVICES

Thus far we have introduced you to the conceptual framework for performance consulting (the performance relationship map). Many techniques, tools, and processes have been provided to use in filling in that map for a specific situation. You may, however, be asking a question like one of the following:

- "How do I get a client to *want* to work with me in this manner?"

- "How do I use these concepts in the situations that I usually get? Or are they only used when you have a project like Gaso?"

- "What do I do after the assessment is finished and we know what actions should be taken?"

In the next three chapters we provide you with some guidance in these areas.

9

Identifying and Responding to Opportunities for Performance Consulting

We believe that one of the most critical tools in the Performance Consultant's kit is that of asking the right questions right. We influence more by what we ask than by what we tell. Therefore, Performance Consultants must become very adept in the skill of asking questions. How are the following sets of questions different in your opinion?

Set 1:	*Set 2:*
What are the most common errors people are making now?	When can you release people to attend the training program?
In your mind, select the individual who is the best salesperson you have. What does that person do when closing a call that is successful?	What three things do you hope people will learn because they attended the training program?
What effect is the economy having on sales revenue?	How many people can attend the program at one time?
What should your turnover rate be?	Which training program would best meet your need?

| Do people have the authority to make the kinds of decisions you are describing? | What support can we expect from you regarding the training? |
| What is the current gross margin? | Will the managers of the (performers) attend the training? |

The questions on the right are biased to assume that training will be occurring; it is important only to determine for whom and when. The questions on the left are free of that bias. They focus on identifying the performance, business, and work environment needs for a given situation. Each of the questions on the left is designed to provide some information that can be placed into the performance relationship map. Each of these questions can be categorized as a SHOULD, IS, or CAUSE question, while the questions on the right are what we refer to as implied TRAINING questions. In the early stages of work with a client, Performance Consultants want to continually ask questions such as those on the left and avoid those on the right.

Let's look more closely at the questions on the left and lay them into a performance relationship map (Figure 9.1) to illustrate how a Performance Consultant continually uses this systemic approach. Because skill in asking the right questions is so integral to success as a Performance Consultant, you may want to test your skill in discriminating between the four types of questions we have been discussing: SHOULD, IS, CAUSE, and implied TRAINING. Exercise 9.1 is designed for that purpose. When you have completed it, compare your responses to the answers that follow the exercise.

Responding Reactively to Requests for Training Assistance

From our work we have learned that people in the HRD and training professions receive calls like the following each week: "When is the next time you will be running the Time Management training course?" or "I would like to have someone from your department come out to the plant and conduct a refresher

**Figure 9.1. Placement of Questions into
Performance Relationship Map.**

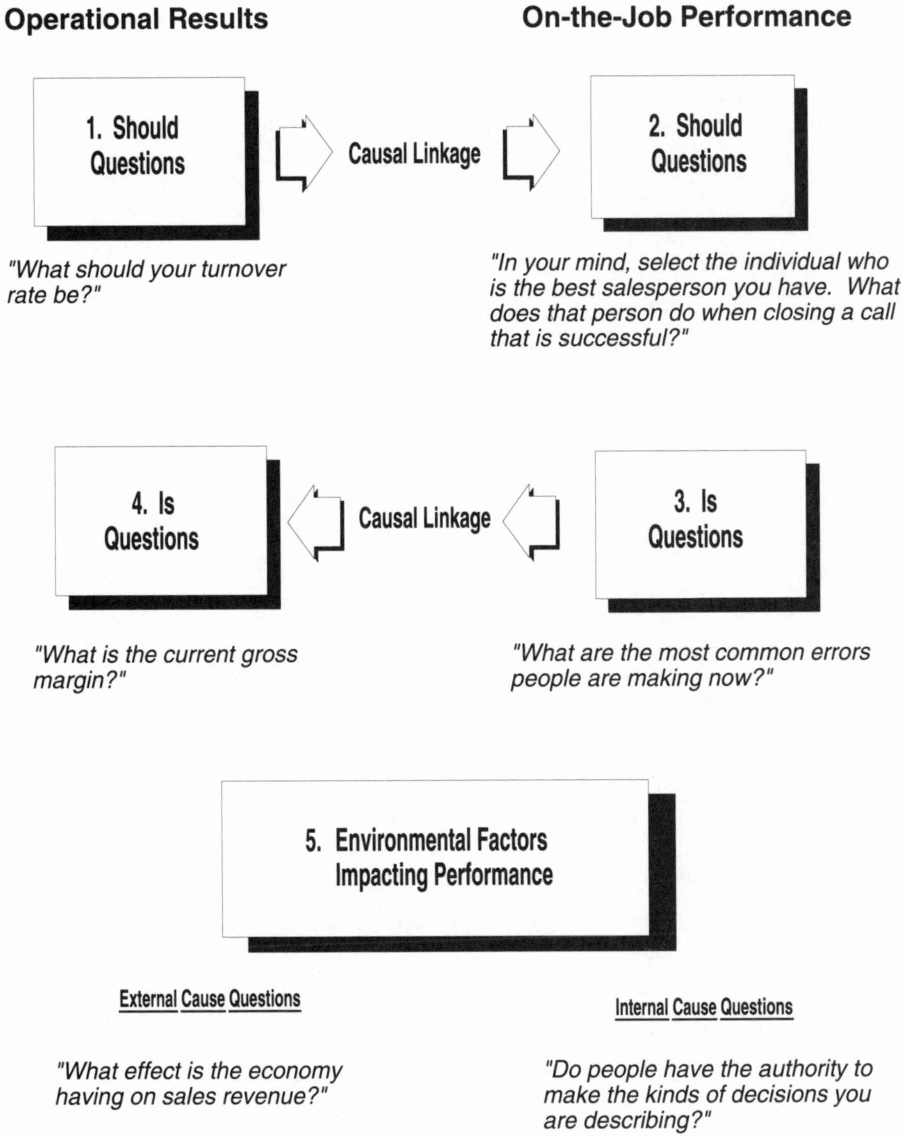

Operational Results   On-the-Job Performance

1. Should Questions	Causal Linkage	2. Should Questions

*"What should your turnover
rate be?"*

*"In your mind, select the individual who
is the best salesperson you have. What
does that person do when closing a call
that is successful?"*

4. Is Questions	Causal Linkage	3. Is Questions

*"What is the current gross
margin?"*

*"What are the most common errors
people are making now?"*

| 5. Environmental Factors
Impacting Performance |
|---|

External Cause Questions

*"What effect is the economy
having on sales revenue?"*

Internal Cause Questions

*"Do people have the authority to
make the kinds of decisions you
are describing?"*

Exercise 9.1. | *DISCRIMINATION EXERCISE: WHAT KIND OF A QUESTION IS IT?*

Instructions:

The following is a list of questions that could be asked of someone who has called with a need for assistance or a problem. Classify each question into *one* of the following categories:

- SHOULD question
- Is question
- CAUSE question
- Implied TRAINING question

_____ 1. What specific outcomes do you want your department to achieve?

_____ 2. What results is your department now achieving?

_____ 3. Could people do what you need if they knew their lives depended on it?

_____ 4. What will participants be expected to do after training is completed?

_____ 5. If we were to have everyone attend the program you are considering, would that be sufficient to correct the problem?

_____ 6. What must employees do differently on the job if your department's goals are to be met?

Compare your responses to the answers we have developed.

Answers

1. SHOULD. This question asks about expected outcomes. The response could be in performance or operational terms.

2. Is. This question asks about actual results.

3. CAUSE. This is a question made famous by Bob Mager, an internationally known consultant and author (with Peter Pipe) of the book, *Analyzing Performance Problems* (1970). The question helps to identify whether the CAUSE of nonperformance is lack of skill or lack of motivation.

4. TRAINING. This could be a SHOULD question if it deleted the phrase "after training is completed."

5. CAUSE. This question is probing to determine if lack of skill and knowledge is the *only* cause for nonperformance, or if other factors must be considered.

6. SHOULD. This question asks what employees must (SHOULD) do differently.

---

program on safety." One way to respond to these questions would be to accept the premise that is proposed (that training is needed and now it is important to determine when and for whom). Another option is to approach this caller using the performance consulting process. This requires that questions be asked to determine if training is or is not an appropriate action. As Performance Consultants we want to engage in a discussion about performance as soon as a request comes to our attention. At the same time we want to be viewed as helpful to this individual, and not as an obstacle. We have found that Performance Consultants must take two steps when these types of calls for service occur:

1. *Determine what kind of need the individual has presented:* Is it a business, performance, training, or work environment need? Is it some combination of those needs? The guideline we would encourage is that you ask questions about the highest-level need you have been given. For example, someone may call and say, "My associates don't seem to prioritize their work. I know you have a course on time management. I'd like to discuss when you could offer it to my group." This individual has provided us with a performance need ("associates don't prioritize their work") and a training need ("I'd like them to attend the course on time management"). We would begin our questioning with the performance need and ignore for now the request for training.

2. *Identify who the caller is:* Is the individual with whom you are speaking inquiring about a need for other people or about a need for himself or herself?

These two determinations occur within the first minute of the call. Once they have been made, you are in a position to respond from a *performance* rather than a training perspective. Figure 9.2 is a decision flowchart to guide you in determining what kinds of questions to ask, based upon the various scenarios in which you might find yourself.

The following describes more completely the decisions in this flowchart:

1. *Is the basic purpose of the call to discuss a training or performance need?* You receive many types of requests and questions in your job; not all of them will be for training or performance needs. This first decision prompts you to determine whether to continue in the flowchart or exit out of it by responding as you would normally do.

2. *Is the caller requesting assistance for others?* If the caller is someone requesting assistance for others, you ask questions of that individual with the purpose of focusing on performance needs. Sample questions are provided for (a) an identified training need and (b) a performance need. You will note that the training need questions are designed to move you quickly into the performance area.

3. *Is the caller the individual with the need?* If the caller is requesting assistance for herself or himself, the process is similar to the one noted above. First, determine if the person is calling about a training or performance need; then begin asking questions such as the ones suggested.

Asking these types of questions, when you are interacting one on one with someone who has a need, can result in substantial savings over time.

A recent example occurred with one of our clients. A manager called and indicated that she wanted all the people in her unit (about twelve) to attend a course in operating a word-processing software package. The course that was requested was two days in length; to respond as requested would have resulted in twenty-four participant days of training. This was a situation where a manager was calling about a *training* need for others. The Performance Consultant responded by asking questions like "What do you need these individuals to do on the job that has led to the conclusion that this program would be beneficial?" and "What do you want them to do that they are not doing now?" In the course of the conversation it was learned that the *performance* need was to have these individuals support others in the organization who were calling for assistance in performing specific functions with the software. Rather than the full two-day course, it was determined that each person required only three hours of training in specific functions! If you would like to practice using this flowchart, complete Exercise 9.2.

Initial Project Meetings

When you are asking callers performance-based questions like those just discussed, it is possible that you and the caller will determine that a more in-depth conversation would be beneficial. In essence you are beginning to qualify the caller (and the situation) into a possible need for performance consulting services. The meeting that is conducted for the purpose of discussing a need in depth is the initial project meeting. This meeting, which can occur either over the telephone or face to face, is designed to further explore the situation. The outcome you seek from such a meeting is *not* a commitment to conduct training; rather, you want a commitment to more fully assess the situation in order to ensure that the true needs of the client will be fully addressed. In other words, you want an agreement that allows you to perform some, or all, of the assessment services described in Part Two of this book. Remember, to operate from a performance perspective, you need to be able to completely fill in the performance relationship map for a specific situation. What is the probability that one individual, in one meeting, will have *all* the information that is required by this map? However, to *tell* someone that an assessment is required is not very collaborative. What you want to do is to raise the awareness of the client that additional information is needed; this is done through the use of SHOULD-IS-CAUSE questions.

Figure 9.2. Flowchart for Determining Questions to Ask in Responding to Requests for Assistance.

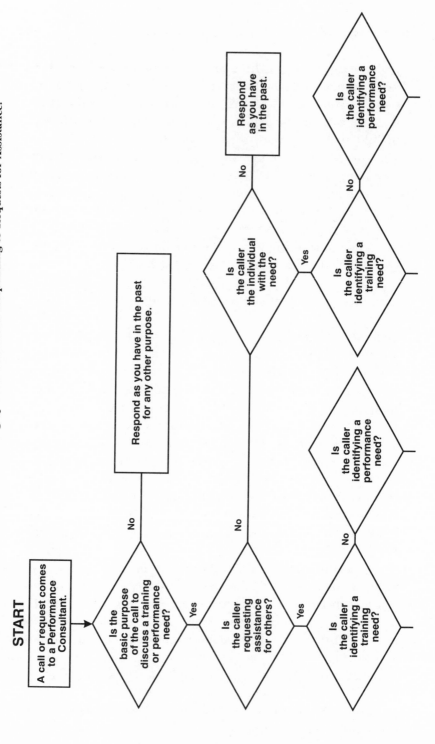

Yes

Affirm that you will be able to assist the individual but require more information. Then ask a question like one of the following:

- *You indicated that these performers would benefit from a training program in the area of (fill in the subject or topic). What have you observed them do or not do that has led to the conclusion that they would benefit from this type of program?*
- *It would be helpful to learn more about why you believe these individuals would benefit from this training. What do you want them to do that they are not doing now?* (Go to the performance need questions to continue the discussion.)

Yes

Affirm that you will be able to assist the individual (if this has not been stated yet). Indicate that you do, however, require more information to ensure that any action taken will result in the needed performance change.

- Ask SHOULD probes such as:
  - *What do you want these individuals to do that they are not doing now?*
- Ask IS probes such as:
  - *What are these individuals doing or not doing that concerns you?*
- Ask CAUSE probes such as:
  - *How long has this problem been in evidence?*
  - *(If performance used to be good) Is anything different that could have contributed to this problem?*

Yes

Affirm that you will be able to assist the individual but require more information in order to ensure that any program is, in fact, a good option for the need the individual has. Then ask a question like one of the following:

- *You indicated that you are interested in attending a training program in the area of (fill in subject or topic). Tell me a little more about your job and the situations you face that require these types of skills.*
- *It would be helpful to learn more about why you believe this program would be helpful to you. What do you want to be able to do differently that leads you to the conclusion that this course would be of help to you?* (Go to the performance need questions to continue the discussion.)

Yes

Affirm that you will be able to assist the individual (if this has not been stated yet). Indicate that you do, however, require more information to ensure that any action taken will result in the needed performance change.

- Ask SHOULD probes such as:
  - *In what ways do you want to change your performance?*
- Ask IS probes such as:
  - *What are you currently doing or not doing that you wish to change?*
- Ask CAUSE probes such as:
  - *Has anything changed in your job recently that makes these skills more important than they used to be?*

Exercise 9.2. *RESPONDING TO CALLS FOR ASSISTANCE*

Instructions:

Four situations have been provided. Consider that you have picked up the telephone and the caller has made the statement that is shown. Determine three things for each of these situations:

1.   The type of need or needs identified by the caller

2.   The role of the caller (whether the individual is calling for others or for himself or herself)

3.   The first question you would ask

Then compare your responses to the suggestions that follow this exercise.

1.   "I'd like to get some of my supervisors into the course you have on leadership; how do I do that?"

   Needs: _____ Business   _____ Performance   _____ Training

   _____ Work environment   _____ None of these

   Caller: _____ Calling for others   _____ Calling for self

   Initial question I would ask:

2.   "There is a great deal of friction between the shifts in my unit. I'd like to discuss with you what could be done to alleviate that situation."

   Needs: _____ Business   _____ Performance   _____ Training

   _____ Work environment   _____ None of these

   Caller: _____ Calling for others   _____ Calling for self

   Initial question I would ask:

3.   "Who do I contact about tuition refunds?"

   Needs: _____ Business   _____ Performance   _____ Training

   _____ Work environment   _____ None of these

Caller: _____ Calling for others   _____ Calling for self

Initial question I would ask:

4. "I would like to go to the 'Effective Writing' workshop described in the training catalog. When is the next time you will be running it?"

    Needs: _____ Business   _____ Performance   _____ Training
           _____ Work environment   _____ None of these

    Caller: _____ Calling for others   _____ Calling for self

    Initial question I would ask:

Suggested Answers

1. *Need:* Training   *Caller:* Calling for others

    Example of an initial question: "What do you want your supervisors to be doing that has led to the conclusion that they would benefit from a course on leadership?" (SHOULD question)

2. *Need:* Performance   *Caller:* Calling for others

    Example of an initial question: "Could you describe what you mean by 'friction'? What are people doing that has you concerned?" (Is question)

3. *Need:* None of these   *Caller:* Calling for self

    Example of an initial question: This individual has not expressed a training or performance need; rather, she or he just wants some information about a benefit. This would be managed in whatever manner is normative for your department.

4. *Need:* Training   *Caller:* Calling for self

    Example of an initial question: "It would be helpful to learn more about why you believe this program would be beneficial for you. What do you want to be able to do differently or better in the area of writing?" (SHOULD question)

Although the overall outcome of this initial project meeting is to gain an agreement to do some type of assessment, additional purposes may be relevant. Consider the following list:

- To gain additional information about the business, performance, and work environment needs of the individual

- To determine what the individual knows, or does not know, about the situation

- To identify who else, besides the individual with whom you are meeting, should be considered as a client

- To confirm the results the individual wants from any work that is done

- To position yourself as a Performance Consultant, working in a collaborative manner with the individual

- To move the individual away from thinking that training alone will resolve the problem

To successfully conduct an initial project meeting, you need to determine the objectives for the meeting and then thoroughly plan for it. There is a lot riding on this meeting, so the key to a successful initial project meeting is to prepare the right questions to ask the client. The right questions are SHOULD-IS-CAUSE questions that focus on what SHOULD be happening, what IS happening, and the CAUSE for the difference.

There are two reasons for asking SHOULD-IS-CAUSE questions. One is to determine what the client knows about the problem, but the second is to increase the client's awareness about what is *not* known regarding the situation. Our experience has been that when there truly is a business and/or performance need, clients can provide operational data and data regarding the business need with relative ease. However, they often have difficulty responding to questions about performance needs and the causes of performance gaps (work environment needs). It is your responsibility to ask the questions that will assist a client in describing performance. It is also likely that thoughtful questions will result in a client response like the following: "I don't know the answer to your question, but it is something we should find out before moving forward." You can acknowledge that "I don't know" answers to some questions are to be expected. In fact, they are welcomed, because "I don't know" answers signal a need to conduct a performance assessment.

We have been referring to this as a meeting (singular), but in actuality there may be meetings (plural). It is possible that in the initial project meeting you will ask questions the client is not able to answer; however, the client may acknowledge others who could provide this type of information. An action that may result, therefore, could be a second meeting with additional individuals being present. It has been our experience that the initial project meeting process can continue for two or three meetings. The goal, however, is to eventually determine that additional information is required; forming an agreement to work together for the purpose of completing a performance assessment is still the goal.

Process for an Initial Project Meeting

Successful initial project meetings require that you prepare the SHOULD-IS-CAUSE questions you plan to ask prior to the meeting. We have also found that successful initial project meetings follow a process that we will briefly outline here.

- **Confirm and Agree on the Purpose of the Meeting.** Certainly, you and the client have already agreed upon the general purpose of the meeting. However, at the start of the meeting, it is wise for you to reaffirm the purposes and check with the client for any additional purposes.

- **Summarize Your Understanding of the Situation.** Here, you briefly summarize previous discussions, particularly if you already have some information about the situation.

- **Ask SHOULD-IS-CAUSE Questions.** This will be the major portion of the discussion with the client. If you have had proactive discussions with the client, you will ask about the business, performance, training, and work environment needs that were previously mentioned. When more than one need has been identified, ask questions about the highest-level need first. In other words, if the client has mentioned both business and performance needs, begin by asking about the business need. If the client has mentioned both training and performance needs, lead off by asking questions about the performance needs. The highest-level need is the one of greatest concern to the client.

Whether you start with a SHOULD question or an IS question is somewhat dependent upon the nature of your previous conversations. If the client has indicated that there is a need for something to be done in the future, you may want to begin with SHOULD questions. For example, if a manager calls and says, "We are launching a new product in the next year and have aggressive sales goals to meet," you would likely begin your questioning by understanding the operational (sales) SHOULDS (goals).

However, if the previous conversations with a client focused on current problems, you may want to begin with IS questions. For example, if a supervisor calls to inform you of conflict between work teams within his unit, your questions may want to begin by identifying performance (work team conflict) in an IS manner (what is currently occurring).

In essence, you begin your questions at the place where your client is and move on from there. The problem arises when the *only* need that has been identified is a training need. For example, let's suppose that a client has called to say that she would like to discuss conducting a communication course for her employees. In this case, the only information that has been provided is that there is a need to deliver a training program in the area of communication. You do not want to reinforce the belief that such a course is required. Therefore, you would want to avoid questions like "How many people do you want to attend this program?" What you *do* want to ask are questions that move you into the performance and business areas. One way of doing this is by asking a question such as "You indicated that your employees need a course in communication. What have you observed them doing that has led you to conclude that a training program would be beneficial?'' This question moves you into a performance (IS) mode. You have moved out of the training "box" into a performance "box" with one question. Eventually, these questions will lead to SHOULD questions as well as to identification of any linkage to operational issues.

■ *Indicate What Is Known and Not Known About the Situation.* As the client is responding to your SHOULD-IS-CAUSE questions, you are mentally placing the answers on a performance relationship map. This way, you are able to identify what is known and not known about the situation. Of course, you are also taking notes so that you will be able to recap what you have learned during this discussion. You now use the performance relationship map and your notes to comment on what is known and not known regarding the problem. You indicate that more information is needed if the business and/or performance needs are to be resolved and you suggest how to move ahead to obtain the necessary information.

■ *Form a Contract for the Performance Assessment.* If you have agreement that it would be beneficial to obtain additional information, you then negotiate the specifics of an assessment contract. Negotiation of this type of contract is the subject of Chapter Ten; therefore, it will not be discussed here.

■ *Agree on Actions to Be Taken by Each of You.* At this time you briefly summarize the items that have been agreed upon and indicate that you will put this agreement in a memo to be sent to the client.

As we stated, preparing for an initial project meeting is key to its success. Preparation primarily consists of development of the SHOULD-IS-CAUSE questions you want to ask the client. If you would like to practice doing this, complete Exercise 9.3. This exercise is based upon a situation with which we were involved some time ago. We have fictionalized the name of the company to Lone Star Telecom. In this situation you are the Performance Consultant and have received a call from a client. What ques-

Exercise 9.3. PREPARING QUESTIONS FOR AN
INITIAL PROJECT MEETING

Situation

You have just received a phone call from the general manager of the customer services department of Lone Star Telecom. She has indicated that there is a training need within the six customer service centers. (Refer to Figure 9.3, which depicts the organizational structure for this department.) The reason for her concern is that over the past several months she has seen the following trends:

1.   For the past six months, sales have been below objectives.

2.   The service representatives do not seem to be working as a team. While a service representative is dedicated to one specific unit (for example, Collections, Residence, or Business), these representatives are to take calls from any of the units when it is very busy. This does not seem to occur, according to the general manager.

The general manager indicated dissatisfaction with the current situation. She has noticed that the Lone Star Telecom list of courses describes a team effectiveness workshop. She would like to have this workshop conducted for everyone within each of the six customer service centers.

She is also interested in a selling skills workshop for the service representatives but wants to have the team effectiveness workshop implemented first. Before hanging up, you and the general manager agree to meet one week from today to discuss the training need in more detail.

Instructions

What questions would you plan to ask this general manager in the initial project meeting? Questions should be developed for each of the needs she has identified:

1.   Sales are too low (business need)

2.   Service representatives are not working as a team (performance need)

Because the business need is the highest-level need, you will begin the questioning by discussing that need. Form SHOULD, IS, and CAUSE questions for each need. Performance relationship maps (Figures 9.4 and 9.5) are provided as a guide to use in creating your questions. When you have formed as many questions as seem appropriate, compare your list to the ones in Figures 9.6 and 9.7.

tions would you ask for the needs that were identified in the call? Fill in the questions you would ask and then compare your questions to the ones we have listed following this exercise.

Some Tips on Asking Questions

In reviewing the questions we developed, we have used some techniques that we would like to bring to your attention.

Transitioning from Business to Performance Questions. When you are asking questions about a business need, such as sales being too low, it is relatively easy to identify operational questions to ask—for example, "What should sales be?" and "What are they currently?" It is more difficult to move into performance questions. It is vital to do this, however, because these are the questions that help to identify any causal relationship between operational results (sales) and what people must do to accomplish those results.

We have learned that one of the best ways to make the transition into performance questions is to focus on exemplary performers. You will note that in the questions we developed for Lone Star Telecom, we inquire about whether one of the six customer service centers is doing better in sales than the others. If this is the case, we ask, "What are the service representatives doing in that unit that is different? What are the supervisors doing? How is that different from what supervisors in the other five units are doing?" It is quite probable that the general manager will not be able to answer our questions; we are asking for a description of the performance of service representatives who are geographically distant from this individual. What we hope *will* occur, however, is that the general manager will acknowledge the value of the question and will want to find out that information. In essence, she will want to partner with us for the purpose of a performance assessment.

Asking Cause Questions. In CAUSE questions, we tend to begin with a very open question ("What are the reasons for the gap?"). This gives the general manager the opportunity to respond in

Figure 9.3. Lone Star Telecom Customer Services Department.

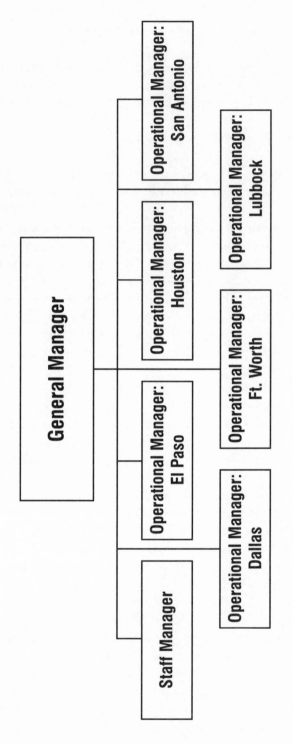

Typical Center

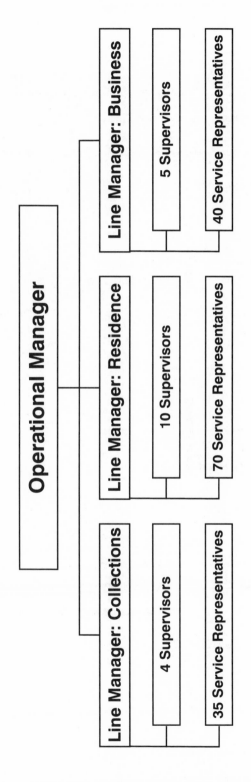

Operational Manager

Line Manager: Collections
4 Supervisors
35 Service Representatives

Line Manager: Residence
10 Supervisors
70 Service Representatives

Line Manager: Business
5 Supervisors
40 Service Representatives

**Figure 9.4. Performance Relationship Map:
Forming Questions for a Business Need.**

Business Need: Sales are too low.

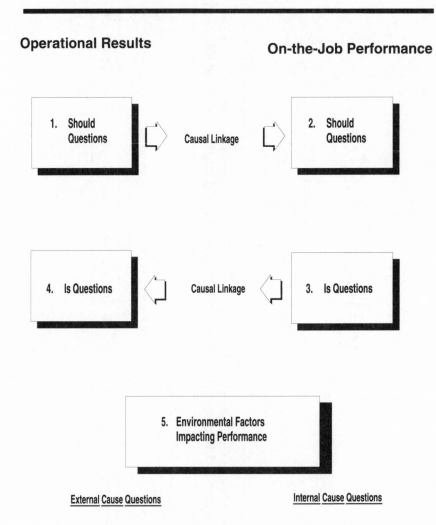

**Figure 9.5. Performance Relationship Map:
Forming Questions for a Performance Need.**

Performance Need: Service representatives are not operating as a team.

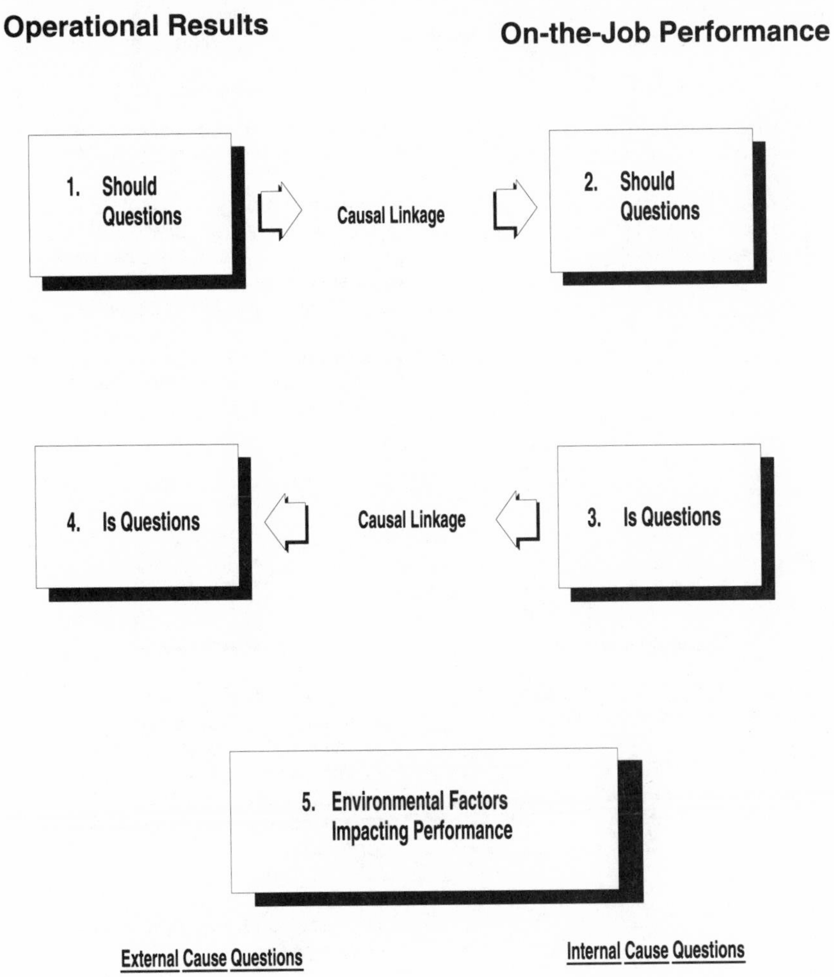

Operational Results   On-the-Job Performance

1. Should
   Questions   Causal Linkage   2. Should
                                                  Questions

4. Is Questions   Causal Linkage   3. Is Questions

5. Environmental Factors
   Impacting Performance

External Cause Questions   Internal Cause Questions

Figure 9.6. Suggested Questions for Lone Star's Business Need.

Business Need: Sales are too low.

Operational Results   On-the-Job Performance

| 1. Should Questions | Causal Linkage | 2. Should Questions |

1. *What should sales revenue be for each service center?*
2. *What are the sales revenue goals for service representatives?*

1. *What should service representatives be doing (on the job) to obtain their sales goal?*
2. *Is there a customer service center that is at or above sales objectives? (If yes): Think about the best service representatives in that unit. What are they doing on the job to obtain their sales goals?*
3. *What should the supervisors be doing to help service representatives meet sales goals?*

| 4. Is Questions | Causal Linkage | 3. Is Questions |

1. *Currently, what is the sales revenue for each service center?*
2. *Currently, what is the sales revenue for service representatives?*

1. *How does a typical service representative handle a sales situation with a customer on the phone?*
2. *What are service representatives typically doing or not doing that is contributing to the problem of lower sales revenue?*
3. *What are typical supervisors doing to help service representatives meet sales goals?*

5. Environmental Factors Impacting Performance

External Cause Questions

1. What are the primary causes for current sales being below goal?
2. To what degree is any of the following a contributing factor:
   a. Change in competition?
   b. Change in service?
   c. Change in pricing of service?

Internal Cause Questions

1. What, in your opinion, are the reasons for the gap between what service representatives should be doing and what they are actually doing?
2. Are service representatives held accountable for sales? How does that accountability factor into their performance review and merit pay increases?
3. Could service representatives sell as they should if their lives depended upon it?
   (If yes): Why are they not performing as they should?
   (If no): What are they not able to do?

Figure 9.7. Suggested Questions for Lone Star's Performance Need.

Performance Need: **Service representatives are not operating as a team.**

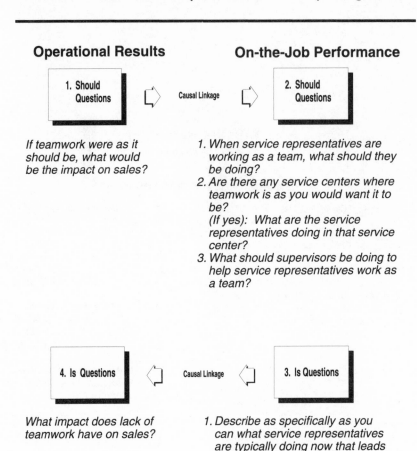

Operational Results

1. Should Questions

Causal Linkage

If teamwork were as it should be, what would be the impact on sales?

On-the-Job Performance

2. Should Questions

1. *When service representatives are working as a team, what should they be doing?*
2. *Are there any service centers where teamwork is as you would want it to be?*
   (If yes): What are the service representatives doing in that service center?
3. *What should supervisors be doing to help service representatives work as a team?*

4. Is Questions

Causal Linkage

3. Is Questions

What impact does lack of teamwork have on sales?

1. *Describe as specifically as you can what service representatives are typically doing now that leads to your conclusion that they are not performing as a team.*
2. *What are supervisors typically doing to help service representatives work as a team?*

5. Environmental Factors Impacting Performance

External Cause Questions

No Questions

Internal Cause Questions

1. *What are the primary reasons for the lack of teamwork?*
2. *Was there ever a time when teamwork was in evidence? (If yes): What do you think has caused the change to the current situation?*
3. *Do service representatives know that they are expected to help each other when necessary?*
4. *How do service representatives know when other representatives need assistance? What is the trigger that alerts them to this situation?*

any manner. However, in our preparation we can often form some specific work environment questions that could be relevant to the situation. If the general manager does not acknowledge these conditions, we will want to probe about them. Asking "Are service representatives held accountable for sales?" is an example of this type of probe.

Guidelines for Sequencing Questions.   We are frequently asked if there is an order in which to pose the questions. It is difficult to be too prescriptive in this area. A few guidelines are:

- Begin with questions about the highest-level need the client has mentioned.

- Ask all questions (SHOULD, IS, and CAUSE) about a specific need before moving into a second need area.

- For each need, begin with SHOULD and IS questions. After establishing that there is a gap between the SHOULD and IS, ask the CAUSE questions. It is these questions that have the highest risk of creating defensiveness in the client; establish some rapport and knowledge about the situation before asking about them.

Contracting for Performance Assessments

As we indicated, the desired outcome from an initial project meeting is an agreement to obtain more information. "Agreement" is a contract for services; "more information" is a performance assessment. In the next chapter we provide more specifics about ways to negotiate for a successful contract.

Summary

1. Asking SHOULD-IS-CAUSE questions needs to be an automatic response by the Performance Consultant to virtually any request for performance or training services. Performance Consultants influence more by what they ask than by what they say.

2. SHOULD, IS, and CAUSE questions can be asked in response to the requests for training assistance that come to the attention of the Performance Consultant; the goal is to reframe the request for training into a request for performance change.

2. Initial project meetings provide an opportunity to raise the client's awareness that more information is required before proceeding. The desired outcome from an initial project meeting is the agreement (or a contract) to conduct a performance assessment.

10

Contracting for Performance Assessment

A key process within any successful consulting project is that of *contracting*. This is not a legal term; rather, it is that phase in the process when a mutually understood and accepted agreement is reached between the Performance Consultant and the client. As Figure 10.1 indicates, a Performance Consultant needs to contract for services on two occasions: (1) when reaching agreement with a client on the assessment that is to be completed (the assessment contract) and (2) when agreeing on what actions will be taken as a result of the assessment (the implementation contract).

Assessment contracts are entered into when there is a need to identify any or all of the information noted in the first four boxes in Figure 10.1. An assessment contract ensures that the information that is to be obtained and reported is the type the client expects and wants. Implementation contracts, by comparison, are negotiated when it is time to turn the assessment findings into actions. Figure 10.1 shows the four major types of actions that can result; implementation contracts identify which of these four action types will be taken and how this will be done. In this chapter, we will discuss the development of assessment contracts; in Chapter Eleven we will discuss implementation contracts.

Figure 10.1. Performance Contracting.

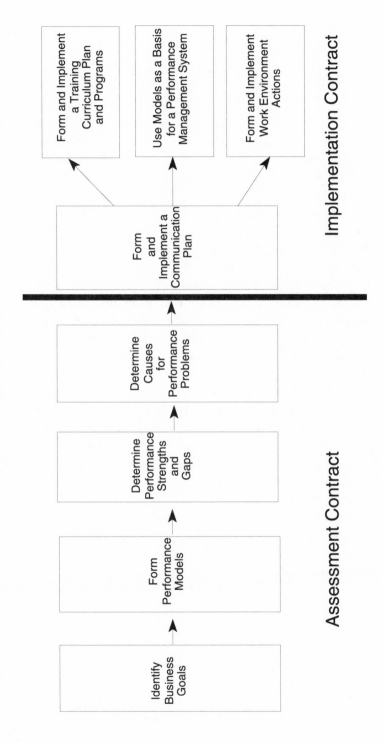

What Is a Contract?

Before we discuss the specifics of an assessment contract, we want to provide some general information on this phase in the consulting process. We find that people often react to the term *contract* by saying that it sounds legalistic. That is not the case.

In his book *The Consultant's Calling*, Geoffrey M. Bellman (1990, p. 213) describes the "living contract" that he reaches with each of his clients. He states, "I attempt to create a contracting process with my clients that is alive and adaptable, not one that is fixed in ink. I encourage trust between client and consultant. I see anything that smacks of mistrust—as defensive legal contracts can do—as damaging to the partnership I want to establish. I favor written communication that records what we decided so we don't forget our responsibilities. I keep files tracking the work the client and I are doing together, but I balk at anything written that suggests we need to protect ourselves from each other."

As Geoff Bellman indicates, contracts are built upon trust. Our experience has been that clients will not enter into contracts with us until a level of trust has been developed. Clients do not want us, in our role as Performance Consultants, investigating the performance of their units if they are uncertain how we will deal with whatever we find. The bottom line is that during the precontracting phase of the consulting process, Performance Consultants must build rapport and trust with their clients. In Chapter One we described some techniques that encourage this trust building, including developing business knowledge relevant to the client and working in a collaborative manner. So a first ingredient to successful contracting is the formation of trust between you and your client.

A second ingredient is also articulated by Bellman when he says that a contract requires "the client and consultant . . . to be mutually clear about what each expects of the other and what each is going to provide the other. Contracting is an exchange of wants and needs going both ways" (p. 213). Again, our experience has been similar to that of Bellman's. In fact, we define a contract as a clear articulation of mutually shared expectations regarding the deliverables and processes to be used in a specific project. Recall that when you are contracting for either an assessment or implementation, you are reaching agreement about something *that does not now exist.* It is no easy task to ensure that both you and the client leave a contracting discussion with the same understanding of what is to be produced.

A third ingredient in successful contracting is that you operate under the premise that a contract is a living agreement. To quote again from Geoff Bellman, "You must attend to [contracting] constantly because it is alive and always moving, changing, and adapting to what is happening. . . . It starts with first contact and is alive, and being renegotiated, throughout the entire consulting relationship. Either person can open a discussion of this living contract at any time" (p. 213). Contracting is a *process* and not a document or "thing." As work proceeds in any consulting effort, learning occurs and problems are encountered that were not envisioned initially. With those changes and new insights, the original contract will need to be renegotiated. It is as though we are removing the layers from an onion; each new layer presents unforeseen challenges and opportunities that must now be incorporated into our plans.

Some time ago, Jim Robinson was working with a large transportation company. The contract called for the development of an individual assessment system. A paper-and-pencil instrument, to be completed by individual employees and others who worked with them, was to be developed. After experience with the paper-and-pencil assessment, a more sophisticated computer-based system would be developed. However, a few weeks into the project, top management became excited about the potential of the computer-based approach and asked that the timetable be moved up several months. The contract needed to be renegotiated to accommodate the compressed timetable and to examine the roles and responsibilities of everyone involved. In fact, as it turned out, Jim and his colleagues took on additional responsibility that was not outlined in the original contract because of the new timeline.

An individual who has added much to the literature on contracting is Peter Block. In his book, *Flawless Consulting: A*

Guide to Getting Your Expertise Used (1981, p. 42), Block clearly indicates how critical contracting is to effective consulting. He states, "I believe the point of maximum leverage for the consultant is probably during the contracting phase of a project. There are possibilities for impact that may be lost for the life of the project, if they are not pursued in contracting. The contract sets the tone for the project, and it is much easier to negotiate a new, initial contract than to renegotiate an old one."

We wish to add a final thought on the contracting process. In this process, you, as a Performance Consultant, are the guide and influencer, and the client is the decision maker. Think of going on a trip in a car; the client is behind the wheel making the turns and you, as the Performance Consultant, are sitting on the passenger side with a map. You will guide the direction of the trip as well as you can, but in the end it is the client's right and responsibility to decide which way to go. It is important to continually remind yourself of this role difference and to act in support of it.

Let's summarize the general guidelines we have stated thus far about contracts:

1.   They are based upon trust.

2.   They articulate mutually shared expectations.

3.   They are living agreements that are continually renegotiated.

4.   They are critical to the success of any project.

5.   They require the Performance Consultant to perform in the role of guide, while the client has the role of decision maker.

The Assessment Contract

In Chapter Nine, we indicated that contracts for assessments frequently are developed at the conclusion of an initial project meeting. The purpose of this meeting is to raise a client's awareness that additional information is both needed and desired; if you are successful in achieving this result, you will find yourself needing to negotiate a contract for assessment services.

A contract for any consulting service should include agreements in the following four areas:

1. The deliverables to be produced
2. The processes to be used in accomplishing the deliverables
3. The roles and responsibilities of those involved in the project
4. The time frame and costs to be incurred

Let's discuss each of these areas in more detail as they relate to performance assessments.

Deliverables. This is a clear articulation of the purpose of the performance assessment and of each of the reports that will be generated throughout the assessment. It is also an agreement about the types of decisions that can and must be made as a result of each of these reports.

Processes to Be Used in Accomplishing Deliverables. This is a mutual understanding of the data sources and processes used in obtaining any or all of the following: (1) SHOULD data, (2) IS data, and (3) CAUSE data.

Roles and Responsibilities. The roles of the Performance Consultant and the client team are clarified here. Typically, Performance Consultants are the doers. They develop the data collection instruments such as interview guides and questionnaires. In addition, they collect the majority of the data, tabulate the data, and form the report of findings, which can include a performance model and identification of training and work environment needs.

The role of the client team, while less active, is still crucial. The client team must legitimize the project and ensure that all those involved understand the purpose and the importance of the project. The client team stresses the need for everyone to cooperate fully during the performance assessment. Frequently, people will be reluctant to share performance information with those collecting the data. The clients can overcome this reluctance by positioning the project as a positive approach to improving both unit and individual performance.

Time Frame and Cost of the Performance Assessment.   This is often a sticky wicket for Performance Consultants. Clients frequently want data within a few days when a few weeks may be required to obtain reliable, credible data. The time to negotiate a timetable is during the contracting process. Certainly, information can be obtained within a few days, but it will be of a limited nature. Clients need to understand what they gain—and what they lose—by collecting data too quickly. The decision regarding the completeness of the data and the time frame is the client's to make. The role of the Performance Consultant is to clarify the advantages and disadvantages of each time option and to influence a decision toward the more reliable approach.

Clarification is also needed regarding the costs for the project. In organizations that use charge-backs, the clients need to know the amount of the charge. Even in organizations without charge-backs, the clients need to have an understanding of any out-of-pocket expenses, such as travel expenses or additional staff, that will be incurred.

An additional element to include in this portion of the contract focuses on the assumptions used to derive the time and cost estimates. For example, perhaps you agree to provide the client team with a report in two weeks. This agreement is based upon the *assumption* that you will be conducting interviews with ten people. What if a client phones you one week into the project and indicates that interest in the project is increasing and you need to interview six other people? If you clearly indicated the assumptions used to derive the time in the original contract, you are now in a strong position to discuss options with the client. It is certainly possible to interview more people, but then more time will be required before a final report can be made. Is this trade-off acceptable to the client? Stating assumptions is even more helpful when it is the cost that will increase. Renegotiating costs can be an uncomfortable process; by placing this discussion into the frame of assumptions and how they have been modified, the discussion is less difficult.

Our research indicates that when there is a business or performance need and the consultant can successfully negotiate a contract with the client team, the probability of a successful performance assessment is high. While the performance assessment does not solve the problem, it does provide the information required to determine the actions that can ultimately resolve the situation. This assessment also creates ownership among key people for the problem and the actions needed to resolve it.

Performance Consulting Tool 6 is a checklist to use when negotiating a contract for performance assessments. When you are summarizing an agreement in a memo, for example, refer back to this checklist to ensure that you have negotiated all items that are relevant and critical to the success of your specific project. If, for some reason, an item was overlooked in the discussion with the client team, note it in your memo as one that still needs agreement. Follow up the memo with phone calls to the clients to discuss that item and to ensure that the document you have sent is an accurate reflection of the client's understanding of the project.

Performance Consulting Tool 6

Checklist for Performance Assessment Contracts

The following is a list of items that should be considered when contracting for performance assessments with clients. Not all of these areas will be relevant to each situation. This list should be viewed as a checklist to assist in determining what to include.

1. Deliverables

_____ a. What specific major questions do you and the client team want to answer with the collected information?

_____ b. What specific decisions will be made from the infor-
             mation that is collected?

_____ c. What will be the format of the final report? Will it be a
             paper document? a meeting? both?

2. Processes

_____ a. What sources of information will be included in the
             assessment?

_____ b. What types of information (that is, quantitative or qual-
             itative) will be collected?

_____ c. What methods of data collection will be used in the
             assessment?

_____ d. How many people will be included in the assessment?

_____ e. Will the identities of people be protected?

3. Mutual Responsibilities

         a. Who will be responsible for:

_____   Designing the assessment?

_____   Collecting the information?

_____   Analyzing the information?

_____   Reporting the information?

_____ b. Who will be responsible for legitimizing the project to
             the target group?

_____ c. Who will be responsible for providing access to nec-
             essary people and information?

4. Time Frame and Costs

_____ a. When will the final report be made?

_____ b. Which costs will be charged to the client's budget?

Which costs will be assumed by the Performance Consultant's budget?

_____ c. What assumptions did you use to derive the fee and time frame?

Documenting the Assessment Contract

It has been our experience that when you are forming an agreement to develop a product that the client team is unfamiliar with, it is best to summarize the agreement in some manner and forward that summary to the clients. In the case of an assessment contract, you are agreeing to obtain information so that decisions can be made. It is important to ensure that you and your clients have identical expectations for what will be done and how it will be accomplished. By putting your agreement in writing, you are helping to ensure that this mutual understanding is present.

Exhibit 10.1 is a sample memo for this type of agreement. This memo is referring to the case study of Lone Star Telecom, which was discussed in Chapter Nine. In that situation, a general manager had called because of concern regarding sales (which were below goal) and lack of teamwork between the service representatives. The general manager requested that the service representatives be provided with training in two areas: selling skills and teamwork.

In the initial project meeting, questions were asked that raised the awareness of the general manager that the business need of declining sales and the performance need of lack of teamwork probably resulted from many factors. In other words, conducting two training programs probably would not solve these problems. The general manager also acknowledged that information, key to the success of this project, was lacking. The memo in Exhibit 10.1 summarizes the contract that was agreed to between the Performance Consultant and the general manager and serves as an example of what might be included in this type of document.

**Exhibit 10.1. Memo Summarizing
an Agreement to Conduct a Performance Assessment.**

TO: General manager, Customer Services Department
FROM: Performance Consultant, Lone Star Telecom
DATE: March 15, 19XX
SUBJECT: Performance assessment

This memo confirms our discussion of yesterday in which we agreed to conduct a performance assessment within the customer services department. The assessment will focus on the service representatives within all six locations.

1. **Deliverables**

   a. As a result of this performance assessment, we will be able to answer the following questions:

   - What performance results and best practices are required of service representatives if the sales goals and required teamwork are to be achieved?

   - What gaps exist between required practices and the current performance of service representatives?

   - How are work environment factors either encouraging service representatives to perform as needed or discouraging them from doing so?

   b. As a result of the information gathered during the performance assessment, we should be able to determine all actions required to change current performance to what is required for sales and teamwork goals to be achieved.

   c. This assessment will require two report meetings:

   - A meeting to discuss the performance results and best practices that have been identified

   - A meeting to discuss the performance gaps and the causes of those gaps

2. **Processes**

   a. To obtain information for the performance model, data will be obtained from successful service representatives and their supervisors, located primarily in the El Paso and San Antonio, Texas, service centers. This information will be collected through one-on-one interviews; it is anticipated that a total of twelve interviews will be conducted. Additional information regarding model performance will be obtained through a review of the literature that will focus on the selling and teamwork practices of successful service representatives.

**Exhibit 10.1. Memo Summarizing
an Agreement to Conduct a Performance Assessment, Cont'd.**

---

b. Once the performance model has been approved, data regarding training and work environment needs will be gathered by sending questionnaires to all service representatives, their supervisors, and managers.

c. Information collected during the performance assessment will be treated as anonymous. No individuals will be personally identified with the information they provide.

3. **Mutual Responsibilities**

a. I will be responsible for all the data collection as well as for the development of the two reports.

b. Your responsibilities will include:

- Notifying each service center of the upcoming performance assessment and why it is important

- Participation in the two report meetings

4. **Time Frame and Costs**

a. I estimate that the two reports will be available on the following dates:

- Performance model: three weeks after the start of the project

- Needs assessment report: four weeks after approval of the performance model

b. The following costs will be charged against your budget account:

Twelve days of Performance Consultant time	$12,000
Questionnaire tabulation	2,500
Total	$14,500

My travel expenses will be assumed in my budget.

If you have any questions about this memo, please give me a call. I look forward to working with you on this project.

Things That Can Go Wrong

It is possible that during the meeting when an assessment contract is being discussed and formed, things may not go as planned. In fact, you should plan on some surprises! The following are some of the most common problems that occur during this contracting phase.

The Client Resists the Process

The client may resist the questioning process by making a statement such as "Why are you asking me all these questions? I thought you were the *training* department, and I have a training need. Are you going to help me or not?"

Recall that contracting for performance assessments often occurs at the conclusion of an initial project meeting. This meeting, described in detail in Chapter Nine, is one where you are asking many questions. It is also typical for this meeting to occur following a request from the client for assistance; you are responding in a reactive manner. Given this scenario, the client may have expectations for what will be occurring in this meeting that are not aligned with your own: you expect to ask questions while the client expects to learn when a training program will be conducted. In this case, the client may stop the process with a question similar to the one noted above.

We have three suggestions for this situation:

1. Indicate that you *do* want to assist this individual and will offer training if that is what the client deems necessary. (Remember, the client is the decision maker.) But also indicate your desire to provide actions that will result in success; you require additional information to ensure that the program the client has identified *will* be sufficient and appropriate to the situation. Then seek permission to continue with the questioning process.

2. If there is an example from the past where a training program was conducted but no change resulted, remind the client of that situation. Indicate your commitment to help ensure that this problem is not repeated in the current case.

3. If the client is adamant in wanting a program and resistant to the questioning process, be prepared to return to the traditional training approach and provide the training that is requested, or be prepared to say no to the client's request.

The Client Resists Additional Data Collection

The client may see no need to obtain additional information, believing that he or she alone has sufficiently responded to the questions that you raised during the meeting.

Again, performance assessment contracts generally result from a meeting in which many questions are asked of the client team. These questions are focused against the performance relationship map. They include questions about what performance SHOULD be, what it IS, and why there are gaps. There are occasions when a client will respond to the questions that are raised in a manner that (for the client) is sufficient. Taking time to obtain additional information is not viewed as valuable; the client wants action now. How do you manage this type of situation? Here are three suggestions:

1. A proactive tactic is to address this problem as soon as you observe a pattern from the client that indicates that the client believes she or he has all the necessary information. Following a reply from a client to a question, inquire whether others in the unit would view things in a similar manner. Or ask who you might talk with to gain additional insight into what the client has said. In other words, don't wait until the conclusion of the conversation to deal with a client's resistance to additional data collection.

2. If the client continues to resist collection of additional information, engage him or her in a discussion of the advantages and disadvantages of taking action without doing any assessment. The advantages are obvious—something is being done. What are the disadvantages? What could possibly go wrong? What about the missed opportunity to gain broader support and buy-in for the actions that do get taken? Another option is to ask if you can negotiate for a minimal amount of time, perhaps one week, to do some assessment.

3. Finally, we encourage you to state in a direct manner the

concern you have about taking action (which often consists
of a training program) based solely on the input of the
client team. You are a partner on the team; you have a point
of view that needs to be presented. However, the client is
the decision maker and has the right to override your concerns. There are occasions when that will occur.

The Client Objects to the Time and Research Needed

The client may be amenable to a performance assessment but
may not want to allow sufficient time to do it reliably or to
permit access to specific sources of information that you believe
are necessary.

In today's organization, time is a very valuable commodity.
There will be occasions when you and the client team may not
agree on (1) how much information should be obtained, (2) the
sources of information to use, or (3) the time in which the assessment will be completed. In this instance, a discussion of the
advantages and disadvantages of the approach proposed by the
client team and the one proposed by you can be helpful. What
are you gaining and losing with either option? Is some combination of viewpoints viable? Ultimately, however, this is the
client team's decision. Your role is to increase the perceived
value for the approach you propose; in the end the client decides
what will be done.

The Client Takes a Passive Role

The client team may agree to the performance assessment but
take a passive role throughout the assessment process. The risk
is that when the findings are reported, such a client may express
limited ownership for the results and limited interest in taking
actions based upon the results.

Some performance assessments you do will require little
time, so maintaining client involvement through the assessment
phase will not be an issue. Other assessments, however, can require months of time to conclude. We have personally been in-

volved in assessments that required six months or more to complete. During this time there are few things for the clients to do; generally, the data gathering is done primarily by you and others who work with you. It is important, however, to form a meaningful role for the clients so they do not "disconnect" from the process. You want to avoid a situation where you and the client team do not meet between the time the performance assessment contract is negotiated and the time the findings are reported.

One suggestion we offer is to have regular updates with the clients throughout the assessment process. These updates should be interpersonal in nature (not only through electronic mail or memo). It is also important to agree that you will contact the client team if you encounter any unusual situations or problems. Continue to keep the client team's interest high during the assessment phase; it will provide dividends in terms of client commitment during the implementation phase.

Summary

1. A contract is an agreement between the Performance Consultant and the client team that is:

    ■   Based upon trust

    ■   An articulation of mutually shared expectations

    ■   Living and open for continual renegotiation

    ■   Critical to the success of the performance assessment

2. In forming contracts, the Performance Consultant is in the role of influencer and the clients in the role of decision makers.

3. Performance assessment contracts include negotiated agreements in four areas:

    ■   Deliverables from the assessment

    ■   Processes to use in completing the assessment

    ■   The roles and responsibilities of those involved in the assessment

    ■   The time frame and cost of the assessment together with the assumptions used to derive each of those items

4. It is advisable to summarize a contract in a memo that is sent to the client team; this ensures that the understanding between the Performance Consultant and client team is mutual.

11

Contracting for Performance Implementation

As discussed in Chapter Ten and reiterated in Figure 11.1, the Performance Consultant must form two types of contracts with a client: (1) contracts used when a decision has been made to do a performance assessment and (2) contracts used when the assessment is completed and a decision has been made to change or improve performance. We will be concerned with this second situation in this chapter.

We define a contract as a clear articulation of mutually shared expectations regarding the deliverables and processes to be used in a specific project. Once a performance assessment is completed, it is time to agree on the deliverables and required actions for changing performance. If all we did was obtain data, Performance Consultants would be of limited value. The ultimate test of a consulting project is how the information is actually used to make desirable changes.

Contracting for implementation begins with the data feedback meeting. This is the meeting when all findings from the assessment (for example, for models or performance gaps) are reviewed. In our experience, however, project implementation is seldom fully contracted for in this meeting. Rather, the contract evolves over a series of meetings that follow the feedback meeting.

Figure 11.1. Performance Contracting.

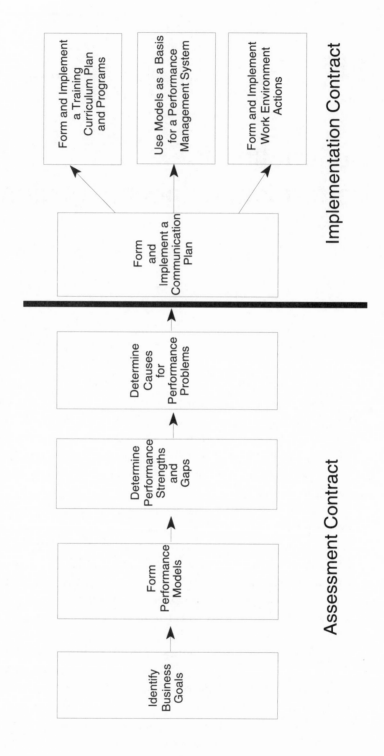

We have also learned that the feedback meeting must be effectively facilitated or there may be no contract for additional work. So, because the contracting process begins in this meeting, we will start there.

Data Feedback Meeting

Data feedback meetings may occur on several occasions, including:

- Following the collection of all information about business goals
- Following the draft of performance models
- Following the collection of information on current performance strengths and gaps and the causes of the gaps

We will focus on the meeting that occurs at the conclusion of the performance assessment, when the next step is either (1) no step at all or (2) a step to change performance in a direction that has been identified as necessary.

Data Funnel

The process of interpreting data and translating it into information that can be used to agree on actions is similar to the funnel displayed in Figure 11.2. As we discussed in our previous book, *Training for Impact: How to Link Training to Business Needs and Measure the Results* (Robinson and Robinson, 1989), you begin with dozens, perhaps hundreds, of facts tabulated from the raw data. These results are indisputable and involve no interpretation at all. For example, computer-tabulated data indicating means, percentages, or frequencies are *results,* or facts.

These results must be put into a user-friendly format so that clients can work with you to interpret them. In this book we have provided you with several format options. For example, in Chapter Six we provided ideas on how to display performance model data, in Chapter Seven we presented options for display-

Figure 11.2. Data Funnel.

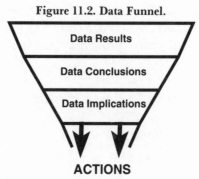

ACTIONS

ing is information, and in Chapter Eight we showed how to display results about the work environment. A vital role of the Performance Consultant is to turn data into information; this requires you to display data results in a user-friendly and helpful manner.

As the funnel in Figure 11.2 indicates, we draw *conclusions* from data results. The funnel narrows because conclusions are usually deductions from many pieces of data. You now began to reduce the amount of information with which you must deal. By forming decision rules like those described in Chapter Seven and displaying the results in matrices, you help clients to draw conclusions about which performance activities or competencies may require development. By displaying work environment results like those in Chapter Eight, you are again making it easier for your clients to observe the patterns and form conclusions about where the problems are most severe.

The final element in the data funnel is the *implications* of the conclusions, or the "so what." Again, the funnel narrows, because you will have fewer implications than conclusions. Often these implications affect the business need that initiated the project; it is important to point this out to the client. For example, in the Gaso example, the low skill of territory managers in counseling station managers and dealers regarding pricing of gas and nongas products will make it more difficult to run profitable stations, and if the stations are not profitable, the company may not achieve its profitability goals. Illustrating this type of relationship between the business goals desired by the client and the performance requirements for employees increases the probability that clients will be dissatisfied with the status quo; doing nothing will be an unacceptable response. Therefore, you should draw these implications. It is even better if you facilitate the feedback meeting so that your clients formulate them.

From implications will come identification of *actions* that are required. What training or developmental actions are needed? What managerial actions must be taken if the work environment is to support the desired performance? When you identify actions for both your clients and yourself, you are entering into the contractual phase of this meeting. As noted earlier, you may actually set up another meeting to discuss actions, because the feedback meeting itself can be lengthy. We have been in feedback meetings that range from a few hours to a full day. The scope of the assessment, the amount of information to be reviewed, and the number of people who need to be present in the meeting will determine how long it takes. If people have spent several hours drawing conclusions and implications from the information that is presented, it may be wise to postpone contracting for implementation actions until another day.

Preparing for the Data Feedback Meeting

Obviously, this meeting is critical. If the meeting does not result in a commitment to take action of some kind, the assessment has failed. In essence, you have learned something, but this learning has been relegated to the shelf to gather dust. The best criterion for the success of a data feedback meeting is an agreement to take some action. You may not achieve all you would want, but you will make progress in addressing at least some of the issues identified in the assessment.

To achieve success, this meeting must be well planned. The first step is to form the purposes for the specific meeting you will be having. Generally, the purposes for a feedback meeting include some or all of the following:

- To review results and form conclusions from them
- To determine opportunities for actions to be taken
- To form an agreement (or contract) about what to do next

It is also important to determine the facilitative style you will be using in the meeting. To what degree does your client expect you to come into the meeting with stated results, conclusions, and recommendations for action? This would be supportive of an expert style, using Block's styles of consulting (1981, pp. 18, 19). Or does your client want to work with the information and be actively involved in forming the conclusions and recommendations? We would strongly advocate the second option as the preferable approach. However, it is important to determine *prior to the meeting* what your client's expectations are and to either influence a change in those expectations or support them in the meeting. Do not surprise your client by coming in with a list of recommendations when the client wanted active involvement, for example.

In preparing for a data feedback meeting, then, it is important to obtain answers to the following questions:

1.   How does the client team prefer the results to be presented? in graphs? in narrative descriptions? both?

2.   Does the information need to be formally presented, using slides and overhead projectors, or is a handout sufficient?

3.   How much time will be allotted to the meeting?

4.   Who will be in attendance in the meeting?

5.   What specific outcomes and agenda should be established for the meeting?

6.   What role will you have in the meeting (for example, are you the facilitator)? What about other individuals—what will their role be in the meeting?

7.   What consultative style (such as expert or collaborative) should be used in the meeting?

8.   Is there any report or information that should be sent ahead to those who will be attending the meeting?

Agenda for a Data Feedback Meeting

While feedback meetings can differ, generally we have found that they follow the same pattern. The following agenda is typical.

■ *State the Purpose and Agenda for the Meeting.* The purpose and agenda, already agreed upon with the client team, are overviewed for everyone in attendance.

■ *Present Findings for Each Major Category or Position and Seek Reactions.* It is important to organize the review of findings in some manner. If, for example, you obtained information on three different jobs, it would be appropriate to review the findings for each position separately. In this way the specific patterns and issues within a position can be identified; as you conclude the meeting, you can show shared patterns and issues across positions.

When you are presenting findings, it is important to seek the reactions of people to what was learned. Are they surprised? Is there anything in the results they cannot agree with? Remember, results are the start of our funnel. If people disagree with the findings, they will never agree to conclusions or implications drawn from those findings. While clients may be disappointed with the findings (the current skill level may be lower than they would like), disappointment is not a bad thing; in fact, it can be a motivator to take action. What we don't want are reactions indicating that a client does not agree with the results. Statements like "I don't know how you could have gotten that finding," *are* a concern. The way to avoid this is to have the client involved from the beginning in decisions regarding the design of the data collection strategy.

■ *Agree on the Conclusions and Implications for Action.* Discuss the conclusions and implications for each position or category separately. We often write these conclusions onto a flipchart. If several clients are present, it will be necessary to poll the group from time to time to determine if they agree with a conclusion or implication someone has stated. To the degree possible, we are seeking consensus.

■ *Complete the Review of Data for All Positions and Discuss Possible Actions.* The process just described needs to be repeated for all assessed positions. When that has occurred, you and your clients can discuss the actions that may be required if the performance issues identified in the data are to be resolved. This is the transition into a contracting discussion—a discussion that frequently is postponed to another meeting. At a minimum, you want to leave the feedback meeting with a commitment to, and a date for, the next meeting.

Contracting for Action Implementation

As Figure 11.1 shows, four potential areas need to be considered when contracting for implementation:

1. A communication plan
2. Training actions
3. The development of a performance management system
4. Work environment actions

Let's begin by discussing what deliverables may be required within each of these areas.

Communication Plan

To date, the work on the project has focused on the assessment phase. Although many people may have been involved in providing information, few of them know of the findings that resulted from that data collection process. It is very important to form a plan by which all those who provided input, together with other stakeholders, learn of the findings from the assessment and of the actions that will be taken.

Over the years we have learned what does *not* constitute an effective communication process:

- Sending a one- or two-paragraph memo or E-mail with a brief statement of findings. Some people will have no recall of the assessment and will wonder what the memo is referencing; others will have many questions and no one to go to for answers.

- A simple request to the people in the feedback meeting to "share this information with others." The messages that result from such a suggestion are highly inconsistent in terms of quality and thoroughness.

- Sending information with no guidelines for its use. One of the worst communication efforts we observed occurred after performance models had been developed. Much time and care had been taken to form these models. When they were completed, they were sent in a three-ring binder with a cover memo to all individuals in the position and their managers. People had no idea what they were to do with these binders. As a result many just tossed them out; others put them "on the shelf." Some people did call our client to ask what they were to do with the information they had just received. Because the communication process was ineffective, limited benefit was derived from the investment made in forming models.

What are some communication options that *do* work? We would offer the following suggestions:

- Cascade the information through the organization or unit by developing managers or other key personnel to present and discuss findings with their employees, with emphasis on the word *develop*. Results from climate or attitude surveys are often communicated in this manner; this cascading approach is particularly effective when communicating a performance model. Remember that a model identifies the results an individual should accomplish on the job together with the competencies and/or best practices for doing so. It is very likely that people currently in the position are neither completing all results nor performing all the practices that are listed. It is important to communicate these "new" expectations in a thoughtful manner, providing people with opportunities to discuss concerns and raise questions. It is also important that the request to perform as described in a model should come from a manager to the employee and *not* from the training department to the employee.

■ Develop a few individuals to facilitate meetings of groups of people in order to discuss the findings from the assessment. In this option, individuals learn of the findings from someone other than their direct manager. Sometimes these meeting facilitators are from the training function; typically, they would be partnered with individuals from the client's organization.

■ Summarize the findings from an assessment in the employee newsletter. We have had clients who did this. In one instance the client actually developed the article and had it published within three weeks of the feedback meeting! The article contained many of the principal findings together with actions that had been agreed upon by the time of the article's printing. The name and telephone extension of an individual who could provide more information or answer questions was also provided.

■ Develop an "executive summary." These are usually a few pages in length and describe key findings and actions. Send the summary to all those who provided data for the assessment.

The keys to a successful contract regarding communication are to determine (1) what specific information will be communicated, (2) who will be responsible for this communication, and (3) the process and time frame by which it will be completed.

Training Actions

Generally, assessments like those discussed in this book *do* identify some training and developmental needs for employees. Recall the findings at Gaso, as described in Chapter Seven, indicating that territory managers had to increase their skill in working with station managers and dealers concerning the financial aspects of the business. Territory managers also needed to learn how to form a business plan with station managers and dealers.

There are times when the scope of an assessment is small. In these instances only one training need may be identified (for example, that managers need development in forming strategic plans). A learning experience is designed or purchased and then made available to those who need it. In other instances, however, many training needs are determined. This is particularly true if you have assessed several positions. In this situation, we have found it beneficial to form an architecture for the training curriculum that will be developed. Figure 11.3 illustrates a curriculum that could be developed for Gaso when all positions have been assessed.

This architecture contains the following elements:

1.   *Performance tracks:* The vertical boxes indicate the performance tracks within the curriculum. For example, if people need to enhance their managerial performance, they would look in the management track; if they want to develop selling skills, they would review the sales track.

2.   *Performer groups:* The horizontal boxes indicate the performer groups for whom the curriculum is intended. Territory managers would look across the top row of boxes to identify the learning experiences that relate to their position. District managers would look across the second row of boxes for relevant learning experiences.

3.   *Learning experiences:* Within each box are the identified learning experiences that correspond to the performer group for each performance track. For example, territory managers who believe they need to develop skill in time and territory management would look in the planning track boxes and select whatever learning experiences are noted. District managers who believe they need to develop coaching skills

Figure 11.3. Curriculum Architecture for Sales Training.

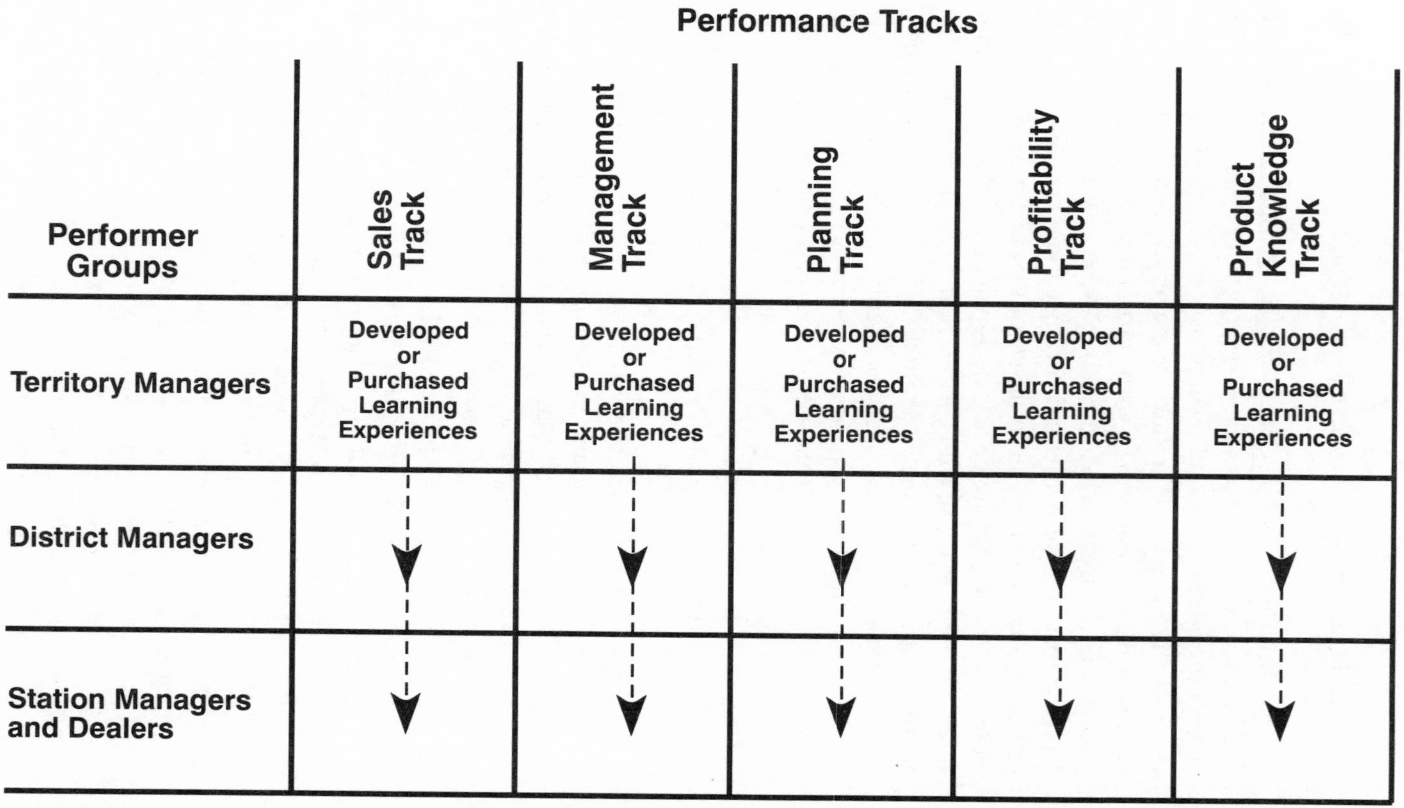

Performance Tracks

Performer Groups	Sales Track	Management Track	Planning Track	Profitability Track	Product Knowledge Track
Territory Managers	Developed or Purchased Learning Experiences	Developed or Purchased Learning Experiences	Developed or Purchased Learning Experiences	Developed or Purchased Learning Experiences	Developed or Purchased Learning Experiences
District Managers	→	→	→	→	→
Station Managers and Dealers	→	→	→	→	→

would look in the management track boxes for possible learning opportunities.

A curriculum architecture such as the one displayed in this figure is developed on the basis of findings from the performance assessment. This type of architecture also makes it apparent when no learning experience has been developed to address a training need. It is important for such an architecture to identify learning experiences *other than leader-led training programs* that can be used to address skill deficiencies. Curriculum architectures should incorporate learning methods such as:

- *Self-instruction:* Any learning experience in which individuals take responsibility for their own learning without relying on an instructor or other leaders. Examples would be the use of audiotapes and instructional packages designed to be completed without assistance.

- *Technology-delivered learning:* Learning in which the learner interacts with a computer or workstation that coordinates various learning components such as text, simulations, video, audio, and/or CD-ROM.

- *Structured on-the-job learning:* Learning that occurs while individuals are working under the supervision of a skilled performer who can observe progress and provide feedback.

- *Performance support system:* An integrated computer program that provides any combination of expert systems, hypertext, computer-assisted instruction, and hypermedia to an employee on demand. Examples include help systems, electronic job aids, and expert advisers.

Once the curriculum is formed, other actions follow, such as actually purchasing and/or designing learning experiences that address priority training needs. In an implementation contract with a client, the specific training actions are identified together with the priorities for addressing them.

Development of a Performance Management System

More and more organizations are viewing the development of a performance management system as beneficial. Often the human resources function, in partnership with individuals from business units, takes a leadership role in developing this system. We define a performance management system as a system that is created and implemented to ensure that the employee performance required by the organization is identified, selected, developed, and rewarded. Books have been written about designing performance management systems; we cannot describe all of those actions here. However, because this is a major initiative that can emanate from a performance assessment, we want to overview what is possible.

Again, we find it helpful to think in terms of architecture; in this instance we compare a performance management system to the architecture of a house, as illustrated in Figure 11.4. The foundation elements for this "house" are composed of:

- Business goals and strategies for the organization (identified very early in our performance assessment)

- The mission and guiding principles of the organization

- The performance required for success (the SHOULDS we identified in the second phase of our assessment)

As you look above the foundation, the various "rooms" in the house become evident. When we construct a real house to live in, we have options as to how many rooms we will put into it. This is also true for a performance management system. What is illustrated in Figure 11.4 are all the possible options. Each of these options, if included, requires that a system and process be created for it and that people be developed to utilize the system as designed. For example, Gaso may want to form a selection system to use when recruiting people into the territory management position. By reviewing the performance requirements for the position, including the attributes that were identified as

Figure 11.4. Architecture for a Performance Management System.

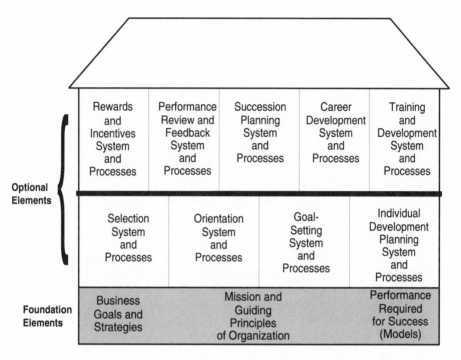

needed, they will determine the selection criteria. As we learned in Chapter Six, one of these criteria is resilience; another is self-confidence. Once these criteria are agreed upon, it becomes important to develop a selection system in which these criteria are assessed in a rigorous manner by everyone involved in the selection process. When the system is implemented, the selection "room" in the performance management system "house" has been built.

A brief description of all the options that can be included in a performance management system follows:

1. *Selection system and processes:* Processes used to select new recruits and to move people both upward and laterally in the organization

2. *Orientation system and processes:* Processes used to orient new employees to the organization

3. *Goal-setting system and processes:* Processes used to establish performance objectives and link them to the goals of the organization

4. *Individual development planning system and processes:* Processes used to identify developmental needs for *individual* employees

5. *Training and development system and processes:* Processes used to identify and address developmental needs for *groups* of employees

6. *Career development system and processes:* Processes used to develop employees for future positions

7. *Succession planning system and processes:* Processes used to ensure a "pipeline" of people ready to be promoted into key positions within the organization

8. *Performance review and feedback system and processes:* Processes used to provide both formal and informal feedback on the performance of individuals

9. *Rewards and incentives system and processes:* Processes used to reward and encourage desired performance

If forming a performance management system will be a part of your implementation contract, then it is important to agree with your clients on the specific performance requirements that will be included in the system and the specific elements, or "rooms," that will be developed in the system.

Work Environment Actions

In Chapter Eight we learned that territory managers at Gaso had skill and knowledge deficiencies that could be addressed through training. An example was the need for territory managers to develop skills to use in counseling station managers and dealers on business plans and on handling personnel problems. But we also learned that the district managers were not providing guidance to territory managers in this area and were not setting an example for counseling station managers and dealers. For this situation to change, the district managers required additional skills; but they also had to be held accountable and rewarded for this type of performance. To date, district managers had been accountable for obtaining results and not for developing their territory managers. Jake Coleman knew that incentives worked and that he would need to change the incentive system if he wanted to modify the district managers' performance.

Clearly, the modification of an accountability and reward system is an action that requires active client involvement and support; this is a change in the work environment that must be agreed upon and included in the implementation contract. The types of work environment actions that we have frequently included in implementation contracts include:

- Modifying the accountability and reward systems (as with Gaso), including an increased emphasis on the need for managers to coach and develop direct reports.

- Modifying work processes that are inhibiting desired performance.

- Enhancing the data processing capabilities of the organization.

- Increasing the parameters within which people can make decisions independently. Sometimes this action requires increasing the limits within which individuals can commit company funds (that is, signing authority).

- Redesigning jobs by removing practices that are not adding value and replacing them with actions and responsibilities that are more supportive of the business goals.

- Taking actions to differentiate the roles and responsibilities of different jobs.

What is the role of the Performance Consultant once decisions have been made regarding work environment actions? That is a question we are frequently asked. If we return to the Gaso example, we recall that Jake has agreed that accountability and rewards for district managers must change to more fully support their role as developers of territory managers. Should Janet be actively involved in designing that new system? or is this something that Jake will manage without her involvement? Will it require the advice and counsel of the compensation department? The answers to these questions are different depending upon the norms within a specific organization, the skill set of the Performance Consultant, and the partnership she or he has forged with the client. In our opinion the optimum answer is that an implementation *team* of people should be formed; the Performance Consultant would be on this team. In this manner the Performance Consultant continues to contribute to the project and brings continuity because of his or her in-depth knowledge obtained during the assessment phase. At a minimum, the Performance Consultant needs to be kept advised of what is occurring relative to modifications of the work environment. As we have indicated, performance has multiple causes. Each action taken to change performance has an effect on other actions, so it is important for communication to occur between everyone who is actively involved in carrying out these actions.

This aspect of contracting is very critical. Virtually any effort to change performance will require some corresponding actions in the systems and management practices of the organization. It is important to recall that achieving performance results occurs only when employees are skilled *and* are working in an environment that encourages and supports the desired performance. When you contract for work environment actions, you are ensuring that this environment will support the performance changes agreed upon with the clients.

Elements of an Implementation Contract

In Chapter Ten we identified the four categories that should be included in a contract:

1. Deliverables (what is to be accomplished?)

2. Actions or processes to be used in achieving deliverables (how will the work be accomplished?)

3. Mutual responsibilities (who is responsible for what?)

4. Time frame and costs of the work

Performance Consulting Tool 7 lists each of these categories, together with a checklist of specific items that could be agreed upon when negotiating implementation contracts.

Performance Consulting Tool 7

Checklist for an Implementation Contract

1. **Deliverables**

    _____ What specific business and performance results are expected from the actions to be taken?

2. **Processes or Actions to Be Taken in Support of Deliverables**

    _____ a. What is the communication plan?

             b. What actions will be taken regarding:

                 _____ Training?

                 _____ Work environment?

    _____ c. Will a performance management system be developed or modified? If so, how?

    _____ d. How will implementation results be measured?

3. **Mutual Responsibilities**

    _____ a. Who will be responsible for ensuring that actions are taken?

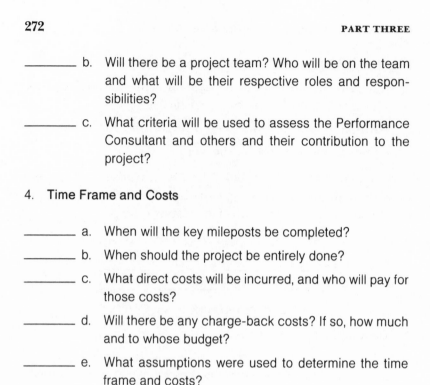

_____ b.   Will there be a project team? Who will be on the team
             and what will be their respective roles and respon-
             sibilities?

_____ c.   What criteria will be used to assess the Performance
             Consultant and others and their contribution to the
             project?

4. Time Frame and Costs

_____ a.   When will the key mileposts be completed?

_____ b.   When should the project be entirely done?

_____ c.   What direct costs will be incurred, and who will pay for
             those costs?

_____ d.   Will there be any charge-back costs? If so, how much
             and to whose budget?

_____ e.   What assumptions were used to determine the time
             frame and costs?

Deliverables

The deliverables section of the contract is particularly important; it specifies the desired performance and business results. At
Gaso the implementation contract would indicate the performance changes expected in both territory managers (that is, to
provide more business counseling to station managers and
dealers) and district managers (that is, to provide more guidance
and coaching to territory managers). It could also indicate the
desired operational results (increased profitability of stations).
When these results occur, the contract will have been fulfilled.

Processes or Actions

The processes or actions that will be taken so that the deliverables will occur are noted in the second section of an implemen-

tation contract. This is where any or all of the following could be included:

- Communication plans
- Training actions
- Work environment actions
- Formation of a performance management system or modification of an existing one

Another important item to include in this portion of the contract is identification of how progress will be measured. How will you and the client know that success is occurring? How will you know if midcourse changes are required? Monitoring progress through some type of measurement effort is critical.

Mutual Responsibilities

In the section of the contract titled "Mutual Responsibilities," the respective roles of key implementation players need to be identified. Will a project team be formed? Will specific people lead each of the major actions in support of the project? For example, will someone lead the team responsible for addressing training needs? Will someone else lead the team responsible for addressing work environment actions? Who will be responsible for communicating what is being done? As a Performance Consultant, it is also important for you to identify what the client expects of you in terms of (1) working style and (2) contributions. We once worked with a client who had more on her plate than time to do it. She asked that we be responsible for reminding her of key deadlines and "stay on her" when she did not fulfill those deadlines. While we might have taken those actions without her endorsement, having her clearly identify this as a part of the working relationship she valued made it easier.

Time Frame and Costs

The time frame is something that needs to be discussed with the client team. What is a realistic target date for a key milepost to be achieved? When do you hope to complete your work? Costs are particularly relevant if they are to be incurred by the client, either in a direct manner through invoices to be paid or as a charge-back to the client's budget. Again, we have found it vital to identify the assumptions under which the time frame and costs were determined. If you anticipate that a performance management system could be formed in six months based upon the assumption that two people will be dedicated to building the system, that assumption should be clearly noted.

Things That Can Go Wrong

It is possible that during a meeting in which an implementation contract is being discussed and formed, things may not go as planned. No matter what is the scope of the work being discussed, you should expect some tense moments and even disappointments. It is important to keep your focus on the big picture rather than on any specific element within that picture. Perhaps management is not committing to all the actions which you believe to be important. However, ask yourself whether they are committing to the overall effort and whether their goals are appropriate for the situation. If they are, then the contract meeting is proceeding successfully.

Certain problems can almost be anticipated to occur at some point during implementation contract meetings; they include client resistance, disagreement, and too-quick agreement.

Client Resistance

As Peter Block indicates, this is a "predictable, natural, emotional reaction of a client against the process of being helped and/or against the process of having to face up to difficult organizational problems" (Block, 1981, p. 113). Resistance in and of itself is not a bad thing; it may indicate that you are on target and that the client is uncomfortable with what is going to be required. An example would be if Jake Coleman at Gaso reacted to the suggestion that district managers need to be held accountable and rewarded for coaching territory managers by saying,

"Just tell them they need to do it. That should be enough." Most likely, Jake would be resisting the magnitude of the work involved in truly changing the performance of the district managers. It is easier to just say "do it" than to get involved in redesigning reward systems. Unfortunately, this approach rarely works.

As a Performance Consultant, it is important for you to do the following regarding client resistance:

1. Recognize it when it is occurring

2. Stop the meeting process and support the clients in expressing their concerns in a direct manner

3. Avoid interpreting the resistance as a personal attack or becoming defensive

Recognize Resistance. Resistance can take many forms. Some of the most common forms of client resistance that occur in a data feedback meeting include:

■   Explaining why something is not possible in the "real world"

■   Moving to theories and hypotheses about why things are as they are (and diverting attention from identifying ways to change them)

■   Silence (withdrawing from the meeting process)

■   Outright verbal attack and rejection of the process

Stop the Meeting Process and Support Direct Expression of Concerns. Once you see that a client is resisting the process, it is important to stop what you are doing and help the client to discuss his or her concerns directly. One method for doing this is to name the resistance in a nonevaluative manner, for example, "You are quiet. What are you thinking?" or "I notice that you continue to give us reasons why the situation is as it is, while we are trying to develop actions." Once you make an observation, it is important to become *silent* so the client can respond to your observation and/or question.

Avoid Interpreting the Resistance as a Personal Attack. Remember that resistance means you are on target with your observations or information. Becoming defensive in response to resistance will not facilitate discussions that could be quite helpful; instead, such a response will close the discussion and make decisions regarding future actions more difficult.

Disagreement

Disagreement is different from resistance. In this case a few alternatives may be under consideration; you support one of them and your client sincerely believes that another could be better. In such an instance, it is important to identify what you *do* agree on. Do you agree on the goal? Are there any actions in support of the goal that you can both agree on? What does each of you value in the option you prefer? It is important for you to realize that the client team is the decision maker. Therefore, if the client team prefers one option and is not persuaded to believe differently, it is their decision to make.

Too-Quick Agreement

Here, a client is quick to agree to anything that is proposed. While on the surface this may seem beneficial, it is seldom a good sign. Quick agreements, without thorough discussion and participation by the client, usually mean that the client wants to conclude the discussion. It also means that the client cannot be counted on for meaningful support; the project could die of benign neglect!

If quick acquiescence occurs, it is important to once again stop the process of the meeting and comment on the behavior you are observing, for example, "You are agreeing to every proposal that is suggested; that makes it difficult to know what your true thoughts are regarding these proposals." Another option is to indicate what the client will need to do if a particular action is taken and then ask the client if she or he is prepared to take those actions and incur those costs. In this instance you are testing the degree of client commitment.

Implementation contracts are a critical part of the performance change process. As a Performance Consultant you *want* to get to, and be a part of, this meeting. It means that the assessment phase is about to pay off and actions are going to be taken. When you take part in this meeting, and later when you are a part of the implementation project team, you have truly moved to the role of Performance Consultant and are in a position to make a difference in your organization's future.

Summary

1. The process of contracting for implementation begins in the data feedback meeting when clients begin to define the actions that will be required to change performance.

2. Implementation contracts specifically identify the desired performance and operational results that form the deliverable portion of the contract.

3. Implementation contracts also indicate the actions that will be taken to achieve this desired performance. Actions typically include some or all of the following:

    ■ Communication plans

    ■ Training actions

    ■ Work environment actions

    ■ Formation of a performance management system or modification of an existing one

4. The role of the Performance Consultant during the implementation phase will vary and is dependent upon the scope of the project, the type of actions being taken, and the client-consultant relationship that has been formed. However, the Performance Consultant is typically a part of the team of people chartered to lead the implementation effort.

PART FOUR

ORGANIZING A PERFORMANCE IMPROVEMENT DEPARTMENT

Up to now we have been discussing how an *individual* can successfully fulfill the role of Performance Consultant. In this final section of the book, we will shift our focus from the individual to the entire department. How must the department (typically referred to as the training department or HRD department) be structured if it is to truly encourage and support the role of Performance Consultant? What accountabilities and reward systems need to be formed? What roles and skill sets will be required of those who are in the department?

In the last two chapters of this book, we identify the key elements of a performance improvement department, noting how they are different from those of a more traditional training department. We will also guide you through the process of forming a strategic plan for a transition from your current situation to the one we espouse.

12

The Six Elements
of a Performance Improvement
Department

Geary Rummler's statement (1983, p. 75), "Pit a good employee against a bad system and the system will win most every time," is relevant to the situation faced by many individuals who truly want to operate as Performance Consultants. Often the very department in which they work makes it difficult or impossible to focus on performance rather than training. Consider these vignettes from client organizations with which we have worked:

> One company's training department operates on a charge-back system, meaning that internal customers must pay for the services they receive from the department. Unfortunately, the *only* service with a fee is delivery of a training program. No fees are incurred for completing the performance consulting services, such as developing performance models, identifying performance gaps and causes, and measuring the performance and operational results from an intervention. This system encourages delivery of training (which yields fees) and not provision of performance services (which does not).

Another organization has the expectation that people of similar titles or levels will work directly with peers; however, trainers often are at a "lower" level in the organization than the clients they are to support. They therefore are precluded from direct access to their clients.

The performance measures for a member of the training department in another organization are based upon the number of training programs conducted and favorable ratings on the reaction evaluation forms. There are no measures for the quality of the client-consultant relationship or the contribution to performance and operational impact.

For ease of reference, in the remainder of this book we will use the name *training department* to refer to functions formed to address the traditional roles of training and development; we will use the term *performance improvement department* to refer to the type of function we believe is required in the 1990s and beyond. Let's look more completely at how a training department is different from a performance improvement department.

Six components of organizational structure separate a traditional training department from a performance improvement department. These are:

1.   The name of the department

2.   The mission of the department

3.   The services offered by the department

4.   The roles of those within the department

5.   The actual organizational structure of the department

6.   Accountability and measures for the department

Training or Performance Improvement: What's in a Name?

Naming a product, service, or function is very important. Consider how much time, energy, and money are spent in determining what to name new products or services as they enter the marketplace. Remember when personnel departments were renamed to be human resources departments? Even companies rename themselves, partly to give evidence of an updated image. For example, Pittsburgh Plate Glass is now PPG Industries and Federal Express is now FedEx.

Names of functions indicate (or should indicate) the purpose of the function. One overall purpose can be to provide products and services that result in learning. Any of the following functional names connote this purpose:

- Training department
- Education department
- Training and development department

Compare and contrast those names with the following:

- Performance improvement department
- Individual and organizational performance department
- Performance consulting department
- Performance enhancement group

Something very different is in evidence. There is no mention of training. The focus is on a different end result—that of improving performance. Just changing the name of the department is a meaningless exercise, however, unless it is supported by several other changes.

What Is Our Mission?

A mission statement is a reason for an organization's existence. The formation of a mission statement is a critical exercise in the life of any function. It should accomplish two things: (1) it should state what the purpose and accountability for the function are and (2) by implication, it should state what the purpose for the function is *not*. Mission statements become a standard against which you can assess requests for services. ("Is it within our mission to do this?") They are also a means of communicating the purpose of the function to both internal personnel and those who are considering employment within the function.

Below are two mission statements from client organizations with which we have worked. How are they different?

> *Mission Statement 1:* "We support the mission and business plan of our company by developing the skills, enhancing the knowledge, and expanding the perspectives of all employees."

> *Mission Statement 2:* "We provide consulting, training, assessment, and measurement services that ensure continuous individual and organizational performance improvement in support of our business plan."

Each of these statements indicates that the function is working in support of "the business plan," which is positive. But look at what each statement indicates should be done to support that plan. In Mission Statement 1, the accountabilities of the department are to develop skills, enhance knowledge, and expand the perspectives of all employees. Contrast that with Mission Statement 2, in which the accountability is to ensure continuous individual and organizational performance improvement. Note also that the services listed are to provide consulting, training, assessment, and measurement services. This implies a broad array of service options, not just the delivery of skill and knowledge programming.

Thus far we have discussed two critical elements that separate training from performance improvement departments: name and mission. Now let's look at a third element: services provided by the department.

Services Provided by Performance
Improvement Departments

Yet another way in which training departments and performance improvement departments differ is in the breadth and types of services that are offered. In traditional training functions, services such as the following are offered:

- Identifying training needs
- Designing and developing training programs and other structured learning experiences
- Delivering structured learning experiences
- Training trainers and assuring the quality of the training delivered by others
- Evaluating training programs at the reaction and learning levels

Performance improvement departments are responsible for those services but add the following to the list:

- Forming performance and competency models
- Identifying performance gaps
- Determining the causes of performance gaps
- Measuring the impact of training and nontraining actions that are taken to change performance
- Consulting with management on business and performance needs
- Proactively identifying performance implications for future business goals and needs

So a performance improvement department provides all the services of a training department but also adds these performance-oriented services.

The Roles of People Within the Department

In order to provide the types of services that have been described, a performance improvement department requires individuals within the department to fill specific roles. It is important to note that we are describing roles and not jobs. A role is a set of related outputs. Most people have one job but work in many roles. Sometimes people refer to roles as the "hats" they wear in a job. Performance improvement departments require roles that are not found in training-focused departments.

In traditional training departments, you will typically find individuals who fill the roles listed below. Many of these definitions are extracted from *Models for HRD Practice* (McLagan, 1989), published by the American Society for Training and Development:

1. Instructor-facilitator: Presents information, directs structured learning experiences, and manages group discussions and group processes

2. Program designer: Prepares objectives, defines content, and selects and sequences activities for a specific intervention

3. Training materials developer: Produces written or electronically mediated instructional materials

4. Training administrator: Provides coordination and support services for the delivery of HRD or training programs and services

5. Evaluator: Forms and reports results from reaction (end-of-course) and learning evaluations

Although performance improvement departments also require people to work in these roles, additional roles are necessary. We have identified four roles as critical to the success of a performance improvement department. These roles, and the definitions we developed for them, are listed below.

1. Client liaison: Partners with management for the purposes of identifying and contracting for performance improvement initiatives that address business needs

2. Performance analyst: Identifies the ideal and actual performance required to meet business needs and determines the causes of performance discrepancies

3. Performance Consultant: Assists and guides management in taking actions in support of performance improvement initiatives

4. Impact evaluator: Identifies and reports the impact of an intervention on individual performance and organizational effectiveness

Each of these two sets of roles requires a set of skills or competencies in order to perform in a successful manner. It has been our experience that these skills are unique enough so that people who are successful in fulfilling the traditional training roles (such as the instructor role) may not be successful (or even want to work) in the performance improvement roles and vice versa. Often a function will require several people in the instructor role but only one or two people to work as client liaisons or performance analysts. It becomes critical, therefore, for the manager of such a function to assess how many people are required to fulfill the various roles, given the mission of the function and the organization's size and performance needs.

While we are describing the role of Performance Consultant, we want to point out that the term can also be used as a job title. So the *job* of Performance Consultant may involve the roles of client liaison, performance analyst, performance consultant, and impact evaluator, in almost any combination. Likewise, we have seen positions with these roles called client liaison managers, performance effectiveness consultants, performance analysts, and so on.

Organizational Structure

Another way in which training and performance improvement departments are different is the manner in which they are structured. As illustrated in Figure 12.1, one common option used by traditional training functions is to organize by roles or positions. In this option one or more designers, developers, instructors, and administrators report to the training manager. When a need arises in any subject area for which the function is responsible, the designer works on it and then transfers the project to the developer, who eventually hands it off to the instructor.

A second structure for a traditional training function is displayed in Figure 12.2. In this option the function is organized by subject matter. Some people are dedicated to management development, while others address sales and marketing needs. Frequently, there are different training functions within the same organization that fulfill each of these subject needs (for example, a sales training function reports to the sales organization or a technical function reports to the manufacturing function). This structure has strong verticalization and limited cross-functional working relationships. In both of these options, the

**Figure 12.1. Organization of a Traditional
Training Department: Option 1.**

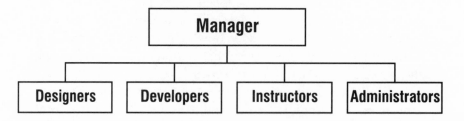

Figure 12.2. Organization of a Traditional Training Department: Option 2.

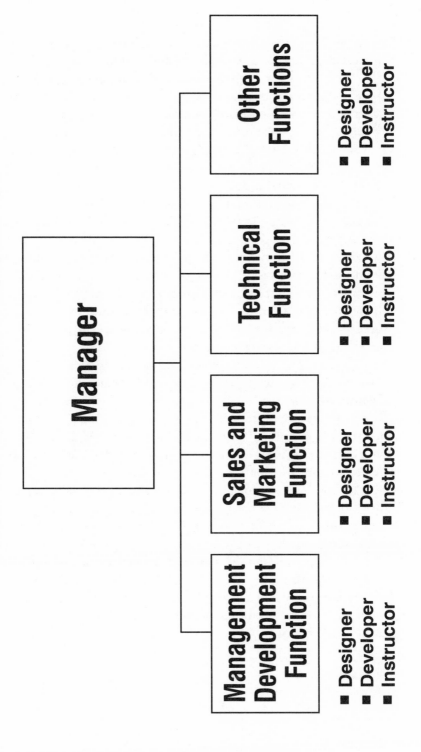

structure focuses on addressing training needs; therefore, positions such as designers, developers, and instructors are required.

By contrast, in a performance improvement department, some people are dedicated to forming relationships with managers within specific business units. These individuals become "experts" in the business of these units and gain the trust of key managers. They attend meetings where business issues are discussed that have implications for people's performance. This option is illustrated in Figure 12.3.

In addition to the training roles of developer and instructor, there are also performance roles of client liaison or consultant and performance analyst. It would be possible to have these functions in different parts of the organization (for example, a performance improvement department can report to the marketing and sales organization and a separate function can report to the research organization). This structure is unique in that the focus is on consulting with business units and working with managers to improve performance.

Figure 12.4 shows another option for a performance improvement department. In this option, certain people within the client liaison group are dedicated to working with management. Once needs are identified, these people will bring in analysts and designers as required. While the client liaison consultants work with specific business units, the analysts and designers have the flexibility to work wherever their services are required.

In both options for the performance improvement department, one thing is constant: the individuals who fill the client liaison role are dedicated to specific business units. This is necessary if they are to truly build a partnership with key managers and gain their trust as valued allies in addressing business needs. In small organizations, it may be possible to have one individual who works as a client liaison to all business functions; in mid- to large-sized organizations, people will likely need to be dedicated to specific business units.

Figure 12.3. Organization of a Performance Improvement Department: Option 1.

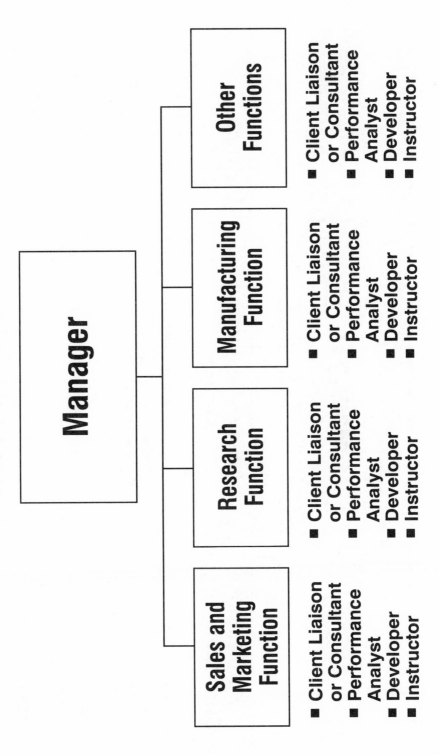

Figure 12.4. Organization of a Performance Improvement Department: Option 2.

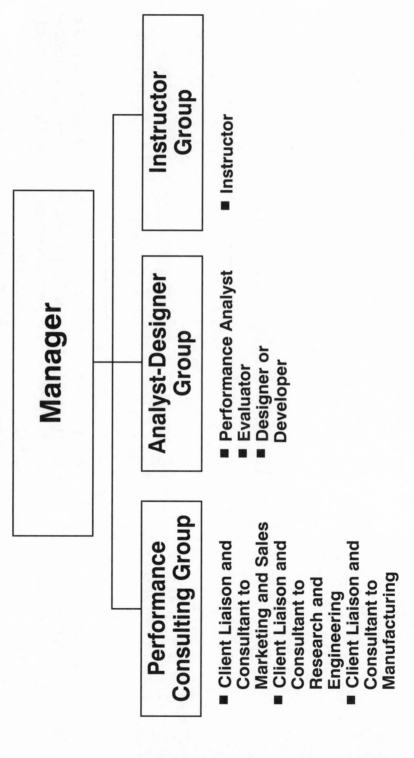

Accountabilities for the Performance Improvement Department

A final area that separates traditional training functions from performance improvement functions is the manner in which the entire function is held accountable. There are measures for the performance of individuals within a function and also measures for the function. It is the latter we will be discussing here.

Often traditional training functions are held accountable for the following measures:

- *Number of instructor days:* Each day that an instructor is in the classroom counts as one instructor day. Generally, higher numbers are viewed as more desirable.

- *Number of participant days:* Each participant in a program represents one participant day. Therefore, if eighteen people are in a one-day program, it has eighteen participant days. Again, higher numbers are valued more.

- *Number of different courses or new courses in a year:* Here, the organization asks the training function to offer a large variety of programs and to bring several new programs on-line each year. Again, "the more the better" is the general rule of thumb.

- *Results from reaction evaluations:* When the reaction evaluations are tabulated, the results are compared against desired goals. Generally, a standard is established (for example, at least a rating of 3.75 or higher on a 5.0 scale) and the results are compared to the standard.

- *Results from learning evaluations:* This is a summary of the tests or performance demonstrations given during training programs. The results indicate to what degree the participants acquired the desired knowledge and skill. Generally, a standard is established and results are compared to the standard.

- *Number of training days per employee:* We often see organizations espousing a goal of "ten days of training per employee per year." Training functions are frequently measured according to their contribution to this goal.

Performance improvement departments may utilize some of the measures just noted but would add the following types of measures:

- *Degree to which skills transfer to the workplace and individual or group performance improves:* In this measure, the function systemically measures the amount of change in individual or group performance associated with its performance improvement projects.

- *Degree to which training contributes to desired operational change:* This is a systematic measurement of the change in operational results associated with projects that the department has been involved in. To what degree has waste been reduced? the error rate declined? sales increased?

- *Quantity and quality of client relationships:* An assessment of both the number of client teams supported in a given year and the quality of those relationships would be determined. The clients become the primary source of data on this measure.

- *Number of performance contracts agreed to in a year:* In this measure, the function is held accountable for contracting with management for changing performance (as opposed to learning). Such contracts are a precursor to actually changing performance and are another way to determine whether the function is focusing on performance more than learning.

We believe that traditional training departments need to reengineer themselves to get into the performance improvement business. In fact, David Brinkerhoff predicts, "The title 'training director' will be all but extinct five years from now" (Filipczak, 1994, pp. 33, 34). In this chapter we have provided the six areas that set apart performance improvement departments from traditional training functions. In the final chapter, we describe how to form a strategic plan to make the transition from where your department is now to what we predict will be the future direction of our field.

Summary

1. In order for Performance Consultants to perform successfully, it is vital for the department or function to which the Performance Consultant reports to be structured to encourage the desired practices.

2. Traditional training departments and performance improvement departments are different in the following areas:

   ■ Name of function
   ■ Mission of function
   ■ Services provided by the function
   ■ Roles of those in the function
   ■ Organizational structure of the function
   ■ Accountability and measures for the function

13

Forming a Strategic Plan for the Transition to Performance Improvement

Our experience is that there are effective and ineffective ways to make transitions. One of the most ineffective we personally witnessed began in a hopeful manner. The president of an organization indicated that he would fully support a change in the way training was done in the organization; he knew there could be a greater return. He chartered a few people to go back to a "plain sheet of paper" and form a new structure. A new plan *was* created, which clearly focused on performance. This new plan had wide-ranging implications for the organizational structure of the function as well as for the geographic locations of various people within the function. Some people moved to new locations as a part of this plan.

Unfortunately, middle- and lower-level management were not brought on board regarding what all the changes in the former training department would mean for them. There was also a lack of role clarity within the department's staff as to who was responsible for various tasks. People were asked to fill new roles and work differently but were provided with minimal guidance in what that meant. As a result, some of the staff worked as Performance Consultants while others continued to work as

Traditional Trainers. In the end, both the clients of this function and the people in it became angry and disillusioned.

If you have determined that your department needs to more fully incorporate the processes and structures associated with a performance improvement function, it is important to plan and execute the transition so that your clients and those in the department will be fully supportive of, and knowledgeable about, the change. It is also critical to form a plan for the transition that the department will be making; this helps to ensure that the transition will be a smooth one.

Strategic Plans for Moving from Training to Performance

We have assisted several training and HRD departments as they strategically planned for their transition. In our work, we have found that the following steps, when followed, result in a strong plan.

1. Identify the current and future desired state for the function

2. Form the framework for the function's purpose:

    a. Mission statement

    b. Vision statement

    c. Guiding principles for the function

    d. Clients and customers for the function

3. Define the business context in which the function will operate:

    a. Identify business goals and initiatives for the organization in the next three to five years

    b. Conduct environmental scan of forces within and outside the organization that will either encourage or challenge the department's plans and fulfillment of its mission

4. Form strategic (three-year) goals:

    a. Goals in support of client requirements

      b.   Goals regarding the department itself

5.   Form tactical (one-year) goals:

      a.   Goals in support of client requirements

      b.   Goals regarding the department itself

6.   Form an implementation plan with milestones

Essentially, the overall process of forming a strategic plan for the department is similar to the one displayed in Figure 13.1. A strategic plan identifies the hopes and visions for the function and integrates them into the business requirements of the organization. In this manner a "win-win" plan is formulated.

In this chapter we will discuss each of the six elements in a plan, providing guidance in forming a strategic plan for moving from a traditional training department to a performance improvement function.

Identify the Current and Future Desired State for the Function

To borrow from the performance relationship map described in this book, the first step in forming a transition plan is to identify your IS as well as the SHOULD that is appropriate for your func-

Figure 13.1. Process of Forming a Strategic Plan.

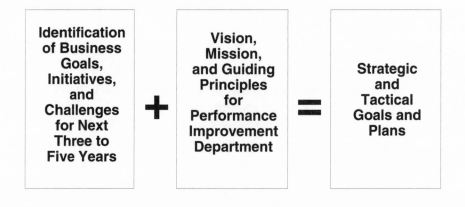

tion. What are the greatest gaps? the smallest? If you are in a department that includes other people, do you all agree on the SHOULD for the future? These are the types of questions that need to be answered in preparation for developing a transition plan.

To assist our clients in this assessment, we suggest that they complete a survey entitled "Mini-Survey: Visioning the Future." This survey appears as Performance Consulting Tool 8. If you are a "department of one," you may want to complete this and also have your manager do so. If there are several people in the department, then each individual should complete the survey. In defining where you want to be in the future, we encourage you to use a three-year time frame. Three years in today's business environment is a very long time! It is also a period of time during which most of the people who are currently in the training or HRD function will be working in that function; in other words, they have a vested interest in participating in the transition process, because it will have an impact upon them.

Performance Consulting Tool 8

Mini-Survey: Visioning the Future

Instructions:

1. Place the letter "I" (for IS) over the point on each scale that you believe best represents how your department currently operates.

2. Then repeat the process, but this time place the letter "S" (for SHOULD) over the point on each scale that indicates where you would like to see your department in the future (three years from now).

3. If you believe you cannot make a selection for current and/or future operation at this time, leave the scale blank.

4. Remember, you are assessing your department and not your own personal working style.

1. Mission of the Department

1	2	3	4	5
Training mission (focuses on identifying and meeting learning needs of employees)	Mostly training mission; some performance mission	Half is a performance mission and half is a training mission	Mostly performance mission; some training mission	Performance mission (focuses on identifying and meeting performance needs of employees)

2. Relationship to Management

1	2	3	4	5
We work primarily as a pair-of-hands to management (managers indicate what they want and we respond)		We work primarily as collaborators and partners with management		We work primarily as experts (we make recommendations and tell management what is needed)

3. Working Style

1	2	3	4	5
Reactive (we react to requests from management with assistance)	Mostly reactive; some proactive	50% of effort is reactive and 50% is proactive	Mostly proactive; some reactive	Proactive (we initiate contact with management to identify potential areas for support)

4. Products and Services

1	2	3	4	5	6
90% training 10% consulting	75% training 25% consulting	60% training 40% consulting	60% consulting 40% training	75% consulting 25% training	90% consulting 10% training

NOTE:

Training   = Design and delivery of structured learning experiences, such as computer-based training or leader-led courses

Consulting = Services not directly tied to learning experiences, such as:

- Identifying current and future performance requirements

- Influencing management to address work environment obstacles to performance

- Working with management to resolve performance problems

- Team-building facilitation

5. Processes That Are Used

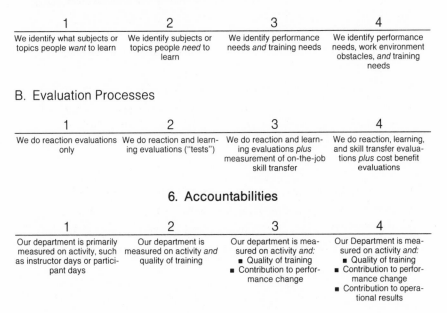

A. Needs Assessment Processes

1	2	3	4
We identify what subjects or topics people *want* to learn	We identify subjects or topics people *need* to learn	We identify performance needs *and* training needs	We identify performance needs, work environment obstacles, *and* training needs

B. Evaluation Processes

1	2	3	4
We do reaction evaluations only	We do reaction and learning evaluations ("tests")	We do reaction and learning evaluations *plus* measurement of on-the-job skill transfer	We do reaction, learning, and skill transfer evaluations *plus* cost benefit evaluations

6. Accountabilities

1	2	3	4
Our department is primarily measured on activity, such as instructor days or participant days	Our department is measured on activity *and* quality of training	Our department is measured on activity *and:* ■ Quality of training ■ Contribution to performance change	Our Department is measured on activity *and:* ■ Quality of training ■ Contribution to performance change ■ Contribution to operational results

Once the appropriate individuals have completed this survey, the data must be summarized. When there is lack of agreement, particularly regarding the future or SHOULD, discussions need to occur so that some consensus is formed. It is important to note that there is no one "correct" place on each scale. We do not believe, for example, that the "correct" future state requires a function that is totally performance-based. It may not be appropriate for some departments in some organizations, and it may not be possible in three years' time. What we do believe is that there must be some movement to incorporate performance-based structures and processes. You and your colleagues will need to decide how much movement is appropriate and possible for you.

One additional note regarding this survey: in order to meaningfully complete it, each individual needs to have some familiarity with performance technology so the difference between a performance approach and a training approach is clear. If you or your staff lack this understanding, it is important to review articles or books on the subject of performance technology prior to completing the survey.

Form the Framework for the Function's Purpose

The next step in the planning process is to form the framework for the operation of your function in the future—in other words, to create the structure that will support your desired future state.

Mission Statement

The first thing to do in forming the structure is to develop the mission statement for your department. In Chapter Twelve we provided a mission statement that supports a performance approach and contrasted it to one that does not. We suggest that you:

1. Form a mission statement that has a maximum of three sentences.

2. Incorporate words or phrases that articulate the following:

   ■ You will be partners with your management.

   ■ You will provide services that enhance employee performance.

   ■ Your efforts will be linked to the business goals of the organization.

3. Avoid words or phrases that indicate that your end goal is to provide training and development services; instead, position training as one of several processes used to meet the goal of performance improvement. In essence, training is a means to an end and not the end itself.

   Examples of a performance mission would be:

   "The mission of our department is to improve organizational and individual performance and pro-

ductivity through internal consulting, training services, and human resource development systems."

"To partner with management for the performance
improvement of individuals and business units by
providing superior products and services that are
innovative, results-oriented, and cost-effective."

Note that the end result of work by each department is
improvement in organizational and individual performance; although the services offered include training, several other services are available.

Vision Statement

A mission statement identifies your reason for being; a vision
statement clarifies how you will operate in the future. It is the
destination to which you are headed. In the future, do you en-
vision that members of your staff will participate in business
meetings with managers so that opportunities to support business and performance needs can be identified proactively? Do
you want your organization to be one that becomes a benchmark
for others because of its obvious contribution to business goals?
What markets within your organization will you support? What
mix of products and services will you provide? Now is the time
to put forward your "dream," tempered by a bit of reality.

An example would be the following type of statement: "In
three years, our department will be viewed as a critical partner
to key managers in the identification of human performance
requirements. On a proactive basis, we will be involved in anticipating human performance requirements and will be held
accountable for improving employee performance in the organization. We will balance our work so that 75 percent of it is in
consulting services and 25 percent is in training services."

Guiding Principles for the Function

Each of us has beliefs and values regarding people, their development, and their performance. Typically, these become unstated assumptions under which we work; we refer to them as

guiding principles. For example, if you believe that adults learn best when they are actively involved in the learning experience, you are biased toward designing experiential learning programs rather than didactic or presentation-type learning formats.

In forming a strategic plan for your department, it is important to make these "unstated" principles explicitly known. To the degree that there is consensus among the staff, the process of making other decisions will be easier. If, however, differences of opinion exist regarding these principles, it is important to discuss and, to the degree possible, resolve those differences.

We have found it beneficial to divide guiding principles into two categories:

1.   Principles regarding the way people learn and develop
2.   Principles regarding the way human performance is developed and changed

The following list shows typical principles for each of these two categories. We do not include them to indicate that they are the "correct" ones; rather, they may provide some ideas to which you can react and respond in forming a list that works for you and your colleagues:

Guiding Principles for the Way People Learn and Develop

People process information in a variety of ways; no one methodology works for all people.

The content that is presented must be job-relevant and close in time to when people need it.

Learning can be fun—it does not have to be boring.

People are more motivated to learn when they understand the

Guiding Principles for the Way Human Performance Is Developed and Changed

The performance expected on the job must be defined and reinforced by employees' managers.

Knowledge and skills are insufficient to cause desired performance to occur; the work environment of the individual must reward, hold accountable, and support the individual so big picture regarding how the learning will benefit them on the job.

that he or she can perform in a specific manner.

People want to do a good job; error is rarely caused by neglect or a conscious choice by the individual not to perform.

People perform best when their performance is measured and they are provided feedback on progress toward meeting their goals.

A process for identifying these principles is to brainstorm with your colleagues. Just get the various ideas down on paper; then discuss what you have, paring the list down to those principles everyone can support.

Clients and Customers for the Function

The last element of the framework to discuss is identification of both the clients and customers for your products and services. As noted in Chapter Two, we define *clients* as the individuals who own the business and performance needs you will be supporting. Typically, these individuals are limited in number and are the people who manage key units, departments, or groups within your organization. These are the individuals with whom you need to form strong partnerships and relationships.

For this discussion we are using the term *customers* to refer to the groups of performers who will actively use your products and services. If you are doing team building, they are the people in the session; if you are conducting a workshop, they are the people who attend it. In essence, customers are the groups of people whose performance is targeted to change.

Let's look at two examples:

> *Situation 1:* You work in a training department and report to the sales division. Your clients may be the

regional sales managers and the vice president of that
department; your customers (including the vice president) are all employees within the sales function.

Situation 2: Your department is located within the
human resources department. In this instance, the
clients may be the president of the organization and
all direct reports to that individual; customers may
be every employee who works in the organization.

Who are your clients and customers now? Who should they
be in three years' time? It is important to focus on who your
clients and customers should be. You may not have a strong
partnership now with these individuals. If that is the case, you
are beginning to identify some strategic goals and opportunities
for your function to forge these relationships.

Define the Business Context in Which
the Function Will Operate

One of the primary characteristics of a performance improvement function is that the function's work is directly supportive
of the business needs of the organization. If this is to be true, it
is vital to define the business goals, initiatives, and challenges
that will be faced by the organization you support.

Identify Business Goals

In order to formulate the strategic plan, it is imperative to determine the business goals, initiatives, and challenges that will
be faced by the organization you support. This information may
already be known to you. If it is not available, however, it must
be obtained. A suggestion would be to use Performance Consulting Tool 1, "Sample Interview Guide: Proactively Identifying
Business and Performance Needs," in Chapter Two. You may
need to adapt it for obtaining business information for your

strategic plan; however, the basis for the type of information you require is included in the guide.

We have found that, generally, five to ten business objectives are identified. They include business goals related to any or all of the following:

- Revenue goals
- Goals regarding market share
- Goals regarding the launch of new products or services
- Goals regarding customer satisfaction and/or quality
- Goals regarding cost containment efforts
- Goals regarding operating profits

We have worked with organizations that also establish specific business goals regarding the work environment and utilization of their employees. For example, one organization with which we have worked includes this goal: "Within three years employees within our organization will evidence a higher degree of satisfaction with their development and empowerment and will have increased motivation to work here." This client intends to use climate survey data as one of the measurements for this goal. Thus, business goals can also focus on internal improvements in the culture and not just on revenue and profits.

One tip: Be certain to obtain information for these goals *from managers*. They own these goals and are the best source of information about them. It is important not to presume to know what the business goals are for our organizations. The managers who are accountable for the business results can do the best job of describing the goals.

Conduct Environmental Scan of Forces Within and Outside the Organization

A second element in forming the business context for your function is the environmental scan (sometimes referred to as a situation analysis). This activity can be very energizing as you and others in the department develop a list of the factors that will encourage and discourage the transition you want to make. It is a critical step in the process, because you are identifying, even anticipating, the factors that may challenge the transition you want to make. Given these potential obstacles, you may want to form either strategic or tactical goals for overcoming them. Additionally, you will want to capitalize on any factors that will encourage your transition into a performance function. Generally, these factors can be placed into three categories:

1. Factors outside your organization
2. Factors outside your department but within your organization
3. Factors within your department

Identifying these factors is generally a brainstorming activity involving the people in the department. Let's look more closely at these types of factors and some examples of each of the three categories.

Factors Outside Your Organization.   These are factors that are outside the business entity to which you report. If you are part of a very large organization and happen to support one major business group within that organization, the factors external to you might be within the larger corporate organization. There can also be factors outside of your company or organization altogether. The types of items to consider when forming this list would be:

■   Forces within the industry of which your organization is a part. For example, if you work in a hospital, you know that there will be many changes in the future relevant to the health care industry. Do you view these changes as a force that will challenge your transition into a performance function or encourage it?

■   What about regulatory practices? certification requirements?

other requirements with which your organization must comply?

■ If you work within a business unit of a larger organization, what is occurring within the larger body that might encourage or challenge your transition? In general, will this transition be reinforced by other entities, or will you be "swimming upstream"? Are there budget issues that need to be considered because of requirements from the enterprise to which you belong?

■ Certainly one force that will *encourage* your transition is the trend within the HRD industry. Organizations that espouse performance improvement strategies are continually placed in the limelight because of their progressive practices. If your organization utilizes benchmarking practices, your management will be continually exposed to this trend.

Factors Outside Your Department but Within Your Organization or Business Unit. Now we are focusing closer to home! Here you want to identify factors that will both challenge and encourage the transition and that are within the organization (or business unit) you are supporting. You may want to consider the following types of factors:

■ Does the organization expect to grow substantially, or will it be in a maintenance mode?

■ How philosophically in tune are key managers within the organization, including your own manager, with the transition you want to make?

■ What kind of credibility and relationships exist between your department and managers in the organization?

■ How satisfied is management with the current status of your function? How aware are they of a need for a change?

Factors Within Your Department. These factors are directly related to the structure and skill set of the people in your department. Again, there can be factors that will encourage your transition as well as factors that will challenge it. For example:

- What kinds of limitations, if any, will you have regarding the number of people on your staff and their individual skill sets? This can be of particular concern early in the transition, when you must continue to support a heavy training schedule while you try to add a consulting focus.

- How supportive is your staff regarding the transition? Do they value it? Are they threatened by it?

- Are there any budget restrictions on training required for your staff and/or external consulting assistance as you make the transition?

Form Strategic (Three-Year) Goals

Now you and your colleagues are ready to put it all together. You have identified the type of function you want to be in the future and have determined the business context in which you need to operate. Given all of this, what do you want to accomplish in three years' time? A suggestion would be to divide these goals into two goal categories:

1. Strategic goals regarding client requirements (external focus)
2. Strategic goals regarding the performance improvement department (internal focus)

We need to set goals in both areas because we must develop our own capabilities (the departmental goals) while supporting the business (client requirements).

We know of no other way to form these goals than to discuss what they should be. Some will be obvious. An example is that of a health services organization with which we worked. This organization was planning to launch a major new service area. In order to support the new service, they were creating a division of more than one hundred people. This was a business need that clearly could benefit from the support of the performance improvement group, which formed this strategic goal for the department: "By 1997 we will have contributed to the successful launch and implementation of our new service. Management will view us as having been a key partner in the project's success." It is important to note that, at the time this goal was formed, management had not even asked for this type of assistance! There was a need to initiate contact and actively market the services of the performance improvement staff if they were to gain the opportunity to work on this business need.

Some strategic goals are not so obvious. These will generate from the synergy of the discussion you have with your colleagues. The following are examples of strategic goals that could be identified for each of the two goal categories we have described:

Client-Focused Strategic Goals

■   A client-focused strategic goal may be to partner with management in order to achieve a key business goal (similar to what was described above).

■   A goal may be to establish partnerships with key clients in the organization. For example, perhaps there are five separate business groups in your organization, each of which is headed by a vice president. A goal could be that within three years, members of the performance improvement department will have formed strong consulting relationships with each of the vice presidents and will be brought in, on a proactive basis, to deal with business needs that affect the performance of people.

■   If the organization will be moving to alternative learning methods, a strategic goal might be: "In three years' time we will have purchased and installed hardware and software so that 25 percent of our training will be delivered through a computer-based self-study approach."

Departmental Strategic Goals

■   Perhaps you realize that a great deal of training delivery will continue to be done in the organization, but that you need to "off-load" some of the training delivery responsibility. Then a strategic goal could be that in three years' time you will have instituted a volunteer facilitator's program and a process that ensures that these facilitators are selected, developed, and made accountable for delivering quality learning experiences.

- Perhaps you need to grow the capability of your staff. A strategic goal could focus on what skills will be developed and for whom. What internal capabilities will be required of your staff that they do not have now?

- Perhaps you want to concentrate on a particular aspect of the performance function. For example, it may be that little has been done in the area of evaluation and measurement. A strategic goal could be that within three years a certain percentage of all projects completed by your function will be measured for behavioral and operational change.

When strategic goals are established, by definition, they become the areas of focus. It is important to avoid overloading the system by having too many strategic goals. Remember, each strategic goal will yield several tactical ones. We suggest having four to eight strategic goals with a client focus and an equal number with an internal focus.

Form Tactical (One-Year) Goals

Once the three-year strategic goals have been identified, it is possible to determine the tactical (or one-year) goals that will support the strategic initiatives. It is also possible to identify strategic goals for which no tactical support will be provided in a particular year. Figure 13.2 is a graphic depiction of this concept.

Each tactical goal should identify:

1. The specific result or outcome that will occur
2. The individuals who "own" the goal (and who are accountable for its accomplishment)

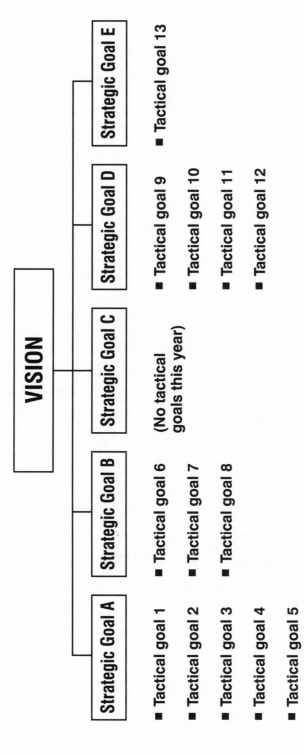

Figure 13.2. Relationship of Strategic and Tactical Goals.

3.   The date when the goal is to be completed

4.   The measurement criteria for determining that the goal was accomplished successfully

Exhibit 13.1 provides an example of a strategic goal with supporting tactical goals.

Exhibit 13.1. Strategic and Tactical Goals for Making the Transition to a Performance Improvement Department.

Strategic Goal:

In three years, the balance of work within the department will be 75 percent consulting services and 25 percent training services (from a current balance of 10 percent consulting and 90 percent training).

Tactical Goal 1:

Form and implement a system to recruit, select, and develop both internal and external people who will design and deliver training programs under the sponsorship of the performance improvement department.

Owner: John
Date: End of year
Criteria: By the end of the year five additional people will be available to the department. They will be fully trained and certified to design and/or deliver training.

Tactical Goal 2:

Complete a cost-benefit analysis of CD-ROM technology to be used in determining whether this technology should be purchased and used internally for educational purposes.

Owner: Susan
Date: Six months
Criteria: Information from the analysis is sufficient to make a "go or no-go" decision.

Tactical Goal 3:

Complete an analysis of current training and educational programs to determine (1) which should be retained, (2) which should be delegated to other training functions, and (3) which should be stopped altogether. Develop and implement a plan based upon the analysis.

Owner: Fred
Date: Three months (plan formed)
         Nine months (plan implemented)
Criteria: The amount of educational and training programming for which the department is personally responsible is reduced by a minimum of 20 percent.

**Exhibit 13.1. Strategic and Tactical Goals for Making
the Transition to a Performance Improvement Department, Cont'd.**

Tactical Goal 4:

Develop a tracking system to monitor progress toward the goal of rebalancing training and consulting services.

Owner: Fred
Date: Three months
Criteria: The tool is simple to use, provides reliable information, is electronic in nature, and yields monthly reports.

Tactical Goal 5:

Develop a list of consulting services that the staff is currently skilled to provide and a marketing effort to educate management about these service areas.

Owner: Susan
Date: Three months (plan formed)
         Six months (plan implemented)
Criteria: Requests for consulting services increase to support the goal of 25 percent of the work to be in this area by the year's end.

Potential Problems in the Transition

We advocate a process of transition rather than leaping from training to performance. In the leaping approach, a date is selected by which the function will become a performance improvement department. Usually this date is within the next twelve months. Several significant actions take place on this date. These actions often include discarding the entire training catalog and reassigning people into new jobs. This process is filled with confusion and trauma. It can also be met with resistance from customers as well as from those in the function itself. We have rarely seen this approach work without much confusion and pain.

The transition approach is supported by the strategic planning process. Three years is a reasonable time in which to expect this type of transition to occur. However, even with the best of plans, there will be problems. Let's discuss what bumps you might encounter during your transition:

1. *Training requests pour in:* While you are trying to spend more time consulting and partnering with management, the "business as usual" requests keep coming in. For some time, it is as though part of your function is in the training world and part in the performance world. Unfortunately, the training portion can continually pull and tug at your resources, leaving little for the performance part. Learning to say no and finding alternatives to delivering the training part of your responsibilities are two options for dealing with this problem.

2. *A history of being viewed as a training function:* If your function's history has been strongly identified with training services, managers will have difficulty understanding the new performance-based approach. They will still look to you when they want a training course. They will not naturally include you in initial discussions about business and performance issues before a decision to have a training program is made. This baggage from the past needs to be overcome. The best method of overcoming this history is by building strong partnerships with managers, *one manager at a time.* If you would like to work at the senior level but currently do not have access, begin where you can gain access. Eventually, word-of-mouth marketing will work in your favor.

3. *People who hang on to the traditional roles:* Sometimes the people who resist the change the most are those in the performance improvement department itself. If people have been successful in the role of the Traditional Trainer, they may have limited interest in changing. In addition, while these individuals are confident in what they need to do to be a successful instructor, they may be uncertain about what is required to fulfill the role of Performance Consultant. When this ambiguity is present, people tend to cling to what they know. Therefore, it is vital to provide people with clarity on their new roles and responsibilities; they also need to be developed and supported so that they can have successful experiences in these roles.

Summary

1. In planning a change from a focus on training to a focus on performance, it is best to plan a transition over time rather than to make a dramatic and sudden shift.

2. Strategic plans that support a transition should include the following:

    ■ Clarification of the desired versus the current situation of the function

    ■ The mission, vision, and guiding principles for the function

    ■ Business challenges and goals that the function must support

3. Goals are formed to address client requirements and also to meet the needs of the performance improvement department.

4. Strategic goals usually require three years to achieve; tactical goals are written in support of strategic goals and can be achieved in one year.

Some Closing Thoughts

In technology today, the word *platform* is used with frequency. People speak of the difference between a DOS platform and a Windows platform, for example. The implication is that with each platform one also gains capabilities and a set of operating assumptions. So it is with our field, where we have the traditional training platform and the performance platform. We have noted that the traditional training platform is designed to address what people *learn,* while the performance platform focuses on what people *do* on the job. In the training platform the end goal is to ensure that people have learned; the performance platform requires the result to be successful on-the-job performance. As we have noted in both the Preface and the Introduction, the traditional training platform does not yield the results our organizations need and demand of us at this time.

We must make the transition to the performance platform

in order to truly represent a value-added service to the clients and employees we support. We have already seen this transition begin within some organizations. A few functions have evolved to the point where Performance Consultants consistently work with management on performance improvement projects. Some departments are just starting the transition; many others are at various stages. Unfortunately, many traditional training departments have yet to make the commitment to move toward performance improvement strategies. We hope this book has provided you with the concepts, techniques, and motivation to get on the performance platform and move beyond training.

Resources

On the following pages are books and workshops that have been identified as resources to consider in order to learn more about any of the following five categories:

1. Assessments

2. Evaluation

3. Consulting

4. Performance technology

5. Implementation of performance change

This is not designed to be a complete list. Also, books continue to be published; depending upon when you are reviewing this section, many additional books and workshops might exist that would be relevant. We are not endorsing these resources as the best or only ones available; rather, our intent is to provide you with a list that can get you started in researching where, and from whom, to obtain additional information. In addition, we have provided the names of four associations that are closely affiliated with the technologies described in this book.

To best use this list we suggest that you:

- Determine which of the five categories are most relevant to you and your development

- Review the list of workshops and books to determine which may be appropriate

- Contact the supplier of a workshop for additional information in order to determine if the program will meet your needs (you may also want to obtain references to check on the quality of the program as others have experienced it)

- Use your own network of colleagues to assist you in identifying good resources for additional development in any of the areas noted above

Assessments

Books

American Society for Training and Development. *Be a Better Needs Analyst.* ASTD Info-Line Collection, publication no. 8502. Alexandria, Va.: American Society for Training and Development, Feb. 1985.

American Society for Training and Development. *ASTD Trainer's Toolkit: More Needs Assessment Instruments.* Alexandria, Va.: American Society for Training and Development, 1993.

Craig, R. L. (ed.). *Training and Development Handbook.* (3rd ed.) Alexandria, Va.: American Society for Training and Development and McGraw-Hill, 1987.

Dubois, D. D. *Competency-Based Performance Improvement: A Strategy for Organizational Change.* Amherst, Mass.: HRD Press, 1993.

Peterson, R. *Training Needs Analysis in the Workplace.* San Diego, Calif.: Pfeiffer, 1992.

Robinson, D. G., and Robinson, J. C. *Training for Impact: How to Link Training to Business Needs and Measure the Results.* San Francisco: Jossey-Bass, 1989.

Rossett, A. *Training Needs Assessment.* Englewood Cliffs, N.J.: Educational Technology Publications, 1987.

Swanson, R. A. *Analysis for Improving Performance: Tools for*

Diagnosing Organizations and Documenting Workplace Expertise. San Francisco: Berrett-Koehler, 1994.

Workshops

Aldrich Associates
265 East Village Road
Shelton, CT 06484
(203) 929-6234

Organizational Review and Needs Assessment

In this workshop, participants will learn how to identify gaps between actual and desired job performance; how to prioritize training needs will also be discussed.

American Management Association
135 West 50th Street
New York, NY 10020-1201
(518) 891-1500

How to Conduct Training Needs Analysis

A step-by-step process for conducting training needs analysis is presented in this seminar. The concepts, methods, and tools needed to analyze and develop programs to meet organizational needs are discussed.

The Center for Effective Performance, Inc.
4250 Perimeter Park South, Suite 131
Atlanta, GA 30341
(404) 458-4080

Criterion-Referenced Instruction

This workshop will prepare you to complete a performance analysis in order to determine the nature and cause of inadequate performance and point to solutions that will solve it.

The Center for Effective Performance, Inc.
4250 Perimeter Park South,
Suite 131
Atlanta, GA 30341
(404) 458-4080

The Training Manager Workshop

In this workshop you will learn how to conduct performance analysis in order to recommend appropriate solutions to performance problems. You will also learn how to conduct goal analysis to translate abstract intents into specific, observable performances.

Clark Training & Consulting
1702 West Camelback Road,
Suite 303
Phoenix, AZ 85015
(602) 230-9190

How to Plan and Conduct Needs Assessments and Evaluations: Tools for Human Performance Analysis

You will learn the skills needed to implement the performance analysis model and the hows, whens, and whats of evaluation to demonstrate the effect of your interventions.

Contemporary Learning Systems
27718 Franklin Road
Southfield, MI 48034
(313) 357-3133

Training Needs Analysis

This seminar presents methods designed to clearly identify the factors that may be interfering with the accomplishment of organizational goals.

David D. Dubois and Associates
2 Rice Court
Rockville, MD 20850-1149
(301) 762-5026

Needs Analysis Assessment and Planning for Competency-Based Performance Improvement Programs

In this workshop you will

learn how to complete needs analyses and planning processes that support the development of competency-based performance improvement programs. You will also be actively involved in learning how to do strategic organizational and business analysis.

Friesen, Kaye and Associates
3448 Richmond Road
Ottawa, Ontario, K2H 8H7
Canada
(613) 829-3412

Training Needs Analysis and Evaluation

Participants learn how to link training priorities to organizational goals and how to conduct a cost-benefit analysis to evaluate the true cost of training.

General Physics Corporation
6700 Alexander Bell Drive
Columbia, MD 21046
(410) 290-2372

Needs Analysis

Participants will be introduced to techniques that will allow them to determine if they have a performance problem, probable causes, and identification of both training and nontraining solutions.

Harless Performance Guild, Inc.
P.O. Box 1903
Newnan, GA 30264
(404) 251-3881

Accomplishment-Based Curriculum Development System (ABCD)

ABCD is a comprehensive and detailed system for training analysis, design, development, and evaluation. ABCD begins with front-end analysis and project alignment and takes the participant through all the steps to the assessment of existing training.

Harless Performance Guild, Inc.
P.O. Box 1903
Newnan, GA 30264
(404) 251-3881

Front-End Analysis

In this workshop you will learn how to clarify client requests for training and other solutions to performance problems and needs. In addition, you will learn how to conduct a diagnostic front-end analysis for projects where existing goals are not being met because of inadequate human performance.

Langevin Learning Services
1990 River Road
Manotick, Ontario, K4M 1B4
Canada
(613) 692-6382

Training Needs Analysis

This workshop offers a practical approach and step-by-step procedures for performing a needs analysis.

Partners in Change, Inc.
2547 Washington Road, Suite 720
Pittsburgh, PA 15241-2557
(412) 854-5750

Performance Consulting: Moving Beyond Training

In this workshop you will learn how to identify four kinds of needs: business, performance, training, and work environment. Additionally, you will learn how to form the data collection strategies needed to obtain required information and then how to report it to your clients so they will want to take all the actions needed if performance is to change.

Practical Management, Inc.
23801 Calabasas Road
P.O. Box 8789
Calabasas, CA 91372-8789
(818) 348-0256

*Needs Analysis, Evaluation,
and Validation*

The objective of this workshop is to help the organization resolve its operational
needs, to learn whether or not
the delivery of training has
been successful, and to determine the contribution made
by training.

R. T. Westcott & Associates
263 Main Street
Old Saybrook, CT 06475
(203) 388-6094

*Needs Analysis Processes and
Evaluation Methods
(NAPEM)*

This train-the-trainer workshop covers over thirty-five
techniques and practices for
determining training needs,
establishing the basis for evaluating training effectiveness,
and achieving a return on the
training investment.

University Associates, Inc.
Consulting & Training
Services
8380 Miramar Mall, Suite 232
San Diego, CA 92121
(619) 552-8901

Training Needs Assessment

In this seminar, new methods
are presented for accurately assessing training needs and
making recommendations for
both training and nontraining
interventions.

Evaluation

Books

American Society for Training and Development. *Essentials for
Evaluation.* ASTD Info-Line Collection, publication no. 8601.

Alexandria, Va.: American Society for Training and Development, Jan. 1986.

American Society for Training and Development. *Measuring Attitudinal and Behavioral Change.* ASTD Info-Line Collection, publication no. 9110. Alexandria, Va.: American Society for Training and Development, Oct. 1991.

American Society for Training and Development. *Tracking Operational Results.* ASTD Info-Line Collection, publication no. 9112. Alexandria, Va.: American Society for Training and Development, Dec. 1991.

American Society for Training and Development. *ASTD Trainer's Toolkit: Evaluating Results of Training.* Alexandria, Va.: American Society for Training and Development, 1992.

Gordon, J., Zemke, R., and Jones, P. (eds.). *Designing and Delivering Cost-Effective Training—and Measuring the Results.* (3rd ed.) Minneapolis, Minn: Lakewood Books, 1993.

Holcomb, J. *Make Training Worth Every Penny: On-Target Evaluation.* San Diego, Calif.: Pfeiffer, 1994.

Kirkpatrick, D. *Evaluating Training Programs: The Four Levels.* San Francisco: Berrett-Koehler, 1994.

Merwin, S. *Evaluation: Ten Significant Ways for Measuring and Improving Training Impact.* Minneapolis, Minn.: Resources for Organizations, 1992.

Phillips, J. J. (ed.). *Measuring Return on Investment.* Alexandria, Va.: American Society for Training and Development, 1994.

Robinson, D. G., and Robinson, J. C. *Training for Impact: How to Link Training to Business Needs and Measure the Results.* San Francisco: Jossey-Bass, 1989.

Swanson, R. A., and Gradous, D. B. *Forecasting Financial Benefits of Human Resource Development.* San Francisco: Jossey-Bass, 1987.

Workshops

General Physics Corporation
6700 Alexander Bell Drive
Columbia, MD 21046
(410) 290-2372

Measurement of Practical Skills

In this workshop you will learn a skill-measurement methodology. Topics include developing the measurement instruments, testing and using the instruments, and applying skills-measurement methodology.

Hale Associates
903 Burlington Avenue, Suite 8
Western Springs, IL 60558-1576
(708) 246-7676

Measuring Managerial Performance

During this workshop, you will learn to measure the effect of programs and practices on management goals and objectives.

Linkage Incorporated
110 Hartwell Avenue
Lexington, MA 02173
(617) 862-4030

Assessment, Measurement, and Evaluation: Demonstrating the Business Impact of Human Resource and Training Programs

In this workshop you will learn practical skills, methods, and tools used in each phase of the assessment, measurement, and evaluation cycle. You will also learn to use quantitative and qualitative evaluation tools and techniques to verify the impact of your programs.

Partners in Change, Inc.
2547 Washington Road, Suite 720
Pittsburgh, PA 15241-2557
(412) 854-5750

Measuring the Impact of Training

This workshop provides you with the processes and skills needed to measure your training initiatives for performance change and operational impact.

R. T. Westcott & Associates
263 Main Street
Old Saybrook, CT 06475
(203) 388-6094

How to Get a Return-on-Training-Investment (ROTI)

This program is designed to train trainers in the process of embedding ROTI processes in existing or newly designed training programs.

Swanson & Associates, Inc.
168 East Sixth Street,
Suite 4002
St. Paul, MN 55101
(612) 292-0448

Using Financial Models to Measure the ROI of Human Resource and Training Programs

This workshop presents tools and techniques for planning, estimating, and tracking training program costs and benefits. You will learn how to apply a systems approach to measuring the business impact of training.

Ziff Institute
25 First Street
Cambridge, MA 02141-9819
(315) 354-4092

Training Evaluation and Impact

This workshop provides proven methodologies and field-tested tools for creating and measuring high-impact training.

Consulting

Books

Bellman, G. M. *The Consultant's Calling: Bringing Who You Are to What You Do.* San Francisco: Jossey-Bass, 1990.
Block, P. *Flawless Consulting: A Guide to Getting Your Expertise Used.* San Diego, Calif.: Pfeiffer, 1981.

Gilley, J. W., and Goffern, A. J. *The Role of the Internal Consultant*. Burr Ridge, Ill.: Irwin Professional Publishing, 1993.

Holdaway, K., and Saunders, M. *The In-House Trainer as Consultant*. San Diego, Calif.: Pfeiffer, 1992.

Workshops

Designed Learning Inc.
1009 Park Avenue
Plainfield, NJ 07060
(908) 754-5102

Advanced Consulting Skills

This workshop is for those organizations and individuals who made the transition from a traditional staff position to consultant. The workshop helps participants learn how to contract with a client, acquire skills to deal with resistance, and engage a client in a discussion about proceeding or not proceeding with a project.

Designed Learning Inc.
1009 Park Avenue
Plainfield, NJ 07060
(908) 754-5102

Staff Consulting Skills

Designed Learning's workshop can help you to develop consulting skills—the key to influencing in the absence of direct control. You will acquire the skills necessary to ensure that your ideas and expertise are implemented to the benefit of the organization.

The Leadership Group, Inc.
Seattle Tower Building
1218 Third Avenue, Suite 1600
Seattle, WA 98101
(206) 382-1276

Developing Your Self for High Impact Consulting

You will learn where and how to apply systemic principles in your day-to-day work to achieve the highest level of impact and effectiveness.

Linkage Incorporated
110 Hartwell Avenue
Lexington, MA 02173
(617) 862-4030

*Consulting Skills for HR
Professionals*

This workshop provides participants with the knowledge and
skills necessary to increase their
consulting role with internal
clients and customers.

NTL Institute
1240 North Pitt Street, Suite 100
Alexandria, VA 22314-1403
(703) 548-1500

Consultation Skills

In this "real world" learning
workshop, you will have a
chance to exercise, analyze, and
refine your consulting skills as
you participate in an actual
consultation. This workshop
emphasizes client contact, contracting, diagnosis, intervention, feedback, and follow-up.

NTL Institute
1240 North Pitt Street, Suite 100
Alexandria, VA 22314-1403
(703) 548-1500

*Integrating Training and Con-
sultation: Design and Practice*

This program presents a model
based on a consultancy approach to training and development. The stages in the
consulting cycle are applied to
the needs assessment and the development of appropriate consulting and training
interventions.

NTL Institute
1240 North Pitt Street, Suite 100
Alexandria, VA 22314-1403
(703) 548-1500

*Process Consultation: A Practi-
cal Diagnostic and Intervention
Approach*

In this workshop you will learn
skills and a conceptual framework for process interventions.
You will learn how to apply a

multilevel process model, utilize a framework of intervention that is consistent with your style and work culture, develop practical intervention skills, and understand when and when not to intervene.

Robert H. Schaffer & Associates
401 Rockrimmon Road
Stamford, CT 06903
(203) 322-1604

Consulting for Results

This workshop is all about making your consulting inputs link directly to the achievement of business results. The workshop builds skills and provides essential insights into the everyday practice of consulting.

Robert H. Schaffer & Associates
401 Rockrimmon Road
Stamford, CT 06903
(203) 322-1604

The Dynamics of Effective Consulting

This workshop covers key topics such as starting up a consulting relationship, avoiding pitfalls, utilizing the strategies and tactics of effective consulting, and learning the breakthrough approach to productivity improvement.

University Associates, Inc.
Consulting & Training Services
8380 Miramar Mall, Suite 232
San Diego, CA 92121
(619) 552-8901

Successful Internal Consulting

You will learn a well-tested consulting sequence—what to do, when to do it, and why it's done that way. You will also learn more about helping the client solve problems rather than solving them yourself.

Performance Technology

Books

American Society for Training and Development. *Basics of Performance Technology.* ASTD Info-Line Collection, publication no. 9211. Alexandria, Va.: American Society for Training and Development, Nov. 1992.

Deterline, W. A., and Rosenberg, M. J. (eds.). *Workplace Productivity: Performance Technology Success Stories.* Washington, D.C.: National Society for Performance and Instruction, 1992.

Fournies, F. F. *Why Employees Don't Do What They're Supposed to Do . . . and What to Do About It.* New York: McGraw-Hill, 1988.

Gilbert, T. F. *Human Competence: Engineering Worthy Performance.* New York: McGraw-Hill, 1978.

Mager, R. F. *What Every Manager Should Know About Training.* Belmont, Calif.: Lake, 1992.

Mager, R. F., and Pipe, P. *Analyzing Performance Problems.* Belmont, Calif.: Fearon/Lear Siegler, 1970.

Rummler, G. A., and Brache, A. P. *Improving Performance: How to Manage the White Space on the Organization Chart.* San Francisco: Jossey-Bass, 1990.

Stolovitch, H. D., and Keeps, E. J. (eds.). *Handbook of Human Performance Technology: A Comprehensive Guide for Analyzing and Solving Performance Problems in Organizations.* San Francisco: Jossey-Bass, 1992.

Workshops

The Rummler-Brache Group
163 Washington Valley Road, Suite 103
Warren, NJ 07059-7121
(908) 469-5700

Improve Performance Through Process Management

The workshop presents the unique three-level framework for improving performance, the methodology for completing a process involvement project, and methods of implementing a successful process management effort in an organization.

Swanson & Associates, Inc.
168 East Sixth Street, Suite 4002
St. Paul, MN 55101
(612) 292-0448

Performance Improvement Workshop

The workshop presents an organizational diagnosis process that provides the actual and desired performance requirements at the organizational, process, and/or individual level that culminates in a performance improvement plan.

Implementation of Performance Change

Books

American Society for Training and Development. *Managing Change: Implementation Skills.* ASTD Info-Line Collection, publication no. 8910. Alexandria, Va.: American Society for Training and Development, Oct. 1989.

Argyis, C. *Knowledge for Action: A Guide to Overcoming Barriers to Organizational Change.* San Francisco: Jossey-Bass, 1993.

Conner, D. R. *Managing at the Speed of Change.* New York: Villard, 1993.

Jacobs, R. W. *Real Time Strategic Change.* San Francisco: Berrett-Koehler, 1994.

Kirkpatrick, D. L. *How to Manage Change Effectively: Approaches, Methods, and Case Examples.* San Francisco: Jossey-Bass, 1985.

Mohrman, A. M., Jr., Mohrman, S. A., Ledford, G. E., Jr., Cummings, T. G., Lawler E. E., III, and Associates. *Large-Scale Organizational Change.* San Francisco: Jossey-Bass, 1989.

Workshops

Being First, Inc.
1242 Oak Drive, DWII
Durango, CO 81301-7516
(303) 385-5100

Facilitating Large Systems Change

This program presents the Change Process Model and helps you to develop a pragmatic change plan. You will also develop the skills and knowledge to carry out the change plan.

Linda S. Ackerman, Inc.
Optimal Performance Institute
1130 Besito Avenue
Berkeley, CA 94705
(415) 549-0717

Managing Complex Change

With this workshop you will gain a deeper understanding of the different kinds of change occurring in organizations and the appropriate strategies to successfully handle each of them. You will also learn how to plan for and manage the steps in the change process.

NTL Institute
1240 North Pitt Street, Suite 100
Alexandria, VA 22314-1403
(703) 548-1500

Facilitating and Managing Complex System Change

This workshop is designed to help you plan and successfully manage fundamental, sometimes traumatic, changes associated with start-ups, restructuring, downsizing, affirmative action, and other complex cultural transformations. You will leave this learning experience better prepared to plan, initiate, and manage change.

ODR, Inc.
Building 16
2900 Chamblee-Tucker Road
Atlanta, GA 30341
(404) 455-7145

Building Resilient Organizations for Turbulent Times

Presented in this workshop is a conceptual foundation in the critical dynamics of organizational change and the principles and techniques that comprise the MOC™ methodology. Participants will learn when and how to administer and interpret the results of diagnostic and planning tools.

ODR, Inc.
Building 16
2900 Chamblee-Tucker Road
Atlanta, GA 30341
(404) 455-7145

Managing Organizational Change: Tactics of Implementation

The Managing Organizational Change (MOC™) methodology for implementing change projects is presented in this workshop. In addition to learning the MOC™ methodology, you will learn to identify and contribute to the productivity of key players, manage employee resistance to change initiatives, and increase management support for tactical implementation plans.

Ridge Associates, Inc.
10592 Perry Highway,
Suite 201
Wexford, PA 15090
(412) 934-1770

Managing the Human Side of Change

This workshop provides the knowledge, skills, and strategies needed to institute changes with minimal negative effects; the workshop also develops skill in using a change management "toolkit" to build commitment to the desired changes.

*Robert H. Schaffer &
Associates*
401 Rockrimmon Road
Stamford, CT 06903
(203) 322-1604

Change Acceleration Workshop

The purpose of this workshop is to help management teams with a vital mission achieve their goals faster, better, and with greater bottom-line impact.

University Associates, Inc.
Consulting & Training
Services
8380 Miramar Mall, Suite 232
San Diego, CA 92121
(619) 552-8901

Facilitating Organizational Change

In this workshop, you will learn how you can anticipate and reduce resistance to change efforts. One focus of this program will be on learning why most change efforts fail and on developing strategies to better ensure the success of change efforts.

Associations

*American Society for Training
and Development (ASTD)*
1640 King Street
Box 1443
Alexandria, VA 22313-2043
(703) 683-8100

*Human Resource Planning So-
ciety (HRPS)*
41 East 42nd Street, Suite 1509
New York, NY 10017
(212) 490-6387

*International Society for
Performance Improvement (ISPI)*
1300 L. Street NW, Suite 1250
Washington, DC 20005
(202) 408-7969

*Society of Human Resource
Management (SHRM)*
606 North Washington Street
Alexandria, VA 22314-9797
(703) 548-3440

Glossary

Business needs: The operational goals for a unit, department, or organization. These are typically expressed in quantifiable terms (for example, "Reduce waste by 5 percent").

Cause question: A question designed to determine (1) why a business or performance problem exists and (2) why performers would not perform as desired if they were developed to do so.

Client: The individual or individuals who own the business, performance, and work environment needs being supported by the Performance Consultant in some manner.

Consulting: A synergistic process that maximizes the expertise of the consultant and the client.

Consulting role: The style or approach used by the consultant when working with a client. It can be either (1) pair-of-hands, (2) expert, or (3) collaborator.

Contract: A clear articulation of mutually shared expectations for the deliberations and actions to be taken during a project.

Human performance technology: A systemic approach to analyzing, improving, and managing performance in the workplace through the use of appropriate and varied interventions (American Society for Training and Development, 1992).

Is question: A question designed to determine the actual operational or performance situation.

Performance Consultant role: The role of addressing performance requirements in support of business needs.

Performance needs: The requirements concerning what people must do on the job if the organization's business goals are to be achieved. These are typically expressed in behavioral terms (for example, "Salespeople must overcome objections").

Performance relationship map: A graphic illustration of the interrelationship between business, performance, training, and work environment needs.

SHOULD question: A question designed to determine the desired operational or performance state.

Traditional Trainer role: The role of addressing learning needs through the delivery of leader-led and mediated programming.

Training needs: The skill and knowledge that people must acquire if they are to perform successfully.

Work environment needs: The systems and processes within the work environment of the performer that must be aligned to support the required performance.

References

American Society for Training and Development. "Training Basics: Basics of Performance Technology." *INFO-LINE*, Nov. 1992, *9211*, 1-32.

Baldwin, T. T., and Ford, J. K. "Transfer of Training: A Review and Directions for Future Research." *Personnel Psychology*, 1988, *41*, 63-105.

Bellman, G. M. *The Consultant's Calling: Bringing Who You Are to What You Do.* San Francisco: Jossey-Bass, 1990.

Block, P. *Flawless Consulting: A Guide to Getting Your Expertise Used.* San Diego, Calif.: Pfeiffer, 1981.

Broad, M. L., and Newstrom, J. W. *Transfer of Training.* Reading, Mass.: Addison-Wesley, 1992.

Csoka, L. S. *Closing the Human Performance Gap.* Report no. 1065-94-RR. New York: The Conference Board, 1994.

Dixon, G. *What Works at Work: Lessons from the Masters.* Minneapolis, Minn.: Lakewood Books, 1988.

Filipczak, B. "The Training Manager in the '90s." *TRAINING*, June 1994, pp. 31-35.

Foshay, W., Silber, K., and Westgaard, O. *Instructional Design Competencies: The Standards.* Iowa City, Iowa: International

341

Board of Standards for Training, Performance and Instruction, 1986.

Gilbert, T. F. *Human Competence: Engineering Worthy Performance.* New York: McGraw-Hill, 1978.

Henkoff, R. "Companies That Train Best." *Fortune,* Mar. 22, 1993, pp. 62–64, 68, 73–75.

Hutchison, C., Shepherd, J., and Stein, F. *Instructor Competencies: The Standards.* Batavia, Ill.: International Board of Standards for Training, Performance and Instruction, 1993.

Kouzes, J. M., and Posner, B. Z. *The Leadership Challenge: How to Get Extraordinary Things Done in Organizations.* San Francisco: Jossey-Bass, 1987.

McLagan, P. A. *Models for HRD Practice.* Alexandria, Va.: American Society for Training and Development, 1989.

Mager, R. F., and Pipe, P. *Analyzing Performance Problems or "You Really Oughta Wanna."* Belmont, Calif.: Fearon/Lear Siegler, 1970.

Rackham, N. *Account Strategy for Major Sales.* Aldershot, England: Gower, 1988.

Regalbuto, G. A. "Recovery from Occupational Schizophrenia." *Training & Development,* May 1991, pp. 79, 80, 83–86.

Reich, R. "Change: Old Work to New Work." *Intercom,* Jan. 1994, *6*(1), 1, 3.

Robinson, D. G., and Robinson, J. C. *Training for Impact: How to Link Training to Business Needs and Measure the Results.* San Francisco: Jossey-Bass, 1989.

Rummler, G. "Geary Rummler: Training Still Isn't Enough." *TRAINING,* 1983, *20*(8), 75–76.

Rummler, G. "Performance Is the Purpose." *TRAINING.* Minneapolis, Minn.: Lakewood, 1989.

Steinburg, C. "Partnerships with the Line." *Training & Development,* Oct. 1991, pp. 28–35.

Vogt, J. F., and Murrell, K. L. *Empowerment in Organizations: How to Spark Exceptional Performance.* San Diego, Calif.: University Associates, 1990.

Index

The Authors

Dana Gaines Robinson is president and James C. Robinson is chairman of Partners in Change, Inc., a consulting company they founded in 1981. It was almost inevitable that Jim and Dana Robinson would become partners in an HRD consulting business. They met when Dana was the training manager for a Philadelphia bank. She purchased the training program "Interaction Management" from Development Dimensions International (DDI) and wanted to measure it for impact. Not being certain how to do this, she called and asked DDI if they could assist— and they sent Jim! This was in 1976, when measuring impact from training was infrequently done. The results were as follows:

1. The program *did* have tremendous impact. The bank management provided Dana with substantial resources to continue the training.

2. Dana and Jim began to speak to various training groups on the subject of measuring impact, using the situation they had collaborated on as an example.

3. Dana and Jim began to date and married in 1982.

351

Dana is a recognized leader in the areas of performance technology and impact measurement. She is also recognized for her skills in forming performance models and for assisting training and HRD functions that want to make the transition to the performance business. Her clients for these services include The Coca-Cola Company, Georgia-Pacific Corporation, The Prudential, Shell Oil Company, and Bell Atlantic.

Dana is a frequent speaker at national training conferences, including the American Society for Training and Development (ASTD) and TRAINING Conferences. She also speaks and works in a global manner; to date she has worked with organizations in Canada, The Netherlands, Chile, Mexico, and New Zealand. She has a bachelor's degree in sociology from the University of California, Berkeley, and a master's degree in psychoeducational processes from Temple University, Philadelphia.

Jim is also a recognized leader in the area of HRD and performance technology. His career began as a line manager with Agway Inc.; while there he moved into the HRD profession when he became Agway's training director. For several years he was vice president of DDI and is the chief architect of its most successful training program, "Interaction Management."

Jim is a frequent speaker at major training conferences, including ASTD and National Society for Performance and Instruction conferences. His consultation often focuses on positioning the HRD function so that its efforts are linked to business needs and will result in measurable impact. His clients include CP Rail System, Owens-Corning Fiberglas Corporation, Hewlett-Packard Company, and Bell Atlantic. Jim has a master's degree in adult education from Syracuse University and a second master's degree in genetics from the University of Wisconsin.

When they are not working, Jim and Dana enjoy time with their family, which includes five (soon to be six) grandchildren. And, even though they each travel approximately 100,000 miles a year on business, they love to travel on their holidays. Between them, they have visited every continent in the world. Highlights have included going on a camera safari in Kenya and exploring New Zealand. Ireland, Hong Kong, and Singapore are destinations they have planned for upcoming trips.

Berrett-Koehler Publishers

BERRETT-KOEHLER is an independent publisher of books, periodicals, and other publications at the leading edge of new thinking and innovative practice on work, business, management, leadership, stewardship, career development, human resources, entrepreneurship, and global sustainability.

Since the company's founding in 1992, we have been committed to supporting the movement toward a more enlightened world of work by publishing books, periodicals, and other publications that help us to integrate our values with our work and work lives, and to create more humane and effective organizations.

We have chosen to focus on the areas of work, business, and organizations, because these are central elements in many people's lives today. Furthermore, the work world is going through tumultuous changes, from the decline of job security to the rise of new structures for organizing people and work. We believe that change is needed at all levels— individual, organizational, community, and global—and our publications address each of these levels.

We seek to create new lenses for understanding organizations, to legitimize topics that people care deeply about but that current business orthodoxy censors or considers secondary to bottom-line concerns, and to uncover new meaning, means, and ends for our work and work lives.

See next page for other books from Berrett-Koehler Publishers

Other leading-edge business books from Berrett-Koehler Publishers

Moving from Training to Performance

Dana Gaines and James C. Robinson

COPUBLISHED with the American Society for Training and Development and edited by the authors of the best-selling *Performance Consulting, Moving from Training to Performance* features chapters by some of the most highly respected professionals in the training and performance fields. It offers practical, action-oriented techniques for making the transition from training to performance, and shows how today's performance improvement departments can take a more active role in helping organizations meet their service and financial goals.

Paperback, 300 pages, 7/98 • ISBN 1-57675-039-6 CIP •
Item no. 50396-259 $29.95

Analysis for Improving Performance

Tools for Diagnosing Organizations and Documenting Workplace Expertise

Richard A. Swanson

ANALYSIS FOR IMPROVING PERFORMANCE details the front-end work essential to the success of any performance improvement effort. In clear language and easy-to-follow steps, Swanson shows how to do the rigorous preparatory analysis that defines and shapes successful performance improvement efforts, and maps the critical steps for insuring that a performance improvement program will meet real business needs and objectives.

Paperback, 298 pages, 9/96 • ISBN 1-57675-001-9 CIP
Item no. 50019-259 $24.95

Hardcover, 7/94 • ISBN 1-881052-48-6 CIP • **Item no. 52486-259 $34.95**

Evaluating Training Programs

The Four Levels

Donald L. Kirkpatrick

A COMPREHENSIVE step-by-step guide to evaluating training programs-from the creator of the "Kirkpatrick Model," the most widely used approach for evaluating training programs in industry, business, government, and academic institutions

Paperback, 250 pages, 1/96 • ISBN 1-881052-85-0
Item no. 52850-259 $24.95

Hardcover, 11/94 • ISBN 1-881052-49-4 CIP
Item no. 52494-259 $32.95

Available at your favorite bookstore, or call (800) 929-2929